Crime and the Media

Crime and the Media

The Post-modern Spectacle

**Edited by David Kidd-Hewitt
and Richard Osborne**

Pluto Press

LONDON • EAST HAVEN, CT

First published 1995 by Pluto Press
345 Archway Road, London N6 5AA
and 140 Commerce Street, East Haven,
Connecticut 06512, USA

British Library Cataloguing in Publication Data
A catalogue record for this book is available from the British Library

ISBN 0 7453 0912 7 hbk

Library of Congress Cataloging in Publication Data
Crime and the media: the postmodern spectacle/edited by David Kidd-
Hewitt and Richard Osborne.
     p.   cm.
   Includes bibliographical references and index.
   ISBN 0–7453–0912–7 (hb)
     1. Crime in mass media—Great Britain. 2. Crime and the press—
Great Britain. 3. Mass media and criminal justice—Great Britain.
I. Kidd-Hewitt, David. 1944– II. Osborne, Richard.
P96.C74C76   1995
364—dc20   95–37981
                                                                CIP

Designed and produced for Pluto Press by
Chase Production Services, Chipping Norton, OX7 5QR
Typeset from disk by Stanford DTP Services, Milton Keynes
Printed in the EC by WSOY, Finland

Contents

Acknowledgements

With much love to Jan, Paul, Rachel and Shelley.
David Kidd-Hewitt

This book is especially for Harriet Jane Osborne-Crowley.
Richard Osborne

Tables

Preface

The recent debates about the mass media's influence on crime and, in particular, violent crime, signify a deeprooted crisis in the cultures of late capitalist countries. Crime is a central preoccupation of politicians, the mass media and of popular entertainment, but the theoretical debate about the relationships between crime and the mass media remain locked in paradigms of effects and quantification. As recent studies have shown however these assumed effects are not at all easily demonstrable.[1] At the same time there is a large body of commonsense opinion that accepts that the mass media are responsible for encouraging, or creating, crime. There is an odd correspondence with post-modern theory in this assumed omnipresence of the mass media and of its universalising effects. The society of the image, the globilised media village, are sometimes taken as given within post-modern theory and this shift short-circuits the problems of media power and representation in the same way as crude populist critiques of television's total dominance. Sociological theory, media studies and criminology have mostly ignored this area of interaction between crime, criminal justice and media representation since the patterns of connection do not conform to the discrete analytic approaches historically favoured by these disciplines. That is to say that it is no longer possible to discuss crime without talking about the media, and vice versa. The essays in this book set out to examine the complex questions that surround both media representations of crime, and criminal acquisition of media images and the spectacle that constitutes the relationships between crime, the criminal justice system and the mass media. In this respect we would have to say that if the O.J. Simpson trial did not exist then a media God would have had to invent it in order to symbolise the contradictory reality we are addressing.

What begins then as a set of relatively straightforward questions, like, 'How is crime reported in the mass media?', 'What effects does this reporting have on viewers?' or 'Does media portrayal of crime encourage crime?', leads inexorably to a set of sociological problems that dwarf the initial approach. Drawing on criminology, media studies and post-modern theory these essays aim to set out a paradigm within which such problems can be considered. Questions of race, gender, class and power intersect with traditional ideas of media dominance and the forms of social control that are exercised through media agendas and ideological representations of social realities. David Kidd-Hewitt sets out the criminological history of the debate and the kinds of questions that have structured it. Richard Osborne then examines the nature of the current debates in relation to the electronic media and its place within post-modern society, that elusive nomenclature for describing the present conjuncture.

Richard Sparks grounds these arguments in a discussion of how television constructs and reinforces a moral universe within popular culture. Jim Pines then analyses the representations of race within the genres of crime shows in the electronic media and their changing significance in a post-modern, pluralistic universe of shifting identity and morality. Paula Skidmore considers the key media issue of child sexual abuse and the discourses of power, ideology and representation that surrounds this arena of news media production. Sue Lees considers a similarly difficult and contentious area when she examines the media coverage of what is now known as 'date-rape'. The problematic of gender dissects the whole discussion of crime and the media, masculinity being an unspoken but defining category of the realities of crime, a crisis of identity which is hidden in the functionalist discussion of crime as natural.

A.E. Stephenson-Burton shifts the debate to a discussion of the massive, and under-reported, reality of white collar crime, where the media agenda of immediacy and simplicity generates a blanket of indifference to fraud and criminality within the elite power structures of society. Mary Eaton analyses the representations of women police officers within popular culture and their effects and influences on 'canteen culture', or in other words the interaction of the fictional and the real. This intertextuality is also the subject of Paul Mason's piece on the modes of presentation of prison life within the electronic media. Noel Sanders examines the post-modern spectacle of self-created media disappearances, the minor celebrity seeking stardom through abduction and absent media presence. Finally Rikke Schubart takes a careful look at the horror movie, audience reactions and the debate about engendering violence and media effects. Her consideration of violence and its effects points to the heart of the failures of commonsense appraisals of media effects and a recognition of the shifting media universe we now all occupy.

Note

1. Gauntlet, D., *Moving Experiences: Understanding Television's Influence and Effects* (Leeds: Institute of Communications, 1995).

1   Crime and the Media: A Criminological Perspective

David Kidd-Hewitt

The world of crime is readily before us for the taking.[1]

Media portrayals of crime and violence have become part of the spectacle of everyday life.

We have become voyeurs of 'factual' programmes that 'entertain' and frighten us with reconstructions of violent crimes and amaze us with the sheer audacity of wily confidence tricksters.[2] We view all manner of police — uniformed, undercover, secret or special, in partnership, groups, organisations or as loners. We see them as cosy, ill disciplined, tough, violent, reasonable, idiosyncratic, racist, sexist, quirky, honest and corrupt. We encounter personal lives, lives '*on the Job*', the clash of gender tensions and sexual dilemmas.[3]

The tools of academic debate are slowly evolving in their attempts to encapsulate and analyse many of these features of the crime and media spectacle, whether it is viewed on film, television or on the pages of a newspaper. The first part of this introductory chapter is intended, therefore, to explore what may be called 'the criminological approach' to the study of crime and the media.

Crime and the media: a criminological approach

The academic world has engaged in interesting and often idiosyncratic struggles with the concept and nature of the mass media and in particular the psychological, sociological and criminological implications of its presence and influence.

This has primarily featured four main areas of questioning:

1. Whether the mass media, particularly television, through depictions of crime, violence, death and aggression, can be proven to be a major cause or important contributory factor of criminal or deviant behaviour.
2. Whether the mass media, particularly the press, construct and present our social world in ways that distort reality, and unjustly stereotype

particular groups or individuals, labelling them as 'outsiders', elimi-
nating their credibility, and in the process exploiting and furthering
their own privileged access to powerful state institutions.
3. Whether the mass media engender 'moral panics' and cause people
   to be fearful by over-reporting criminal and violent events and
   looking primarily for sensation above accuracy.
4. Whether 'real' crime and fictional crime impact on the viewer in
   the same manner, particularly in the electronic media.

The issue of 'mass media-generated fear' as a specific domain of concern
has, for some, become a freestanding area within its own right and both
criminology and media studies have, in recent years, concentrated on
debating the realism or otherwise of fear which is seen to derive from
the portrayal of crime in the mass media.[4]

In order to locate and explore the criminological approach to the crime
and media debate it is necessary first to acknowledge that the 1970s saw
a collection of key texts emerging which confronted the selection, presentation and effects of media portrayals of crime, deviance and social
problems.[5] In retrospect these can be seen as pivotal studies which
constituted a watershed in the development of British criminology.
Influenced by a series of five symposia at York University in the late
1960s new, radical approaches to criminology and related issues began
to surface. This is often referred to as the development of 'New Criminology'.[6] The authors involved were closely concerned with progressing
an enormous and ambitious agenda that had begun in essence some
decades previously, influenced by American criminology and key
theorists such as Edwin Lemert, Howard Becker and David Matza.[7]

However, the study of crime and the media within criminology has
become fixed within a pattern of inquiry which often relies upon the
ritualistic reproductions of key concepts developed in these texts, such
as 'moral panic' and 'deviancy amplification'. These approaches frequently
go beyond or misrepresent the original intentions established, for
example, by Cohen in his seminal work, *Folk Devils and Moral Panics*.[8]
'Moral panic', together with its further articulation in *The Manufacture
of News*[9] and *Policing the Crisis*,[10] left such significant and substantial
foundation stones that they are constantly mistaken for the final edifice
instead of notable developments to be built upon.

As Richard Sparks perceptively notes:

Cohen's original formulation of the term was a modest and descriptive one, beginning by simply noting an observed tendency ... one
danger in attaching too much weight to this idea would be that ...
it elides all such 'panics' under a single heading, representing them

as a consequence of some (hypothetically universal, endlessly cyclical) feature of social life, namely panickyness.[11]

As a result, the context and significance of Cohen's study has frequently been overlooked and often turned into a pastiche – a mods and rockers soap episode cited by sociology and criminology students without the full sense of its place in the continuity of the media's long association with 'the manufacture of news'.[12] Similarly, the 'career' of the mugging label is extracted from Hall et al.[13] and paraded as another key feature of the crime and media connection – a self-contained paradigm that is endlessly reproduced as self-explanatory, when on the contrary it is an extremely complex socio-political issue.

What the debate seems to require is a greater awareness of its ancestry and from this to derive an ability to *rediscover* the pivotal nature of seminal works that characterised the 1970s *'new criminology'*, carrying the sociological implications thus established through to 1990s' concerns with the post-modern relationship between the media and crime.

Crime, morality and the media

From the 1920s to the 1950s family studies and 'correct' socialisation patterns were the primary focus of study for many psychologists and sociologists. The middle-class models of educative ideals and deferred gratification were the yardsticks against which the majority of young people were thought best judged. The media's concern with 'problem youth' both in the UK and the US was based on perceived 'bad influences' and 'disorganised' neighbourhoods which gave rise to teenage gangs and an increase in juvenile crime from both sexes.[14] Steve Chibnall reminds us that the official UK statistics indicate an increase of 250 per cent in the number of adolescents going to prison between 1939 and 1947.[15] There was of course the massive disruption of family life across the period of the two world wars. The criminologist Hermann Mannheim referred to the 'wartime darkening of the picture as far as juveniles were concerned'.[16]

Disaffected youth were designated 'social problems' and what they read and saw was regarded as problematic if its moral content was in the least suspect. To quote Mannheim again: 'Shelter life and black-out together with many empty houses offered ideal opportunities for pilfering and sexual misconduct.'[17]

Connections between crime, morality and the media were, at this time, a matter of concern in the form of horror comics, radio and film.

Horror comics

In the 1930s, apprehension was expressed in the US by various organisations such as the American General Federation of Women's Clubs, and a variety of church bodies, about a perceived growth in depictions of crime, violence, sex, sadism, and vampirism in the comic industry.

Concern grew during the 1940s, culminating in a 1949 inquiry entitled the Joint Legislative Committee to Study the Publication of Comics. Evidence by the psychiatrist Frederic Werthem[18] indicated that whether the stories depicted were set in space, western cities or in the jungle the depiction of criminal and violent acts influenced and frightened children during their formative years and warped people's minds.

These concerns, as expressed by Werthem, were important in establishing a debate particularly amongst psychologists, which has not changed a great deal as the media has expanded into television, film and video. How far are such spectacles contributory factors in producing violent, criminal and, perhaps, sexually promiscuous people?[19] In the case of horror comics, Werthem had no doubt that they were extremely significant.

Mannheim, acknowledging this early 'moral panic' over the dissemination of horror comics,[20] suggested that three stages have characterised the criminological assessment of this and other media such as film, radio and television.

1. Direct causation. This develops the Werthem position of laying significant blame at the feet of the media for a great deal of juvenile delinquency. It also supports the educative influence of the media, in that children copy crimes and deviant behaviour they have read about or seen on the screen.
2. Positive function. This position claims that any 'copy-cat' behaviour is outweighed by claims that children *need* horror. Claims are made that it provides a 'safety valve' or supports 'vicarious enjoyment':

   > According to it, the reader or watcher of brutal acts of violence, of sex orgies, or whatever outrageous material press and cinema may choose to place before them, far from wishing to do the same would rather lean back happily and passively and let those actively engaged take his place. Looked at in this way, horror tales and crime films were not only not dangerous but positively useful as crime-preventing agencies.[21]

3. Misrepresentation. This does not refute the two categories above but points to the irresponsible nature of media in over-representing

violence and pursuing sensationalism. This results in stereotyping people as promiscuous, violent and criminal and is often racist and sexist in portrayal. It also accuses the media of making heroes out of villains which, within limits, this position sees as acceptable. Making villains too attractive, however, can lead to copy-cat implications.

Other features of this position point to inaccurate caricatures of law enforcement agencies as 'weak, stupid or brutal'.[22] Also of concern is that crime appears to pay too often in many media portrayals. Although as Kinsey, Lea and Young note regarding contemporary television:

> The mass media present stereotypical depictions not only of crime but also of policing. It would perhaps make a rather untidy television drama if the denouement usually showed the culprit getting away once again, but this would be closer to the truth.[23]

Radio's influence

Radio has not been systematically studied in terms of its connection with representations of crime and possible influences referred to in the 'direct causation' category. Certainly from the 1920s the radio was becoming extremely important as a medium of communication and entertainment. As a purveyor of fear and fright it would from time to time come up against criticisms, but not within any systematic study emanating from psychiatrists or psychologists as had occurred with horror comics and which would continue to characterise film and later video portrayals.[24]

One programme which eventually transferred to television and represents the early days of crime story portrayal on the radio in the UK was *Dick Barton, Special Agent*. This began in October 1946 and was one of the longest-running radio serials of the time. It did, however, come under fire from the Chief Constable of Gloucester who saw the programme as irresponsible. Chibnall records how *The Police Chronicle* in 1948 supported the Chief Constable in attempting to ban Dick Barton as representing 'crime propaganda'.[25]

In contrast to this the American criminologist, Richard Quinney, credits radio, and *The Lone Ranger* programme in particular, as making a greater contribution to engendering a law-abiding influence than at first might be countenanced:

> Three nights a week we sat by the radio listening to the latest adventures of the masked man in his pursuit of badmen and criminals.

My world was made real by this frontier character. Now, confronting this earlier world, I am able to gain a better understanding of crime in America.[26]

Most of the condemnation from 'experts' in pursuing the crime and media link was, however, directed at the cinema.

Film crooks and copy-cat behaviour

The academic world had begun, early on, to engage in debates with the claimed all-pervasive and persuasive nature of the mass media and in particular the sociological and criminological implications of its presence and influence as represented by the cinema. For example, Professor Cyril Burt in his 1925 study, *The Young Delinquent*,[27] mirrors many of the current concerns which moral entrepreneurs bring to the fore in relation to the perceived 'bad' influence of television, video and film.

Indeed, Burt's work is an early and significant example of the 'copy-cat' claims laid at the door of the 'crook/crime' genre of the contemporary film spectacle as well as TV crime shows. First he examines whether the 'manoeuvres of film-crooks'[28] act as educators to young people, thereby inspiring copy-cat behaviour.

The concerns expressed below closely reflect, for example, those expressed about the film *Child's Play III* as possibly influencing the two ten-year-old children who were convicted of killing Jamie Bulger in 1993. More recently the Hollywood film *Natural Born Killers* (1994) has also been cited as a potential stimulus to young people prone to aspirations of serial killing. Burt's view in 1925 was as follows:

'Crook-films', it is said, are as popular as detective novelettes; the topic of crime has a special appeal to the young imagination; and if a boy or girl has seen a representation of a cracksman breaking into a house, or a hooligan battering the police, or an adventuress proffering her love as the price of giddy pleasures, then, it is supposed, the child may be irresistibly inspired to re-enact in real life the fictitious example set before him.[29]

Burt is not convinced this is a problem other than in 'the dull or the defective',[30] the embarrassing terminology of the day now defunct and turned into 'vulnerable children with high psychiatric morbidity', or perhaps 'neuropsychiatric vulnerabilities'.[31] Although, the writer Michael Medved in his 1992 study *Hollywood vs America* has no qualms about referring to the young audience for violent films as 'drooling, hormone-addled, violence prone sub-literate adolescent males'.[32]

Today, the concern over film extends to the technology of visual imagining, particularly video technology, that reaches directly into the home.[33]

Thoughtless frivolity and fun

It is in the realm of the post-modern spectacle that Burt provides an interesting precursor to the current debates. In his pre-television, pre-video, pre-tabloid newspaper world of pre-war delinquents he recounts that:

> The main source of harm, however, has been as yet unmentioned. It is in the general and more elusive influences that the real danger of the cinema lies. ... Throughout the usual picture-palace programme, the moral atmosphere presented is an atmosphere of thoughtless frivolity and fun, relieved only by some sudden storm of passion with occassional splashes of sentiment. Deceit, flirtation, and jealousy, unscrupulous intrigue and reckless assault, a round of unceasing excitement and the extremes of wild emotionalism, are depicted as the normal characteristics of the everyday conduct of adults.[34]

Compare this to Charles Laurence's account in 1994, when describing the film *Natural Born Killers*. The contemporary versions of 'reckless assault', 'storms of passion', 'thoughtless frivolity and fun' and 'unscrupulous intrigue' are clearly conveyed:

> The film portrays the killing spree and rise to tabloid fame of Mickey, the psychopath ... and his teenage lover Mallory. It opens with a stunning massacre at a truck stop, and follows the demented couple along their murderous path to arrest and jail. It is then that the media arrive in the form of a 'trash-TV' news show, which turns them into heroes. The couple kidnap the host of the show during an in-jail interview, and use him as a hostage for the bloodsoaked, live-on-TV jailbreak that brings the action to a climax.[35]

In a similar vein to Burt, Lawrence argues for recognition that this depiction adds to 'soil already thick with the roots of dangerous social ills'.[36]

Massive research efforts in this area have not produced clear evidence for or against such behavioural claims. Simon Carey, a psychologist who has reviewed the profusion of such studies, comments:

> the only possible conclusion which can be drawn from a thorough review of the huge number of scientific studies designed to test such theories gives victory to neither those who believe that mass media violence does harm nor to those who believe it does not.[37]

There is overall a tension between popular opinion and academic research. Popular opinion will constantly answer 'Yes' to the direct causation category on the basis that 'common sense' demands that there *must* be a connection. For example, the BBC's *Late Show* commissioned a Mori Poll in May 1994 to provide the basis for a discussion of the potential effects of screen violence in causing real violence. Unlike academic researchers, popular opinion was unambiguous. Melvyn Bragg opened the debate with the question: 'Is the screen the most significant, even the crucial factor triggering violence in children?'[38]

Some of the results of the poll were presented as follows:

- *Do you think that violence among children under 16 has increased, decreased or stayed the same?*   81 per cent said *increased.*
- *Do you feel that there is a link between this increase and violence on television and video?*   82 per cent said *yes*

In addition, the overwhelming popular view of a connection between screen violence and real violence was given academic credence by the child psychologist Professor Elizabeth Newson who stated: 'I think sometimes there are good reasons for panicking and I think this is a moment when one should be frightened.'[39]

The programme went on to show, however, that the issues are far from clear-cut and the academics taking part reflected the wider social scientific literature which provides no clear evidence. For example, the comment made by J.D. Halloran in 1978 still holds good today for many researchers: 'No case has been made where television (or the other media) could be legitimately regarded as a major contributory factor to any form of violent behaviour. At most they play a minor role.'[40]

Difficulties persist in experimental research that attempts to simulate the 'real world' under laboratory conditions. Fieldwork provides a 'better' approximation but is very difficult to administer without introducing bias and experimenter expectations. In *Aggression* Albert Bandura acknowledges that: 'Experimental conditions therefore can cover only a limited range of those found in society, and usually the weaker forms.'[41]

Correlation studies are fought over as to their significance or otherwise when results appear to show that those who view a great deal of television are as likely to be violent or deviant as those who view very little. Indeed, it appears that the closest one can arrive at a final, conclusive statement that sums up the psychological position is provided by Schramm et al.:

For some children under some conditions, some television is harmful. For other children under the same conditions, or for the same children under other conditions, it may be beneficial. For most children under most conditions, most television is probably neither harmful nor particularly beneficial.[42]

Criminal careers and the dramatisation of evil: the sociological tradition

The sociological tradition has concentrated primarily on the ways in which the media provide us with perceptions and social constructions about the world we inhabit. In this area the concern has not been so much whether behavioural role models purveyed by the media are likely to stimulate inappropriate 'copy-cat' behaviour amongst young people or indeed those of mature ages (although this is an important area) – rather it is often the reverse. That is, whether the media tend to engender false and damaging images about particular segments of the populace, for example young people. The accusation is one of stereotyping certain people, perhaps by reason of their age, appearance, ethnicity, gender, family background or geographical location.

Stuart Hall, for instance, refers to the process of manufacturing *public images* by the media and others in positions of power:

> A 'public image' is a cluster of impressions, themes and quasi-explanations, gathered or fused together ... the presence of such 'public images' in public and journalistic discourse feeds into and informs the treatment of a particular story. Since such 'public images', at one and the same time, are graphically compelling, but also stop short of serious, searching analysis, they tend to appear *in place of analysis* – or analysis seems to collapse into the image.[43]

For example, a lead story in the *Sunday Times* of 5 February 1995 is headlined:

> The "savage generation" hits Britain.[44]

This follows the publication of a report by a clinical psychologist who had been looking at official crime rates for violent crime by children aged from 10–13 and 14–16. The story continued: 'Psychologists, magistrates and educationalists say a growing core of aggressive children is to blame, nurtured by the rise in single-parent families, the availability of drugs and violent videos.'[45]

References are then made to the 'public image' of the film *A Clockwork Orange* as indicative of an inevitable truth – that a cult of violence is being enjoyed by young people as young as ten years old. Contextualising the article within a failing criminal justice system, fraught teachers unable to cope, a youngster admitting to smashing car windscreens, the breakup of traditional family life and inadequate parenting skills, there can be little doubt in readers' minds that it is single-parent families that are producing the majority of violent young people who are now termed 'the savage generation'. As a concluding flourish, an author of children's books has the last word: 'Since the Eric Cantona incident I have watched young boys directing kung-fu kicks at people in the streets. Television has brought this type of incident into their homes and made it acceptable.'[46]

A significant role played by contemporary sociologists such as Geoffrey Pearson and Steve Chibnall[47] has been to illustrate how the media regularly feature and fuel concerns about the 'pathological' nature of the younger generation. There is a cycle of media-generated concern that regularly re-visits the younger generation to spell out the gloom and violence likely to come from our disenchanted offspring – the spectacle of the 'youth problem', as is the case with *A Clockwork Orange* – withdrawn from view, yet still used to sustain a post-modern nightmare of youth violence.

Deviants, labels and public reaction

The sociological approach within criminology therefore is concerned with revealing the attitudes that the media might generate or reinforce amongst its viewers or readers as a whole, for example fear, anxiety, terror, hatred, admiration, prejudice, intolerance, bigotry, bias, racism. It is a concern to demystify the processes of media *selection* and media *presentation* in order to expose the simplistic view that the media merely report 'the facts', that they merely reflect society as it is.

The sociological tradition of 'challenging' the media's perception and reporting of deviant and criminal events and of drawing the processes of media production and spectacle into critical academic paradigms is relatively new. It primarily reflects the concerns of young post-war sociologists resolute in their goals to wrest criminology from its well-established pre-war determinist framework of analytical individualism and to turn criminology from the study of mere law infraction to that of law and norm infraction.[48]

> We read of murders and drug-taking, vicars eloping with members of their congregation and film stars announcing the birth of their illegitimate children, football trains being wrecked and children being stolen from their prams, drunken drivers being breathalysed and accountants fiddling the books ... indeed, so much space in the mass media is given to deviance that some sociologists have argued that this

interest functions to reassure society that the boundary lines between conformist and deviant, good and bad, healthy and sick, are still valid ones.[49]

Stanley Cohen provides a clear account of the agenda that was thus created for a transition into a new British criminology:

1. A re-constitution of criminology as part of 'the sociology of deviance' and its reintegration into mainstream sociology.
2. An elevation of social control (or 'societal reaction') as a question of central concern and a consequent adoption of a structurally and politically informed version of labelling theory.
3. A determination to 'appreciate' deviance in the senses of granting recognition to the deviant's own subjective meaning and of not taking for granted the control system's aim of eradicating deviance.
4. An emphasis on the political nature of defining and studying crime and deviance.[50]

As a result of this 'agenda', much was accomplished in the rethinking of criminology. In the case of crime and the media, the 1970s saw the emergence of the five pivotal studies which have subsequently informed the sociological tradition in this area.

The first study, J. Young's 'The role of the police as amplifiers of deviancy, negotiators of reality and translators of fantasy',[51] developed the key concepts of 'newsworthiness' and 'deviancy amplification'. It demonstrated the relationship that exists between social control agencies and media 'fantasies' that trigger such agencies to over-react and further stereotype deviants – in this case, the marijuana smoker living in West London. It demonstrates that 'moral panics' engendered by media fantasies amplify the deviant act until there is: 'a translation of stereo-types into actuality, of fantasy into reality'.[52]

The respectable image of the police is set against the degenerate image of the bohemian and polarised by the media into a clear-cut account of good versus evil represented thus:

HIPPIE THUGS – THE SORDID TRUTH: Drugtaking, couples making love while others look on, rule by a heavy mob armed with iron bars, foul language, filth and stench, THAT is the scene inside the hippies' Fortress in London's Piccadilly. These are not rumours but facts – sordid facts which will shock ordinary decent family loving people.[53]

What becomes clear from Young's study is the speed with which the media can represent or, as claimed in this case, misrepresent an 'outsider life-style' and simultaneously create a social problem; and then develop

from that presentation a 'moral panic' which leads to increased social
control action from the police, thereby engendering more media
coverage of 'sordid druggies' and so on.

The second key study is S. Cohen's *Folk Devils and Moral Panics*.[54]
The concepts of 'moral panic' and 'deviancy amplification' have been
enshrined in this work that examined the mods and rockers phenomenon
of the 1960s.

Cohen is credited by John Muncie as producing the first *systematic*
empirical study of media amplification and its public consequences.[55]
It certainly strengthened the growing tradition of unpacking the media's
role in reporting certain events and revealing how they are able to
construct their own version of reality. In doing so, Cohen claimed to
demonstrate a 'deviancy amplification spiral'. This builds on Young's
concerns at the speed and power the mass media possess to create
disquiet, to declare and signal a 'social problem'.

Confrontations *did* occur during Whitsun 1964 at Brighton between
youths respectively designated mods or rockers. Cohen notes: 'The Mods
and Rockers didn't become news because they were new; they were
presented as new to justify their creation as news.'[56] It was the
comparison of the 'news' with his own inventory of what occurred and
the panic engendered by the way in which the confrontations were
reported that Cohen outlines in some detail.

This study began to clarify sociological concern with 'the manufacture of news' as a precursor to the creation of a 'moral panic'. It also
pointed to the importance of the symbolic nature of youth cultures.
Whether Teddy boys, mods, rockers, punks or skinheads, there is a
symbolic threat attached by the media to such perceived uncontrolled
autonomy. 'They need to be brought back into line' was the moral
crusade mounted by the media and other moral entrepreneurs.

The media therefore were seen initially to 'over-report' the confrontations with regular use of phrases such as 'beat up the town',
'orgy of destruction, 'seige', 'battle', 'screaming mob', 'attack'. The image
of innocent holiday-makers struggling to escape from marauding hordes
about to take over Brighton was clearly conveyed. The moral panic and
subsequent amplification spiral ensued:

> It should be noted throughout, that the amplificatory effects of the
> control culture were fed back into the mass media, which further exag-
> gerated them, thus producing another link in the sequence. If the
> policemen did not see themselves as 'the brave men in blue' fighting
> the evil mob, nor the magistrates themselves as society's chosen

mouthpieces for denouncing evil, these polarizations were made in their behalf by others.[57]

It is clear from Cohen's work that sociological concern within criminological studies was now firmly directed towards exposing the media as purveyors of particular social constructions of social reality rather than as objective reporters. The concern is with serious misrepresentation and the control culture impact that flows from such misrepresentations. In other words, 'the manufacture of news'.

In 1973 Stanley Cohen and Jock Young edited a book entitled *The Manufacture of News*.[58] This was a comprehensive attempt to mobilise this growing sociological tradition of demystifying and unpacking the ideological frameworks that inform a range of institutions, the print media in particular. It also symbolises the growing concern with the study of 'deviance' as opposed to merely 'law infraction'. This volume clearly established:

- the mass media as a sociological challenge, that is what explicit or implicit views of society can be ascertained which are generated by media organisations? How do they select and present information?
- notions of deviance and social problems that are manufactured, generated and revealed by the mass media;
- the role of the mass media in moulding and legitimating the shapes and forms of societal control culture. Do they influence control culture and hence control agents, for example the police?

Overall, this was a significant attempt to suggest analytic models of analysis that would aid our sociological understanding of the mass media.

The Mass Manipulative and the Commercial Laissez-faire models .

These two analytical models should be seen as extremes of a continuum – polarised and opposing. They represent traditions of media operation in the selection, presentation and likely effects of their output on the public. They are *both* capable of encapsulating right and left political positions through which a second structure of selection, presentation and effects flows and can be viewed. 'Selection according to "structured ideological biases" is at the heart of the Mass Manipulative model but in the Commercial model ... the criteria are seen to be more *intrinsic* to the material.'[59]

Mass Manipulative model	*Commercial Laissez-faire model*
Selection/Presentation/Effects	
• structured ideological biases (*manufactured*)	• locating human interest and the unusual (*discovered*)
• status quo defended, power and interest rule	• competitive enterprise, public demand rules
• concealment of selected news and information	• fact-finding exposés and honest revelations
• high concentration of ownership aids control culture manipulation and consensual models	• concentrated and experienced ownership aids the efficient presentation of the real world and conflict models
• public as an atomised mass (*passive absorbers*)	• public as discerning consumers (*judicious receivers*)

As a means of 'testing' media portrayals of crime and deviance these models provided a critical sociological starting point. In terms of the polarity the models represent the authors comment:

> Our own position ... is at neither extreme. In playing down the more melodramatic effects of the media as portrayed in the Manipulative versions – partly because of a liberal democratic opposition to censorship and control – the Laissez-faire position exaggerates the impotence of the media. Clearly the media must have some influence.[60]

A crucial gap in the literature was filled in 1977 by S. Chibnall's *Law and Order News*.[61] This book is credited as the first to provide a study of crime journalism in Britain.

Apart from its very valuable historical documentation of the growth of 'law and order' news in the press, Chibnall has been able to extract from his study of the working relationships between crime journalists and the police what he refers to as 'the professional news imperatives of journalism'. It is the evaluation of these imperatives that has been important in informing the sociological tradition of crime and media studies since the late 1970s. This also helps to advance Cohen and

Young's analysis concerning the selection criteria used for newsworthy items.

Chibnall explains that there are 'at least eight professional imperatives which act as implicit guides to the construction of news stories'.[62] These are:

1. Immediacy   (speed/the present).
2. Dramatisation   (drama and action).
3. Personalisation   (culture of the personality/celebrity).
4. Simplification   (elimination of shades of grey).
5. Titillation   (revealing the forbidden/voyeurism).
6. Conventionalism   (hegemonic ideology).
7. Structured access   (experts, power base, authority).
8. Novelty   (new angle/speculation/twist).

Chibnall also provides further professional imperatives that lead to what he terms 'at least five sets of informal rules of relevancy in the reporting of violence ... They guide journalists' treatment of violence by asserting the relevance of:[63]

1. Visible and spectacular acts.
2. Sexual and political connotations.
3. Graphic presentation.
4. Individual pathology.
5. Deterrence and repression.

By being aware of these 'journalistic rules of relevancy', the rationales for the selection and treatment of features relating to the coverage of violence, for example, are better understood. As our main source of crime information the mass media need to be revealed as powerful creators and interpreters on our behalf. Chibnall has added significantly to the sociological tradition within criminology that continues to expose this fact.

The last 'watershed' publication of the 1970s which developed the now growing array of *challenges* to the media from sociology, concerning its responsibilities to inform with integrity rather than merely push for sensational portrayal, is that of Hall et al. *Policing the Crisis*.[64] This study can be seen as bridging the 1970s and the first half of the 1980s in several important ways:

1. It advances the sociological debates regarding the media's portrayal of violent crime from the scholarship of the 1970s in a way that begins

to inform the new debates about the fear of crimes that have been taking place since the 1980s.

2. It brings in the crucial feature of a comparative framework by siting the moral panic about mugging that occurred in the UK within its American context. Observers in the 1980s and 1990s look towards America far more now in terms of media and crime relationships of all kinds.

3. It includes a clear account of the scapegoating of black youth both here and in the US together with an analysis of the ideological and political frameworks that enabled this to occur, and continue to occur.

4. It clarifies the connections which are seen to exist between the media and control culture agencies and attempts to reveal their power base. It also adds a strong socio-economic context to the debate.

The authors followed 13 months of press and 'official' coverage between August 1972 and the end of August 1973 of the 'new' crime of mugging. They witnessed the 'get tough' ideology emerging from this period and specifically noted how crucial the media's role was in promoting a call to new regimes of law and order. The media had already spent some considerable time during the 1960s covering what was seen as spiralling crime in the US and, as is usually the case, using its horror of the American scene to warn Britain of the tendency for all things American eventually to cross the Atlantic. As Hall et al. pointed out:

> When the British Press reported on American cities, the already forged connections between black unrest, inter-racial tension, the spreading ghettoes and crime tended to be reproduced in that form … It reproduced *the idea of American mugging* for British consumption.[65]

Their point is that the press had educated the public so effectively that the Pavlovian reaction to a mugging headline was *not* 'a particular kind of robbery occurring on British streets' but rather 'general social crisis and rising crime'.[66] As John Muncie so succinctly puts it: 'Their explanation of the moral panic is firmly placed in the context of deteriorating material conditions in the inner-cities, worsening race relations and the development of a law and order state.'[67]

The longer-term agenda is identified as the stigmatisation of young, black West Indian males as representing the most likely embodiment of '*the mugger*', what Hall et al. refer to as '*a false enemy*'.[68] Through the application of a Marxist analysis they conclude that the symbol of the black mugger becomes part of the capitalist state's transformation of the deprivation of class in general into a specific division involving racial differences:

It provides the separation of the class into black and white with a material basis, since, in much black crime (as in much white working class crime), one part of the class materially 'rips off' another. It provides this separation with its ideological figure, for it transforms the deprivation of class, out of which crime arises, into the all too intelligible syntax of race, and fixes a false enemy: the black mugger.[69]

The media are seen by Hall et al. as integral to sustaining this image of 'a false enemy'.

At another level of crime and media representation, the reality of changed policing roles across the 1970s and into the 1980s in the TV cop shows had slowly but surely replaced the George Dixon figure with a variety of harder, grittier, confrontational police. They were depicted as more adversarial and without illusions about 'the enemy' or that they were engaged in a war.

Keith Ellawell, the Chief Constable for Cleveland, was reported in the *Daily Mail* in 1992 as lamenting the lost bobby in a rather nostalgic fashion: 'People are not as frightened of breaking the law as they were 30 years ago. The rosy-cheeked bobby on his beat is now a thing of the past.'[70] Television had realised the demise of the 'rosy-cheeked bobby' by the 1960s when *Z Cars* took to the small screen, followed by *Softly Softly* and *The Sweeney*.

Similarly in the US, throughout the 1970s in particular, TV portrayed the organisational sophistication of the police through programmes such as *SWAT*, and *Police Story*. Their gritty characters were predominantly undercover cops or at least the non-uniform variety that would have given George Dixon apoplexy – such as *Starsky and Hutch* and *Baretta*. Quirky (unlikely) partnerships such as *McMillan and Wife* and *Cagney and Lacey* provided cosy moments for those missing the Dixon mould. Other, more consensual models using the individual police person were *The Gentle Touch*, *Police Woman*, *Get Christie Love*, *Columbo*, *Kojak*, *Cannon*, *Barlow at Large* and, for the nineteenth-century buffs, *Sergeant Cork*. Women as the velvet glove against the male iron fist became a clear portrayal into the 1980s.[71] Trow reminisces thus:

> Policemen were nice men ... I think it was the friendly comforting face of George Dixon ... with his 'Mind how you go', and his 'Look after dear old Mum' which strengthened the security I felt and made sense of the American conviction that our policemen were indeed wonderful.[72]

Sparks feels that moving away from the 'domestic parables' of Dixon to confronting more complex environments in TV crime fiction is functional: 'Television crime fiction brings retribution into the midst of flux and anxiety. In subordinating complex institutional conflicts to the restoration of natural justice it also offers a certain consolation, as Adorno noted.'[73]

The media as purveyors of fear, consternation and dread: the post-modern spectacle

The inner-city disturbances that occurred during 1981 in the UK brought a new dimension to the mass media's ability to bring the spectacle of riot and disorder directly into viewers' homes.

In his report to the Home office concerning the 'serious disorder in Brixton',[74] Lord Scarman began by commenting on the issue of media spectacle as follows:

> the British people watched with horror and incredulity an instant audio-visual presentation on their television sets of scenes of violence and disorder in their capital city, the like of which had not previously been seen in this century in Britain ... the petrol bomb was now used for the first time on the streets of Britain ... These young people by their criminal behaviour ... brought about a temporary collapse of law and order in the centre of an inner suburb of London.[75]

The significance of this media spectacle was clearly to provide people with eyewitness accounts of more confrontational violence than had ever been seen before. Howard Tumber comments:

> Every day people saw petrol bombs being thrown, fires raging, buildings damaged, and police and youths seriously injured. It was a crisis, and the box in the corner of the room seemed to be bringing the message that civilisation was breaking down and that social order was disintegrating.[76]

Tumber also makes the point that the trivia of local round-up style news programmes were shaken into dealing with a serious analysis of the inner-city phenomenon and providing explanations for what people had witnessed. It was at this point that the sociological tradition vied for position alongside the psychological. The copy-cat factor was a major feature of debates by psychologists. In addition claims were made that more violent television and films had acted as catalysts. Issues of social deprivation, saturation policing and media amplification spirals were contributed by the sociologists, whilst every politician who wanted publicity was able to obtain it by proffering a cause that damned their political opponents.

However, Tumber reasserted that no change had occurred in the debates concerned with potential links between watching television and committing delinquent acts. Far more evidence exists to identify unemployment as a prime factor in delinquent or violent behaviour. He quoted Halloran's conclusion that:

> most of the psychologists, sociologists and criminologists who have taken delinquency as their main topic of research or study do not appear to regard television or any of the other media as a major cause – or even as an important contributing factor to the development of delinquent behaviour.[77]

What was clearly emerging, however, was a concern about the fear of crime. Selective newspaper reporting and television documentaries, fiction, films and videos stood charged with portraying far more violent crimes, usually on women and the elderly, than are statistically likely to occur. For example, Keith Soothill and Sylvia Walby in their study *Sex Crime in the News* comment: 'The regular presence of the sex fiend on the front page is a phenomenon of the 1970s and 1980s.'[78]

They are not objecting to the news coverage of rape, which they see as a positive move, but the *nature* of that coverage that misdirects women to fear primarily 'stranger-danger' rather than attacks by members of their family or by acquaintances.

Fear of crime information was primarily gathered by successive *British Crime Surveys* during the 1980s. These show a very large gap between people's fear of being a victim and their chances of being that victim.[79] This has engendered a new debate about the 'fear of crime' problem and why there should be such a disparity between, for example, what women fear and the so-called 'reality' of those fears:

> Women's fears are seen variously as a knee-jerk reaction to media coverage of crime; a consequence of their physical and social vulnerability; a generalised response to an underlying, illogical fear of rape and sexual assault; or conversely, a rational reflection of the abuse they experience in the privacy of the home.[80]

Media coverage of crime has certainly been shown to play a significant role in generating such fear.

Schlesinger et al. in *Women Viewing Violence*[81] showed that women identify strongly with the dangers of being physically attacked. *Crimewatch UK*, the foremost 'real' crime reconstruction programme on British television, certainly stands accused of contributing significantly to increasing their audience's fear of personal attack.[82] Indeed, the television presenter of *Crimewatch UK* regularly concludes the programme with the advice: 'Don't have nightmares, do sleep well!'[83] However, the spectacle of violent crime which forms the bulk of the programme's content has rendered this a hollow 'catch-phrase' – a parody of concern.

Crimewatch UK signalled a new television spectacle when, from June 1984, it began to alert the viewing public to a range of crimes that they might help the police to solve. By 1990 the programme claimed it was a direct cause of 251 arrests from 686 cases which resulted in 171 convictions.[84] At the same time, its style of dramatic reconstructions has treated the viewing public to a vast number of portrayals of violent acts in the process of its 'crime solving'.

The programme, however, has been at pains to distance itself from both the tabloid press style of crime reporting and TV cop shows, seeing itself in a responsible partnership with the police to solve crimes and achieve natural justice. Its style of portrayal is nevertheless very close to crime fiction portrayal.[85] For example, in 1985 they reported on 'Mr Cool', so named because of his icy calm and well-turned-out appearance whilst carrying out armed robberies. He threatened to kill people but so far had not done so. He was also a kidnapper. Some of the dialogue of the reconstruction where he held an assistant building society manager under threat of violence ran as follows: 'In a minute we're going back round the front. If you try to run away or say anything I may not kill you, but you won't be able to walk again because I'll shoot you in the back.'[86]

Nick Ross and Sue Cook then recount how:

> An actor named Steve Hodson was chosen to play the part of Mr Cool for our film. Not only did he look very much like the description of the robber, but he could also recreate the silky smooth menacing manner almost perfectly. The resemblance was so striking that, as the Abbey National manager and the Flying Squad team waited for Steve to arrive on the day the filming was to begin, Peter Chapman [the building society manager], who was looking out of the window, suddenly froze. 'That's him', he shouted, pointing to the actor. Steve Hodson was delighted he looked the part until detectives jokingly asked him his movements on certain dates since August 1984. He need not have worried. While we were filming in Brentwood, Mr Cool himself was robbing another building society on the other side of London.[87]

Finally the programme detailed the Mr Cool number to ring if viewers had any information to help in the case.

It is an interesting development, however, that through the medium of such programmes the quantity of violent attacks and deaths that one is likely to witness in non-fiction reconstructions are put into context by the presenters thus: 'each monthly *Crimewatch* features more violence than some police officers will encounter in their lifetimes'.[88]

Taking *Crimewatch UK* as 'real-life' construction leads viewers to a paradigmatic confusion in which Mr Cool, *Reservoir Dogs*, the Yorkshire Ripper, football fans and terrorists all occupy the same pathological universe as they themselves inhabit. The fear of crime and the media's reassurance that something is being done constitute a closed world of threat and reinforcement which imprison the viewer.

This truly signals the era of the post-modern spectacle.

Notes and references

1. Quinney, Richard, *Criminology Analysis and Critique of Crime in America* (Boston: Little Brown & Co. Inc., 1975), p. 265.
2. Ross, N. and Cook, S., *Crimewatch UK* (London: Hodder & Stoughton, 1987), pp. 90–7.
3. See Eaton, M., 'A Fair Cop? Viewing the Effects of the Canteen Culture in *Prime Suspect* and *Between The Lines*', Ch. 8 in this volume.
4. Sparks, R., *Television and the Drama of Crime: Moral Tales and the Place of Crime in Public Life* (Buckingham: Open University Press, 1992), pp. 78–98.
5. Young, J., 'The role of the police as amplifiers of deviancy, negotiators of reality and translators of fantasy: Some consequences of our present system of drug control as seen in Notting Hill', in Cohen, S. (ed.) *Images of Deviance* (Harmondsworth: Penguin, 1971); Cohen, S., *Folk Devils and Moral Panics: The Creation of the Mods and Rockers* (London: MacGibbon & Kee, 1972); Cohen, S. and Young, J. (eds), *The Manufacture of News: Deviance, Social Problems and the Mass Media* (London: Constable, 1973); Chibnall, S., *Law and Order News: An Analysis of Crime Reporting in the British Press* (London: Tavistock Publications, 1977); Hall, S., Critcher, C., Jefferson, T., Clarke, J. and Roberts, B., *Policing the Crisis: Mugging, the State and Law and Order* (London: Macmillan, 1978).
6. Cohen, S., 'Footprints on the sand: A further report on criminology and the sociology of deviance in Britain', in Fitzgerald, M. et al., *Crime and Society* (London: Routledge & Kegan Paul, 1981), pp. 220–47.
7. Lemert, E., *Social Pathology* (New York: McGraw-Hill, 1951); Becker, H., *Outsiders: Studies in the Sociology of Deviance* (New York: Free Press, 1963) and Matza, D., *Delinquency and Drift* (New York: Wiley, 1964).
8. Cohen, S., *Folk Devils*
9. Cohen, S. and Young, J. (eds), *The Manufacture of News*.

10. Hall, S. et al., *Policing the Crisis*.
11. Sparks, R., *Television and the Drama of Crime*, p. 65.
12. Young, J., 'The role of the police as amplifiers'.
13. Hall, S. et al., *Policing the Crisis*.
14. Mannheim, H., *Comparative Criminology II* (London: Routledge & Kegan Paul, 1970) pp. 596–7.
15. Chibnall, S., *Law and Order News*, p. 55.
16. Mannheim, H., *Comparative Criminology*, p. 597.
17. Mannheim, H., *Comparative Criminology*, p. 597.
18. Werthem, F., The Seduction of the Innocent (London: Museum Press, 1955).
19. Barker, M., *A Haunt of Fears* (London: Pluto Press, 1984).
20. Mannheim, H., *Comparative Criminology*, pp. 600–5.
21. Mannheim, H., *Comparative Criminology*, p. 601.
22. Mannheim, H., *Comparative Criminology*, p. 603.
23. Kinsey, R., Lea, J. and Young, J., *Losing the Fight against Crime* (London: Basil Blackwell, 1986) p. 37.
24. Possibly the most famous case is that of Orson Welles' presentation of H.G. Wells' *War of the Worlds* on American radio in 1938. This panicked a significant proportion of the population into a belief that invaders from Mars had landed in the US.
25. Chibnall, S., *Law and Order*, p. 55.
26. Quinney, R., *Criminology*, p. 4. See also Quinney, R., 'There's a lot of folks grateful to the Lone Ranger: With some notes on the rise and fall of American criminology', *The Insurgent Sociologist*, 4, Fall 1973, pp. 56–64.
27. Burt, C., *The Young Delinquent* (London: University of London Press, 1925).
28. Burt, C., *The Young Delinquent*, p. 144.
29. Burt, C., *The Young Delinquent*, p. 144.
30. Burt, C., *The Young Delinquent*, p. 145.
31. Bailey, S., 'Fast forward to violence: Violent visual imaging and serious juvenile crime', *Criminal Justice Matters*, 11, Spring 1993, pp. 6–7.
32. Medved, M., *Hollywood vs America: Popular Culture and the War on Traditional Values* (New York: HarperCollins, 1992).
33. Bailey, S., 'Fast foward to violence', p. 7.
34. Burt, C., *The Young Delinquent*, p. 148.
35. Lawrence, C., 'The Arts: Our worst nightmare', the *Daily Telegraph*, 28 October 1994.
36. Lawrence, C., 'The Arts'.
37. Carey, S., 'Mass media violence and aggressive behaviour', *Criminal Justice Matters*, 11, Spring 1993, p. 8.
38. Bragg, M., BBC2 *The Late Show* Mori Poll, May 1994.
39. Newson, E., BBC2 *The Late Show*, June 1994.
40. Halloran, J.D., 'Mass communication: Symptom or cause of violence', *International Social Science Journal*, XXX, 4, 1978, p. 827.
41. Bandura, A., *Aggression: A Social Learning Analysis* (Englewood Cliffs, NJ: Prentice-Hall, 1973), p. 64.

42. Schramm, W., Lyle, J. and Parker, E., *Television in the Lives of our Children* (Oxford University Press, 1961), quoted by S. Carey, 'Mass media violence', p. 9.
43. Hall, S. et al., *Policing the Crisis*, p. 118.
44. The *Sunday Times*, 5 February 1995, p. 2.
45. The *Sunday Times*, 5 February 1995.
46. The *Sunday Times*, 5 February 1995.
47. Pearson, G., *Hooligan: A History of Respectable Fears* (London: Macmillan, 1983) and Chibnall, S., *Law and Order News*.
48. Taylor, I., Walton, Paul and Young, J., *The New Criminology: For a Social Theory of Deviance* (London: Routledge & Kegan Paul, 1973).
49. Cohen, S. (ed.), *Images of Deviance*, p. 9.
50. Cohen, S., 'Footprints', p. 221.
51. Young, J., 'The role of the police'.
52. Young, J., 'The role of the police', p. 28.
53. Quoted in Young, J., 'The role of the police', pp. 35–6.
54. Cohen, S., *Folk Devils*.
55. Muncie, J., *The Trouble with Kids Today: Youth and Crime in Post-war Britain* (London: Hutchinson, 1984), p. 2.
56. Cohen, S., *Folk Devils*, p. 46.
57. Cohen, S., *Folk Devils*, p. 172.
58. Cohen, S. and Young, J. (eds), *The Manufacture of News*.
59. Cohen, S. and Young, J. (eds), *The Manufacture of News*, p. 15.
60. Cohen, S. and Young, J. (eds), *The Manufacture of News*, p. 339.
61. Chibnall, S., *Law and Order*.
62. Chibnall, S., *Law and Order*, p. 23.
63. Chibnall, S., *Law and Order*, p. 77.
64. Hall, S. et al., *Policing the Crisis*.
65. Hall, S. et al., *Policing the Crisis*, p. 21.
66. Hall, S. et al., *Policing the Crisis*, p. 23.
67. Muncie, J., *The Trouble*, p. 82.
68. Hall, S. et al., *Policing the Crisis*, p. 395.
69. Hall, S. et al., *Policing the Crisis*, p. 395.
70. The *Daily Mail*, 3 March 1992, p. 15.
71. Centre for Research on Criminal Justice, *The Iron Fist and the Velvet Glove* (California: CRCJ, 2nd edn 1977).
72. Trow, M.J., *Let Him Have It, Chris: The murder of Derek Bentley* (London: HarperCollins, 1992), p. 82.
73. Sparks, R., *Television and the Drama of Crime*, p. 29.
74. Lord Scarman, *The Scarman Report: The Brixton disorders 10–12 April 1981* (Harmondsworth: Penguin, 1982), pp. 13–14.
75. Lord Scarman, *The Scarman Report*.
76. Tumber, H., *Television and the Riots* (London: British Film Institute, 1982), p. 43.
77. Tumber, H., *Television and the Riots*, pp. 48–9.
78. Soothill, K. and Walby, Sylvia, *Sex Crime in the News* (London: Routledge, 1991), p. 156.
79. HMSO: *British Crime Surveys*, 1982, 1984 and 1988.

80. Painter, K., 'The "Facts" of Fear', *Criminal Justice Matters*, 19, Spring 1995, p. 25.
81. Schlesinger, P. et al., *Women Viewing Violence* (London: British Film Institute, 1992).
82. Schlesinger, P. and Tumber, H., '"Don't have nightmares: Do sleep well!"', *Criminal Justice Matters*, 11, Spring 1993, p. 4. See also Schlesinger, P. and Tumber, H., *Reporting Crime: The Media Politics of Criminal Justice* (Oxford: Clarendon Press, 1994).
83. Ross, N. and Cook, S., *Crimewatch UK*, p. 158.
84. Schlesinger, P. and Tumber, H., '"Don't Have Nightmares"' p. 4.
85. Schlesinger, P. and Tumber, H., 'Fighting the war against crime: Television, police and audience', *British Journal of Criminology*, 33, 1, Winter 1993, pp. 19–32.
86. Ross, N. and Cook, S., *Crimewatch UK*, p. 97.
87. Ross, N. and Cook, S., *Crimewatch UK*, p. 97.
88. Ross, N. and Cook, S., *Crimewatch UK*, p. 158.

2 Crime and the Media: From Media Studies to Post-modernism

Richard Osborne

One of the wonders of the electronic age: robbing a bank without leaving home.

Taylor and Saarinen.

Post-modernism is the form in which advertising has taken over the whole of our culture in reverse; knowledge, art and literature have become means of selling us ourselves instead of illuminating our condition. Intellectuals sell post-modernism to the academy and themselves to the media.

Richard Osborne

Crime and media reporting

The historical problems of crime reporting and images of crime, in print and electronic media, have always been seen as minor questions on the fringes of other disciplines, an addendum to the mainstream concerns of established academic discourses. Until recently the central reality of crime and its reporting were taken for granted within stable, democratic capitalist societies, where crime was conceived as outside the moral limits of the ordinary, which meant that crime reporting was unproblematic, moralistic and unifying in its agreed disapproval. Throughout the 1960s and 1970s a radical criminology grew up which was critical of this consensus but, in the main, criminology and media studies accepted the intellectual status quo in relation to crime reporting and only with *The Manufacture of News* (1973) and later *Policing the Crisis* (1978) did a critical paradigm for considering crime and the media emerge.[1] As we enter the era of an image-saturated society in which all knowledge and culture are supposedly created in the media, theoretical debate has not kept up with the transitions. Furthermore it is clear that most discussion of crime and criminology, even if it is 'new' criminology, is gendered in its universalising assumptions about the order of social reality. The crisis of crime that besets the western world, both as a sociological phenomenon,

25

and as a media-televised state of fear, it is argued, is inherently masculine in its origins and definitions. In her study of decaying inner cities and the crime waves that accompany the slide into structural unemployment and transitions in gender roles in Britain, Beatrix Campbell argues that: 'The crisis of crime as a crisis of masculinity was an equation that was evaded in the great debates about crime and the community in the eighties and nineties.'[2]

Criminology has not really taken the questions of either gender or the mass media on board however and, for example, one recent widely used American introduction to criminology, *Crime and Everyday Life*, does not have even a subheading on the mass media or on gender. *Crime and Society*, a standard Open University criminology textbook, likewise has no serious discussion of crime and the mass media.[3] For criminology the concern is with the causes of, and measures to alleviate, crime. Classical criminology and positivism have proved supremely unable to deal with the post-1970s implosion of criminality, popular culture and media transformation. Media studies, when not concerned with the hoary old question of ownership, has been too interested in theoretical concerns with image, symbol, narrative and representation to look at basic problems like 'real-life' crime reporting. In the endless debates about media effects it has been violence which has occupied the central ground rather than any other sort of crime, thereby obscuring any serious analysis about the representation of crime. Whilst much of media studies has worried about the effects of television on 'mass' or 'post-modern society' little attention has been paid to the steady growth of a media discourse about criminality. Given that crime in advanced capitalist countries is now a major problem, if not spiralling out of control and, in America in particular, violent crime is rampant, it seems odd that media studies has so comprehensively ignored the topic.[4] Whilst media studies is always aware of the debate about the social construction of news and reality, and the persuasiveness of mass media, it has avoided the theoretically messy problem of analysing representations of crime because it brings to the fore that relationship of image to reality (or referent) that it is now impolite to mention in post-modern circles. Media studies has discovered a fear of crime, particularly in relation to women and violence, and has discussed crime as entertainment on television but it has not developed any particular tools for thinking these relationships. Too much media studies is text and narrative bound and accepts the post-modern elision of representation and reality without a flicker of empirical resistance. (Indeed, the existence of a theoretical object 'post-modern society' is somewhat uncritically accepted as well, but here we can only consider the effects of such an acceptance, not analyse the epistemological status of such an abject.)

At the same time the old criminological concerns with the causes and consequences of crime have been broken down by the fragmentation of societies, by the effects of the fear of crime, by drug wars which themselves invade the social fabric at all levels and by the seeming inability of any governments to control social, or national, developments. It is not an exaggeration to speak of a crisis in criminology. Suddenly the question for criminology is what it means to be caught up in this post-modern maelstrom of perpetual disintegration and renewal, of fragmentation and fear, of struggle and contradiction and of seemingly random violence and criminality at all levels of society. The simple definition of crime as wrongdoing is in disarray, particularly in relation to the powerful and to the political classes. As we know all definitions of crime are simply socially constructed norms and realities enforced by symbolic and legal powers; as those social norms disintegrate before our eyes it is little wonder criminology finds itself in the dock.[5] The criminalisation of the poor in Britain and in America, the refusal of sociological critiques of neo-conservative antistate policies and the inherent individualism of much criminology has led to a situation in which criminology seems to have little to say about a complex transformation in the social definitions of crime and criminality.

The response to what is a crisis in the discipline has been that criminology and social studies have recently produced the notion of the 'under-class' in an attempt to deal with the theoretical complexity of post-modern society and to shore up the crumbling intellectual edifice of normative analysis. Where the outsider criminal would have stood as the folk devil in media stereotypes of the 1960s and 1970s now whole sections of society have had to be symbolically expelled in order to maintain a normative model of society. This exclusion can be seen as a necessary repression at the symbolic level in order to sustain the myth of a rational society, but it makes a nonsense of critical theory, rehabilitation, equality or media objectivity. In fact crime is the great unifier in making everyone a victim and all viewers equal in their potential victimness, but the 'under-class' are criminology's answer to the real fragmentation it cannot think within classical paradigms. Put another way media discourses about crime now constitute all viewers as equally subject to the fragmented and random danger of criminality, and in so doing provide the preconditions for endless narratives of criminality that rehearse this everpresent danger. What makes criminality the perfect metaphor for post-modernism is precisely the way that media narratives encode crime and disorder as the representation of fragmentation rendered coherent, which is perversion made popular as control. The appeal of crime narratives, the insecure security they generate through fear and pleasure, counterpoints the fear of the 'under-classes' that stalks most of popular culture, the old mob disguised as 'joy riders', 'drug dealers', 'football holigans' and the rest. The crisis of the family, of social authority, of employment and education all find their expression in the pathology of crime and the media, in the state of mediachosis that seems to infest post-modern society.

Baudrillard notoriously defines post-modern society as one in which the image–reality–representation problematic is no longer in operation, as we know reality is now hyperreal, we live in an age of the simulacrum. Image and reality are somehow as one and the distinction between what the media shows, and the reality it represents, is collapsed, or imploded into a one-dimensional universe which is image saturated and simultaneously freefloating and authentically unreal. Like cybertech theory these theoretical positions so presuppose their own freefloating conditions of existence that they cannot be understood except in their own terms, as descriptive states of an alienated intelligentsia that no longer wants to think its own material conditions of existence. It is a theory for the age of television which refuses external realities in much the same way that television discourse ultimately does, its own technological complexity makes possible a reality at a second remove which makes self-referentiality not only attractive but logically necessary. The hyperreal merely refers to the cycle of the production and consumption of images in which viewers become as expert as producers at thinking in images and learn an unconscious structure of signifying practices which allows them to negotiate narrative as self-identity. Unfortunately the real often reappears as crime and it is as the victim of crime that the viewer renegotiates the hyperreal as real-life reconstruction. It is this, not simply the loss of meaning, that can often produce the melancholy that Baudrillard ascribes to post-modern systems: 'Melancholy is the fundamental tonality of functional systems, of the present systems of simulation, programming and information. Melancholy is the quality inherent in the mode of disappearance of meaning, in the mode of volatization of meaning in operational systems.'[6]

Baudrillard brilliantly captures the nihilistic mood of post-modern times but his notions of the simulacrum are rather reminiscent of Macavity: the Mystery Cat, 'For when they reach the scene of crime – *Macavity's not there!*'[7] Confronted with the globalised concentration of real economic and media power that satellite systems represent, post-modern theory is simply not there when it comes to explanatory power. Power relations and economic systems have certainly shifted in the last two decades but media cyberpower is not a substitute for an analysis of real material conditions of existence, and the crime that may be a consequence of them. Unemployment, for example, is rather more freefloating than most of its practitioners would prefer and as a material constraint often conjoins with the reality of crime to make redundant notions of consumerism and spectacle. Criminality is a real choice in a world where power systems have not disappeared but have dispossessed many of any access to either the image or the reality of citizenship. This is the other side of the dialectic of post-modern development in which technology has replaced labour on a globalised scale and television viewing has replaced work as a defining condition of being.

Academic culture is never particularly interested in the complexities of the ordinary or in the pressures of popular culture on its own discourses but the wider culture itself is obsessed with a film like Oliver Stone's *Natural Born Killers*, which is commonly assumed to have caused direct copy-cat murders and to glorify the sort of screen violence it supposedly sets out to expose and denounce.[8] Ironically Oliver Stone himself berated both the media and intellectuals in general whilst busily promoting his film and discussing on TV chat shows the kind of popular culture it portrays. Popular culture is undoubtedly obsessed with crime, and particularly violent crime, and television has developed this obsession with the forbidden into endless narrative strategies whose unconscious attraction to the viewer is a critical question in this area. There is something obsessive in the media's, and the viewers', love of such narratives, an hysterical replaying of the possibility of being a victim and staving it off. An analysis of this obsessionality demands a critical psychoanalytic as well as cultural understanding, however, so that without a theory of the subject there cannot be a theory of the viewer. The culture of narcissism has also become a culture of talk-show shock-horror that parades endless deviance as entertainment, the personal as magnified and fragmented repetition.

It is a perversely post-modern question as to why crime is so popular, so threatening and so entertaining all at once, and why television and other media never tire of every aspect of crime reporting and reconstruction. The further question has to be why the pace of integration of different facets of crime representation is so rapid and why an air of inexorable and fascinated fatalism enfolds all presentation of crime, from murder to drugs. Historically perhaps it was Mario Puzo's *The Godfather* which began the development of endless interplay between real-life crime and media crime, the sort of intertextuality that led

Frank Sinatra to threaten Puzo with libel charges over the portrayal of a singer in the book and the Mafia to congratulate Puzo on his portrayal of them. Puzo, in a properly post-modern moment, claims not to have known anything about the Mafia and to have dreamt up the idea in a supermarket.[9]

The kind of best seller that *The Godfather* became is indicative of the developments that brought us the post-modern spectacle; it began as a fairly standard book and transformed into a multimedia spectacle that ended up redefining popular culture's view of the Mafia and organised crime. *The Godfather* film also did much to strengthen already existing stereotypes about the Mafia, the Italian 'family' and corrupt political systems, a parody of the straight world that has been replayed as farce in Berlusconi's Italy. As Hegel would undoubtedly have said 'All that is real is on television.'

The O.J. Simpson trial has also clearly demonstrated that the worlds of television, news, entertainment and criminal justice have now all inter-penetrated one another to the extent that the actions of the media are themselves cited as legal grounds within a murder trial. At the same time the whole jury has had to be incarcerated in a place of safety where the media supposedly cannot influence them. This has not stopped at least two jurors from being disbarred for trying to make money from the trial, one for secretly writing a book about the trial.[10] The two Amercian stations that run live coverage of the trial, CNN and Court TV, have reported huge increases in viewing figures, publishing books about the trial is already an industry in its own right and spin-off merchandising is estimated to be worth $200m.[11] This kind of activity is richly symbolic of the way in which the criminal justice system has become a hostage to the global media systems which devour deviance as a prime element in the infotainment business, and do so through indi-viduals bringing to them the commodity of crime narratives. Understanding these systems of meaning and systems of commerce in which crime stories are a commodity is the problem that delineates the debate about how crime is understood and responded to within post-modern society. Tracing the historical development from mere moral panics to live media criminal spectacle and media-generated justice is the primary task of this debate.

Crime has moved from being a subspecies of tabloid journalism to the very heart of our electronic media culture and there it more and more centrally generates narratives about our social order and social pathology. Whilst the media can be seen as a system that produces social conformity in delimiting what is acceptable and unacceptable behaviour, its current representations of crime interestingly produce dysfunctional imagery in its search for crime drama and dramatic crime. Although the 'normal' functioning of society is taken for granted in the media, crime has become one of the overarching metaphors of the real social crisis that besets advanced capitalist countries and one of the deepest forms of social neurosis that infests post-modern cultures. In reinforcing the hysteria that exists in popular culture about crime, by redeploying the police stereotypes of crime and criminals, this media amplification appears to have reached critical mass, to be ready to implode into the fear society that is slowly emerging in the US. We live in what some criminologists call, with a penchant for the obvious, a 'risk society' in which crime is controlled, or attempted to be controlled, through negative, rational and oppressive means, which often include a greater role for criminologists. Or as Beck puts it: 'Social integration is enhanced through a communality of fear which joins the communality of need as a socially binding force and basis of solidarity.'[12]

Alongside the themes of the 'under-class' in media representations there is always the problem of identity and race, the threat of the other; from Puerto Ricans to blacks the subliminal images of threat and violence were all aired during the Los Angeles riots, and often on live TV. The stereotypical association of young black men with crime and violence is well enough documented and runs through crime fiction narratives as well as news reporting. This deeprooted phobia was mobilised in the defence of the police who were videoed beating Rodney King: they felt threatened by him as he lay on the floor and thus, despite the 'real-life' video evidence, they were acquitted. The actual image and its signifying power conflicted with predetermined images and structures of feeling. Image and representation are linked to patterns of cultural framing that systematically encode certain power and social relationships, crime representations tend to reinforce those reactionary cultural devices whatever the 'objectivity' of the image. Reactions to crime representations are deeply irrational and that is what makes the media's love of crime so dangerous. The fear of crime, and the cynicism that underlies the crime-fest in the media breeds depoliticisation, fatalism and a further erosion of the public sphere and repressive surveillance of the 'under-classes'.

Unwittingly perhaps Oliver Stone in *Natural Born Killers* has touched upon this nodal point of post-modern anomie and ignited the complex issues which are posed in the real-life murders of Nicole Brown Simpson and Ronald Goldman, and the subsequent media trial. Significantly, and semiotically, the real corpses in this trial pose deep problems for theorists of the hyperreal and the post-modern and however much one talks about the freefloating imagery of spectacle there is always a last instance in which there is a corpse and a crime. This return of the real may well be undermined in this case however as O.J. Simpson may eventually be found innocent because of his media immortality, a fact which further problematises the whole sociological understanding of crime and the media. The symbolic and imaginary power of a media superstar cannot be underestimated and the infamous live broadcast of O.J. cruising down a highway with innumerable police cars in pursuit only reinforces the psychological difference such personalities invoke. O.J. Simpson's existence as a media superstar may well outweigh the facts that are assembled against him in that his media after-image can quite legitimately be used as evidence that he cannot be guaranteed a fair trial.

This dialectic between 'real' crime and media representations of crime is one that constantly undermines complacent sociological and criminological descriptions of present social realities and constantly drags one's attention back to the hyperreal. The recent spectacular collapse of Britain's Barings Bank, on the back of a virtual reality disaster in theoretical derivatives, further emphasises the electronic media's obsessions and its active role in creating crime stories. Before any evidence was to hand the world's electronic media had created the story of Nick Leeson, the man who broke the bank of Barings. The story had all the relevant aspects of a best seller — rags to riches, royalty, rich people, crime and exotic locations; it will undoubtedly be a best-selling book. The fact that other individuals could have been involved has little effect on the media's crime story; once it enters the popular cultural lexicon, mere facts cannot hope to compete. This best-selling intertextuality is the very narrative nub of the post-modern crime and media debate and the infotainment value of almost any story is what produces the inevitable elision of reporting and entertainment. Television news over the last decade has steadily moved towards the entertainment format, despite its 'live footage' and 'hard news', and crime news, including terrorism, has all of the newsworthiness that such programmes demand. We know that half of all news on the electronic media is crime news, and that the agenda by which it is reported and understood is a restricted and stereotyped one, and that that predominance is also seen in entertainment programmes.[13]

The economic and symbolic power of the media obviously constrain and delimit the kinds of crime that are portrayed and discussed within the media agenda and that agenda is itself the key issue in theorising crime and the media. In television's endless search for profitable narratives, real-life reconstructions of crime come high on the list of post-modern possibilities. Live footage and real-life reconstructions are actually very cheap television and one does not have to be a Marxist to see the invisible hand of the economy driving the telemarket towards ever more technology-led downmarket broadcasting. The live televising of trials is only the most recent development in the crime/media nexus, followed by 'live' arrests, 'live' documentaries of the police in action and the ultimate spectacle, which has already been suggested, will have to be live executions on TV. The chat show programmes that have suggested this would then naturally have discussions with the members of the family and victims to draw out the symbolic electronic justice.

This normalised surrealism of 'real crime' television points then to the complexities of attempting to theorise the relationship between criminal justice and the media, made all the more difficult by the fact that both are systems of power and social definition which are central to our post-modern societies as well as being institutions of great power with historically antagonistic aims. The criminal justice system seeks to preserve a discourse which produces truths and final judgements of facts whilst the mass media, and particularly television, seek to endlessly reproduce, redraw and redefine social reality as flux, as a never-ending narrative of possibility and infotainment. The mass media are commercially oriented information systems to whom audiences are a life blood, the criminal justice system operates as the last bastion of Enlightenment rationality attempting to hold the symbolic universe of statehood in balance. It is a fundamental question of the crime and media debate as to whether the symbolic power of the media has, in complicated and little understood ways, undermined the criminal justice system to the point where it precisely only functions as a pastiche of its former self.

The O.J. Simpson trial will in many ways answer this question. There will be many books, and films, discussing the trial but the central question will remain: whether O.J. Simpson will be judged as a citizen or as a demigod of the media universe to whom other laws apply. The defence lawyers in the case, as befits a post-modern trial, are far more interested in mobilising certain popular cultural narratives about race and success than in addressing the question of evidence. Indeed the doubt they are attempting to create is properly post-modern in the sense that they are disputing the existence, or the possibility, of a legal metanarrative which can explain the causes and timing of the murder. This is just one possible narrative meaning of many they are suggesting: perhaps the Mafia did it, perhaps it was Tarantino making a film and going too far, perhaps Nicole Simpson Brown staged it to get attention and injure O.J., perhaps a racist policeman planted the evidence out of envy of a black superstar. The seeds of doubt that the lawyers so carefully plant are reared in the social unconscious of popular culture which the media so carefully nourish in their re-creation of reality as a multiple narrative, the segmented flow of soap opera possibility. The seriousness that once attended the courts is in real danger of being eroded by the infotainment values of television culture. That in itself is a philosophical problem about the forms of social discourse that circulate in the postmodern world, cynicism and shallowness do not allow for any form of authoritative argument that carries a charisma based on intellectual, or rational, discourse, everyone is an expert, the will of the people is expressed by the (other) Simpson family. Post-modernism's will to power is a populism in which all individual desires and fears, however much they are reflections of dominant media narratives, are taken as legitimate grounds for political stances.

The endless media speculation about the O.J. Simpson trial, its defining as a kind of Perry Mason shoot-out between the main lawyers, reduces it to a soap opera, an imaginary community the viewers can identify with and take sides over. Whatever the legal verdict, there will be an ongoing struggle over media definitions of the events, which Simpson can influence and, like Kennedy's assassination, it will enter the popular consciousness as myth and conspiracy, two other key elements in post-modern consciousness. Like the Frederick West case in Britain, the 'house of horror' murders, and the Jeffry Dahmer serial killer case, the elements of horror, murder, celebrity, sex and perversion transpose the case from routine criminal justice to post-modern spectacle. Compare the media treatment of O.J. with the fact that in the Miami 11th court circuit over 100,000 suspects have had their cases tried whilst standing on a podium inside a prison and linked by video to the court room, justice seen to be done only by electronic distance.[14] Criminal justice struggles to exert itself as a defining power but the symbolic power of the media overturns, or obliterates, the moments of closure that the courts attempt to enforce. There is a huge movement proclaiming O.J.'s innocence, as though the legal trial really is just another form of truth, another potential discourse, identified with the power elite and the political classes.

The conflicts between the criminal justice systems and the media are only recently being addressed and academic discourse, constructed as it is in discrete departmental frameworks, has great difficulty faced with such a critical and interdisciplinary task. More than any other topic crime and the media demand a breakdown of the historical and philosophical divisions between disciplines. Academia's objectivity, its metanarratives of reason and neutrality, are as much under attack as the state's and the legal system's ability to define proper and improper behaviour. As Foucault puts it when discussing the intellectual make-up, or episteme, of the post-modern world:

> Hence the frequent difficulty in fixing limits, not merely between the objects, but also between the methods proper to psychology, sociology, and the analysis of literature and myth … In this way all of the human sciences inter-lock and can always be used to interpret one another: their frontiers become blurred, intermediary and composite disciplines multiply endlessly, and in the end their proper object may even disappear altogether.[15]

The fragmentation of criminology has more or less reached a critical stage since criminality is more and more seen as a 'tactic of subjection', a means of political control, of policing the 'under-class' and of excluding aliens and attempting to defend mythical identities aginst a corrupted world. The role of the media in this redefining of representations of the world, of creating a popular culture which polices the social unconscious and installs paranoia in its images of post-modern society, renders criminological approaches impotent, except to describe a failing criminal justice system's attempts to regulate and contain the unregulatable. One of the few clear statistics in criminal reporting shows that the favourite target of most burglaries is televisions and videos, and it is here that criminology and media studies find their meeting point. This coalescence requires a sociology of the spectacular society in which the medium is no longer the message but the means of barter in a disenfranchised electronic age where the owners of TV stations become presidents and post-communist Mafiosi murder the presidents of TV stations because they take off advertising.[16] Power, crime and economic reorganisation feed the development of the electronic media in an era of deregulation and it is the speed and depth of all these changes that produce the global symbiosis of fear and fascination in the viewer confronted by a world seemingly out of control, and of crime levels that make domestic viewing seem like the safest vantage point.

It is not too much to suggest that the burgeoning symbiosis between crime and the media redefines the social–psychological understanding of 'law and order' and more importantly of its function of social control. The pace of technological development, the globilisation of media systems and the accompanying transformation of civil society into what is fundamentally a televisual society have shifted the moral universe, our sense of self and the criminal justice system's ability to symbolically uphold the image of a coherent, controlling society. Put in terms of criminology itself Morrison argues that: 'Modernist criminology worked from the metaphysics of totalities, whether the "one" of the social contract, or the "one" of nature; post-modern criminology must live in the meta-physics of difference, plurality, multiplicity.'[17]

The basic question in terms of the post-modern media is precisely how does the reorganisation and global structure, the process of media production and consumption, shape and utilise crime as a constitutive part of its business, which is to sell media products and to gather and hold media audiences? Furthermore how does the fragmentation of social experience interface with the globilisation and harmonisation of that media production and consumption, what is the nature of the viewer/consumer relationship to crime and its representations?

Understanding the construction of news making requires an examination of the conscious and unconscious processes involved in the mass dissemination of symbolic goods. Crime for example is clearly a many layered signifying process, one that lies at the heart of our popular cultural functioning, and so is intertwined both with the state, at its highest level, and with individual fears and fantasies at the other extreme. Crime is a signifier of immense power, flexibility, fascination and eroticism. From Agatha Christie novels to *Miami Vice*, from the news to *Pulp Fiction*, narratives about crime and deviance flourish as never before. Decoding this metanarrative of disloyalty to normalcy is one of the keys to unlocking the mystery of post-modern culture and its discontents. As television replaces religion, and what religion there is is televised, it is not surprising that the moral order has to be re-presented in a form that post-modern viewers can understand: detective stories, murder mysteries, real-life crime reconstructions and now, priests-cum-detectives.[18] What Raymond Williams meant by the 'structure of feeling' of an age can clearly be seen in this age as a pathology of criminality and cynicism that is mediated by the electronic media and endlessly reinforced by all kinds of cultural manifestations from *Terminator* to the 'three strikes' policy of new age California.[19]

This general discussion of the shifts in the form and presentation of crime in the mass media, and particularly television, leads to a number of theoretical questions that need to be addressed in terms of the relationships between crime and the media. The most fundamental is whether or not we are entering, or have entered, a media spiral in which the representations of crime and the fear of crime precisely constitute that sphere which has been designated the hyperreal. Here crime as entertainment is as important as 'real-life' crime since the fusion of modes of decoding the two seem to have overcome the binary oppostions that once structured viewers' perceptions. Has the media left behind any possibility of a rational discussion of crime in its endless search for hard copy, narrative excitement and moral panics about what to do about crime?

Is fear and reaction the only possible exit from this competitive frenzy of televised disorder? Is the post-modern viewer in a state of mediachosis, an hysterical, disordered state in which media manifestations and narratives provide a self-referential, and irrational, world view based on paranoia, cynicism and crime? Is the media precisely a means of transcending reality rather than confronting it, and is its symbolic policing of the popular unconscious a recipe for the disintegration of meaningful culture based on human interaction? Or, as one American writer put it:

> The ritual of crime and punishment has become America's great reality avoidance mechanism, its all sufficient substitute for knowledge and thought: let a scapegoat be found, let a culprit be punished, and the public relaxes, confident that the crisis has been surmounted.[20]

Everywhere in modern capitalist countries the power of the commercial mass media becomes ever greater in defining what is significant and access to these primary defining systems is more and more limited by the criteria by which those systems operate. The questions posed by this nascent, if not already existing, reality of media dominance cover every aspect of crime and the criminal justice system. Schematically we can look at some of the areas that need to be developed in an analysis of crime and the media.

Crime and the fear of crime

The rise of a generalised fear of crime has been well enough documented and the questions that stem from it concern almost every aspect of postmodern culture. Is this fear of crime sufficient to produce a state we can designate 'mediachosis', a morbid pathology of insecurity that determines almost all of the viewer's behaviour? Mediachosis can be characterised as

> a state of consciousness characterised by unconscious acceptance of electronically transmitted modes of perception and thought. A state of being in which cynicism, mistrust and paranoia predominate and in which the media, rather than other human institutions, provide acquired cultural perceptions.[21]

The real fear that socialisation is being performed by the media rather than the family has a long lineage but the present state of depoliticised media culture, and its outcomes in social terms, make that argument compelling. The fear of crime appears to drive much of the decline of the public sphere, the ever-increasing surveillance of public space, the easy acceptance of ever more stringent law and order policies and the return of the death penalty and other retributive measures. The fear of crime can be shown in many instances to be irrational but television's power to create an overpowering cultural imagery can be shown to supplant statistical evidence with ease. Fear is both a form of political control and a marketing technique for neo-conservative politics, as well as both a means of selling crime surveillence technology and services. The feeling that the world is out of control, threatening and dangerous is replayed in much popular culture, from *RoboCop* to *Natural Born Killers* and Pat Buchanan's speeches. It seems: 'We are at the mercy of irrational forces, of deranged sex and drug crazed criminals ... Call the Police!'[22]

How we can measure and analyse these socio-pathological effects of the fear of crime and also assess the connection between fear and actual assessments of the risk of crime and public behaviour are key questions to develop. The distortive effect of these fears on popular culture and, more importantly, politics, also needs careful consideration. Ultimately the debate also centres on the post-modern contention that the media is, as it were, all there is, there is supposedly no other to distance the media created world from. Leaving that philosophical question aside for the time being we can consider some of the areas in which redefinitions of crime and the media operate.

Real-life crime and entertainment

The development during the last two decades of 'real-life' crime reconstruction is a very significant area, particularly in terms of the fear of crime. In discussion of the media's ability to create social realities it is obvious that an endless diet of reconstructions of serious crime conveys only one message, that the world is out of control and is threatening. In Britain it was *Crimewatch UK* that introduced this monthly diet of mayhem and fear. Amongst others in America are *Hard-Copy* and *America's Most Wanted*, which make *Crimewatch UK* seem restrained and which mix live footage with recreations of actual, often gruesome, events. The most recent programme *Caught in Camera* is simply videos of accidents and disasters. Perhaps the defining moment of post-modern consciousness is now the car accident, where technology meets the hyperreal, and is then replayed as a video clip. There are fundamental questions here of sensationalism, exaggeration, commercial motivation, viewer identification and the construction of a pathological world-view. Some criminals may well be caught as a result of these programmes, but measuring how many would be caught anyway, or how other sorts of crimes than those presented proliferate, and what other effects the programmes have also need to be considered. The selectivity of these programmes, the agenda they adopt and set, the kinds of media messages they generate all point towards an analysis which suggests that they are creating a popular culture of cynicism and despair, mixed with a neo-fascistic longing for order and retribution. The wider question of the effects of these 'news'-type programmes requires detailed empirical analysis as well as theoretical debate, as does the question of the general perception of the crime enforcement agencies which these sorts of programmes reinforce. The police themselves have moved into a major public relations mode in these kinds of programmes, realising that unless they control the flow of information about crime their social function itself could be under threat, the fear of crime has to be channelled at criminals rather than those theoretically responsible for controlling them. In Britain there was a period when major miscarriages of justice seemed to occur every day and the image of the police was seriously eroded. Although they have recovered somewhat from this the dominant perception of the police has shifted from the traditional total respect accorded to them, particularly amongst ethnic minorities, but the media portrayals of the police are still overwhelming positive, from *Inspector Morse* to *The Bill*. The fear of crime is greater than the fear of an inadequate police force and as long as the police can win the media war through programmes like *Crimewatch UK* their control of the news flow is guaranteed. In other words they have a vested interest in maintaining the fear of crime, as does every neo-conservative politician who needs to swing an alienated electorate behind punitive and retributive political measures.

Violence and the media

This is the single most debated question raised endlessly by effects research which is, of course, inconclusive because of the empiricist approach adopted. How does the presentation of violence in the media affect the behaviour of viewers in the 'real' world? The question is hopelessly muddied because the perception of violence is so overwhelming that discussion of the real levels of violence are both so complicated and comparative they have little purchase on either popular culture or policy making. Popular culture is awash with stylised, brutal, vacuous and often entertaining violence. Murder, and especially serial murderers, preoccupy the media. It is the single most newsworthy kind of crime, simple to understand, endlessly different in its permutations and often ordinary in its gruesomeness. Murder is also the main fodder of crime/detective shows, as well as novels, comics, films and any other variation of narrative strategy that the media can invent. Freud may have ascribed this fascination to the death wish he claimed to have discovered in all human culture but, whatever the deep psychological reason, we know that it is a necessary leitmotif in all crime presentation. The popularity of serial killers signals the kind of cultural pathology we are discussing, it is as though they are the anti-heroes, for they are always men, of our era. Perversion, bloodlust and insanity sell media narratives and *The Silence of the Lambs* seems to have arrived at the perfect formula, a cultivated pyschopath who eats his victims and charms his captors.

Copy-cat violence

From *A Clockwork Orange* to *Natural Born Killers* it has constantly been claimed that violence in the media generates violence in viewers and, in particular, the direct imitation of specific acts of violence or specific crimes, like kidnap or murder. Despite massive media coverage of incidents like the murder of James Bulger and the supposed influence of the *Child's Play* video on the children there is no hard evidence to support such theories.[23] However, the cumulative effect of television watching, of acquiring a culture through the mass media has not yet been properly analysed or thought through. In part this is because the present generation of children are actually the first to live in a total media environment in which large-scale electronic media consumption is the norm. The question of how one proves a copy-cat effect, rather than a predisposition to crime in any case, is rarely discussed, nor is the question of how the media supposedly provoke criminality in general, despite this being a commonly asserted cliche. As Surrette puts it : 'Once more in regard to crime, the mass media are seen taking the rare real world event and making it the more significant, better-known event in the public's perception.'[24]

Clearly the media does affect crime perceptions in many ways, but the concentration on violence obscures both possible positive effects, perhaps cathartic, and more complex effects such as the creation of a long-term world view, or mediachosis. In relation to copy-cat effects Surrette concludes:

> The evidence concerning the media as a crimogenic factor clearly supports the conclusion that the media have a significant short-term effect on some individuals. As shown the effect depends on the

combined influence of social context factors, the media context, and the media content interacting with characteristics of the audience.[25]

Sensitisation and desensitisation

Does a permanent diet of murder, mayhem and violence desensitise the viewer to crime and violence in the real world, or does it produce an acceptance of criminality as merely a part of everyday life? What effects does the whole crime agenda have on the world view of privatised, alienated citizens? Do they in fact believe, and act, as though there is much more crime than there is, living always in fear of imminent disaster and death? Do these attitudes develop into defining statements about, for instance, youth, and in particular black youth? Starting from police stereotypes there is evidence that the media reinforce certain dominant images, upon which adults and police then act and which naturally are then translated into further realities in which people are 'criminalised' rather than becoming criminal. Soccar violence is of course one of these spirals that seems to have no limit to the forms of media spin available, oddly enough for such a minority activity it has been extensively analysed by academics and itself forms a subspecies of crime and media theory.[26] Given that short-term effects, specific effects and political behaviour can be shown to be affected by the electronic media, it seems obvious that a long-term desensitisation to real crime and violence must occur. For the post-modernists this is precisely the victory of the hyperreal over the fleeting remnants of a known reality, but it seems more logical to talk about the development of a common form of consciousness, a mediachosis, which differently affects particular individuals and groups, and into and out of which individuals move in their struggle to define reality through essentially mass media-oriented signifying systems. Emotionality is a key element of consciousness, and the media's ability to produce fear, fascination and obsession in relation to crime and violence is an important area of investigation.

Criminal justice and the media

The central question here is precisely in what ways does the power of the mass media to shape and define reality interfere with the ability of the criminal justice system to dispense justice, however we define that complex latter term. In essence the answer has to be that at all levels the electronic media is capable of redefining the cultural context in which the criminal justice system operates and in so doing transforming both the concepts of justice, of criminality and of retribution. In so far as the media create, and distort, representations of the social and criminal worlds they further and further diminish the possibility of a rational, reality-based analysis of crime and how it could, or should, be dealt with. Even presupposing a return to the real as possible we would still need a policy about criminality as it is lived, rather than represented. As a long-term trend, whether into the world of the hyperreal or not, this is a deeply worrying phenomenon which is mostly met by the criminal justice system with various degrees of indifference or accommodation. Locking up the jury in the O.J. Simpson trial simply reflects an accurate view of the media's ability to set, and control, the ideological, political and individual agenda.

Media technology and the courts

At a more specific level there is the technological question of how criminal justice, police work and even prison life are affected by the new mass media and their offshoots. The American courts already often have cameras and create mass audiences for the more exotic trials, like the Claus Von Bulow case, the Menendez brothers, rape cases, murder trials and the present 'trial of the century'. Again what effect this has on the actual administration of justice is difficult to analyse, but it will become increasingly important and may well follow in Britain and other countries. Police video surveillance and video evidence, as well as TV footage of riots, disturbances and demonstrations is an ever-growing field. The courts now use video evidence, closed circuit cameras, video links to prisons, surveillence films and many other electronic technologies which clearly impact on the administration of crminal justice. How our experience of these events is mediated by the technology is itself a whole new area of research but there is still rather more speculation than hard evidence. The problem of technology and its effects runs throughout the whole debate about media, post-modernism and perception, as well as underlying the structural employment problem that so determines much of the criminal activity generated in post-modern societies.

Pornography and the media

From computer pornography, via the internet, to satellite pornography channels there is an explosion of media sexuality, and profitable exploitation of deviance and deregulation. In reporting sex crimes, however, the media may have changed, but as Benedict[27] and Lees[28] have demonstrated the modes of reporting rape, in particular, have remained locked in a misogynist time warp that demeans the victims as much as the crime. The eroticisation of violence and the spread of pornography as an industry also alters the newsworthiness of sex crimes and redefines acceptable behaviour. In some ways rape has been overshadowed by the recent satanic abuse panics, a media spiral which seems to have less to it than normally meets the eye. Again interest in perversion, crime and conspiracy coalesce in reporting that has all the elements of newsworthiness and bizarreness that any media could demand. A serious area of research here is into those who manipulate and create the primary definitions which allow these stories to make the quantum leap from small-scale social problems to national obsessions.

At the same time, particularly in Britain, there is a prurient obsession with the private sex lives of stars and public personalities, including the symbolic figures of the Royal family. We have already had reconstructions of the private lives of media personalities and of course Madonna has elevated this intertextuality into her own brand of multiple personality reconstruction as an art form. Michael Jackson's permutations and transformations have ended in an almost entirely media-lived orgy of speculation and reincarnation as the heir apparent to the 'King', Elvis. This is the post-modern spectacle of sexuality, stardom, pornography and crime all rendered as a kind of metavideo narrative of soap opera and tragedy. These manifestations demand a theoretical vocabulary that includes the hyperreal but which must ultimately return to questions of the effects of mass media consumption at the social level in lived culture.

Drugs and the media

The drug wars that President Reagan launched in the media and which are now part of the vocabulary of most western law enforcement agencies were part of a process of the creation of the most sustained moral panic the western world has seen since anticommunism, and indeed there is some symbolic connection. Media representations of drugs and drug users exactly fit the demonology that communism used to occupy, an evil irrational force that insinuates itself into the social fabric with the aim of destroying it from within. In all of the media representations of crime none is so irrational as that of the drug dealer, the drug user and of the drugs themselves. 'Crack' has become the sole most potent

signifier in the media's crime vocabulary and its use and spread are
reported exactly like a plague or an epidemic. It is habitually stated that
one taste leads to instant addiction and a life of violent crime, to gang
warfare and street deaths. In the holy media war that is being waged
against drugs, exaggeration and melodrama are the basic staples of all
reporting, whilst for example we know that all police evidence about
the street value of drugs is grossly inflated and the routine facts and figures
about the drug 'problem' are buried beneath media stereotypes. Along
with the rise of the 'crack' epidemic has been the creation of the
'Yardie' myth in Britain, the 'black Mafia' as it is sometimes dubbed.
Yardie gangs have been the object of much speculation, media reporting
and documentaries, as well as a spin-off novel by a black publisher.[29]
Whether they in fact exist or not, other than as loose associations of
criminals, still seems a very open question, as does the existence of the
new 'Russian Mafia' who were supposedly moving into Britain. In the
drug dealer the media finds its perfect figure of evil, the devil reincar-
nated for urban post-modernism, and there is no ambiguity in the
one-dimensional image that is created and re-created in fiction and
news. The police control of this area of information is almost absolute
and there is no one willing to offer different versions of events, to
question the war on drugs is to be on the side of evil. Of course there
is a drug problem but it cannot be considered seriously whilst the
media maintain its extraordinarily melodramatic coverage of every
aspect of drug trafficking and consumption. The linking of the 'under-
class', 'race' and drugs is one of the most odious features of popular
television's unconscious agenda, and it is important to stress that these
patterns of representations are complex, structural features of media
production and consumption that derive from the contexts and pressures
within which commercial media systems operate, and from the culture
that those systems produce and interact with. In that argument we are
posing a profound opposition to post-modern theory which seems to
imply that any outcome is as possible as any other, whereas real patterns
of power and control exert themselves in these kinds of definition of
the crime and media nexus. On the one hand there is the fragmentation, pluralism, parody and what Baudrillard calls 'media cyberpower',
but on the other hand there is an increasingly simple and straightforward
concentration of economic and cultural power in the hands of multinational media empires; thinking about crime and the media has to
operate in the interstices of these power relationships. Whether
community is recoverable from this nightmare world of dislocation,
criminality and what I have called mediachosis is debatable, whether it

be cybercommunity, or the post-technological communitarian world now being presented by 'new age' and other oppositional groups.

There are clearly enormous problems in discussing crime and the media and they are deeply political in the widest sense of the word. It is not easy to be optimistic about the possible development of trends in the media but without clear insight and rapid analysis we are all in danger of sinking into a post-modernist abyss of despair and melancholic cool while the prisons are built and the electric chairs redesigned in a parody of fascism. The idea that the post-modern viewer is a fragmented, decentred subject, a floating identity located in the interstices of mass electronics and subject to the random horror of media crime representations is an appalling and fascinating one, but one that, in the interests of those bodily incarcerated in prison realities, should be resisted.

Constructing a theoretical paradigm for analysing the interrelation of crime and the media must begin with a critique of post-modernist theory and elevate an interdisciplinarity which pays attention to a sociology of institutionalised fragmentation.

Notes and references

1. Cohen, S. and Young, J. (eds), *The Manufacture of News: Deviance, Social Problems and the Mass Media*. (London: Constable, 1973); Hall, S., Critcher, C., Jefferson, T., Clarke, J. and Roberts, B. (eds), *Policing the Crisis: Mugging, the State and Law and Order* (London: Macmillan, 1978).
2. Campbell, B., *Goliath* (London: Methuen and Co., 1994), p. 140
3. There is certain amount of feminist critique of criminology, such as Young, A., *Femininity in Dissent* (London: Routledge, 1990) but very little work in the sphere of the mass media. See below.
4. In the last ten years six substantive works have been published on the topic of crime and the media. Barak, G., *Media Process and the Social Construction of Crime: Studies in Newsmaking Criminology* (New York: Garland, 1994); Ericson, R. et al, *Representing Order: Crime, Law and Justice in the News Media* (Buckingham: Open University Press, 1993); Gunter, B., *Television and the Fear of Crime* (London: Sage, 1987); Schlesinger, P. and Tumber, H., *Reporting Crime: The Media Politics of Criminal Justice* (Oxford: Clarendon Press, 1994); Sparks, R., *Television and the Drama of Crime: Moral Tales and the Place of Crime in Public Life* (Buckingham: Open University Press, 1992); Surrette, R., *Media, Crime and Criminal Justice, Images and Realities* (Spring Grove, CA: Brooks Cole, 1992). In the same period perhaps 200 books have been published on cultural studies in general and probably the same number on Foucault.

5. See Pavarini, M., 'Is criminology worth saving?', in Nelkin, D., *The Futures of Criminology* (London: Sage, 1994).

6. Morrison, W., 'Criminology, modernity and the "truth" of the human condition: Reflections on the melancholy of post modernism', quoted in Nelkin, D., *The Futures of Criminology*, p. 143.

7. Eliot, T.S., 'Macavity: The Mystery Cat', in *The Children's Book of Comic Verse* (London: Piccolo,1978).

8. Panorama made a classic programme, broadcast on 6 March 1995, which covered the case of an American teenager who had watched *Natural Born Killers* obsessively and later murdered his parents in a 'copy-cat' killing. The whole discussion was completely circular but implied that this kind of crime 'was on the increase'. Several other murders have been ascribed to the film in the usual copy-cat fashion but the question is still wide open about particular effects; these murders may well have happened anyway but in some other form. The question of the media's complicity in glorifying violence and in promoting the debate about the film also has to be considered.

9. In Puzo, M., *The Godfather Papers* (London: Heinemann, 1977).

10. The second juror to be dismissed for trying to sell their story to the media, or to profit by their position, was found to be secretly writing a book on the case, fittingly secret computer files were found. The trial has almost run out of alternative jurors and many are predicting a mistrial.

11. Quoted in BBC2's *Court Report* on 2 April 1995.

12. Beck, U., *The Risk Society* (London: Sage, 1992), quoted in Nelkin, D., *The Futures of Criminology*, p. 67.

13. Ericson, R. et al, *Representing Order*. They analyse general media coverage in a recent period in Toronto and establish that crime news constituted slightly less than half of all news coverage on radio. It is noticeable that the amount of crime reporting and moral panics seems constantly to build upon itself, representing a new order of things.

14. Quoted in Surrette, R., *Media, Crime and Criminal Justice*, p. 233.

15. Foucault, M., *The Order of Things: An Archaeology of the Human Sciences* (New York: Random House, 1972), p. 366.

16. Berlusconi came to be prime minister through a new form of political coalition that was based on electronic groupings controlled through his media empire. The head of Moscow TV was assassinated, it was assumed, for being involved in the decision to halt advertising on Russian TV (March/April 1995).

17. Morrison, W., 'Criminology, modernity and the "truth" of the human condition'.

18. *Father Dowling Investigates* is a bizarre modern version of the Father Brown mysteries in which the 'otherness' of the priest returns some of the abstractness of earlier detectives.

19. In a return to what appears to be a kind of Wild West justice, anyone in California who commits a third offence is locked up for 25 years; this produces cases like the one in which a petty criminal received 25 years for stealing a piece of pizza. The symbolic strength of the retribution is clearly out of all proportion to the crime, but the image of the policy is hugely

popular, despite the obvious conclusion that California's prisons may well soon be overrun with petty criminals.

20. Powers. H., (1990) quoted in Barak, G., *Media Process and the Social Construction of Crime*, p. 38.
21. See Osborne, R., *Psychoanalysis and the Media: Postmodernism and Popular Culture* (forthcoming).
22. Rapping, B., quoted in Barak, G., *Media Process and the Social Construction of Crime*, p. 36.
23. See in particular the recently published Gauntlet, D., *Moving Experiences: Understanding Television's Influence and Effects* (Leeds: Institute of Communications, 1995). He surveys all the recent studies of the impact of television and not surprisingly concludes that there is little hard empirical evidence of immediate effects. The wider question of long-term effects, and of unconscious effects in the viewer, is not considered.
24. Surrette, R., *Media, Crime and Criminal Justice*, p. 136.
25. Ibid., p. 140.
26. The analysis of football hooliganism has reached epidemic proportions. There have been at least nine books published since mid-1994 in Britain, these relating to a problem that involves a few thousand individuals (males) at most. But media coverage, because it is already established as a discourse of paranoia, constantly amplifies the events.
27. Benedict, H., *The Virgin and the Vamp: Rape and Criminal Justice* (New York: Oxford University Press, 1992).
28. Lees, S., 'Media Reporting of Rape: The 1993 British "Date-Rape" Controversy', Chapter 6 in this volume.
29. *Yardie* was a runaway success for the new, small black publishers X Press, and part of the cachet, of course, was that the black author claimed inside knowledge, but in an interestingly general way.

Bibliography

Baussioni, M., 'Terrorism, Law Enforcement and the Mass Media', *Journal of Criminal Law and Criminology*, 72.

Carlson, J. (1985) *Prime Time Law Enforcement* (New York: Praeger).

Chibnell, S. (1975) *Law and Order News* (London: Tavistock Publications).

Crandon, G. (1992) *The Police and the Media: Information Management and the Construction of Crime News* (Bradford: Horton Publishing).

Felson, M. (1994) *Crime and Everyday Life: Insights and Implications for Society* (Pine Forge Press).

Fitzgerald, M. et al (1981) *Crime and Society* (Buckingham: Open University Press).

Freedman, W. (1988) *Press and Media Access to the Criminal Courtroom* (New York: Qournum).

Greene, E., 'Media Effects on Jurors', in *Law and Human Behaviour*, vol. 14 no. 5.

Hans, V., 'Law and the Media', in *Law and Human Behaviour*, vol. 14 no. 5.

Kellner, D. (1995) *Media Culture* (London: Routledge).

Kirley, R. and Csikszenthmihalyi, M. (1990) *Television and the Quality of Life: How Viewing Shapes Everyday Experience* (Hillsdale, NJ: Lawrence Erlbaum),

Larson, O.M. (1968) *Violence and the Mass Media* (New York: Harper and Row).

Lotz, R.E. (1991) *Crime and the American Press* (New York and London: Praeger).

Rosenbaum, D. et al (1992) *Crime Stoppers: A National Evaluation of Program Operations and Effects* (Illinois: Evanston Press).

Sacco, V., 'The effects of Mass Media on Perceptions of Crime', in *Pacific Social Review* no. 25.

Sumner, C. (1982) *Crime, Justice and the Mass Media* (Cambridge: University of Cambridge, Institute of Criminology).

Surrette, R. (1984) *Justice and the Media* (Springfield, IL: Charles and Thomas).

Taylor, Mark C. and Saarinen, E. (1995) *Imagologies* (London: Routledge).

3 Entertaining the Crisis: Television and Moral Enterprise

Richard Sparks

I live in mighty fear that all the universe will be broken into fragments in the general ruin, that formless chaos will return and vanquish the Gods and men, the earth and sea will be engulfed by the planets wandering in the heavens ... Of all the generations it is we who have been chosen to merit this bitter fate, to be crushed by the falling pieces of the broken sky.

Seneca, *Thyestes*

Moral disquiet and the media

It seems reasonable to expect that any important social institution or practice should be widely and often passionately discussed. Broadcasting, and especially its depictions of crime and punishment, provides a singular case in point. Its cultural significance is partly defined by the fact that it has indeed attracted incessant discussion, and a fuller assessment of its social impacts requires attention as much to the meanings which have been attributed to it as to the more narrowly conceived task of documenting its actual 'contents' and 'effects'. This chapter thus concerns some of the attempts which have been made to define and describe the impact of television, especially where these register the growth of the television industries with a sense of unease and disquiet as harbingers of unwelcome social change. It is, in short, about words and their organisation into prevailing vocabularies, inasmuch as these surround the depiction of crime on television and lay claim to influence the ways in which it should be perceived. As Cohen comments: 'Words neither "come from the skies" ... nor can they be taken as literal explanations of what is happening. Nonetheless we must still listen to them very carefully ... it is the rhetoric itself which becomes the problem.'[1]

I shall argue here that if we look again at some of the debates and campaigns which have gathered around the medium, especially in relation to 'violence', we can see that these have in large measure been stimulated precisely by a sense of disquiet and uncertainty about the relations between the public and private spheres, and by extension about social order and political legitimacy in the television age.

All this has large implications for our way of conceiving television's social 'effects'. Many commentators start from the premise that television and other media have pacifying, or anaesthetic, even narcotic effects.[2] A powerful, perhaps predominant stand in commentaries on the impacts of mass media envisions a mainly passive audience, seeking distraction.[3] If at the same time the audience is also terrorised[4] this serves only to consolidate the concentration on private pleasures. In the strong versions of this thesis television is 'mind candy' and a 'tool of stupefaction'.[5] Gerbner's position is ultimately of this latter kind.[6] The provocation of fear by television promotes withdrawal, and hence a further dependency on the medium at the expense of other modes of participation and exchange. If it also correlates with a preference for somewhat authoritarian outlooks these are nevertheless not actively pursued. Such views thus generally allege a tendency towards 'depoliticisation.'[7]

In this chapter I suggest that this at best only identifies a partial truth. Television is quite passively consumed at times (when people are tired, when they want to be allowed their own reveries), and generally within private space: but even this form of consumption is probably much less inert than is often depicted. Indeed, my argument is that in reality people are capable of many and varied responses to television, some of them quite at odds with one another, and some of them passionately engaged. I do accept that there are many contemporary social pressures towards forms of privatism: anxiety about the safety and habitability of public space importantly among them. Television often speaks to those anxieties, focusing them, providing a vocabulary for talking about them, at times sublimating them in entertainment. But the private encounter with television can also provide a sort of connection (for some it is one of very few connections) with public life. For that reason the cultural politics of the medium itself takes on a magnified importance, because it becomes one of the main ways in which our kind of society talks about itself and its future. If we want to understand the impact of 'crime on TV' we need to look not only at what is on the screen but also at the talk which surrounds it and which it provokes.

Crime fictions address themselves to the anxieties of their inferred or target audience, by deploying narrative strategies which both evoke and yet contain the world's dangers. The picture is complex, however: the audience, being disparate, are not uniformly entertained or reassured. Those who feel most keenly that the world has become dangerous and disorganised sometimes respond to television's fables with a tale of their own, about the havoc which television has wrought. One way of addressing the question of how and with what consequences anxieties about crime and social regulation are distributed is to look at the character of some of these responses to 'television violence'. Television, as the dominant medium of popular entertainment since the 1950s, has very frequently been taken as an index of (also in some versions as being more instrumentally related to) the state of society and of public morality. Have the campaigns about 'violence' helped form our assumptions about television's effects, or about the deterioration of 'law and order', or the link between the two?

Television and 'social censures'

Sumner (1990) uses the term 'social censures' to describe the crystallisation of ideological categories into object domains with practical moral and political force, but whose purchase on reality is always doubtful. For Sumner censuring (including the making and enforcement of law and the creation of orthodox criminological categories) is always 'a matter of moral-political judgement'.[8]

> Censures are used for a variety of purposes and in a variety of contexts; that is, they are invoked or exist within the course of historically specific social practices. Their meaning is therefore usually fairly flexible, although some may have fundamental and strong roots in the human psyche ... Their general function is to signify, denounce and regulate, not to explain ... Their typical consequence is not an adequate account of a social conflict but rather the distinguishing of 'offenders' from 'non-offenders', the creation of resentment in their targets, or the cessation of the offensive matter. They mark off the deviant, the pathological, the dangerous and the criminal from the normal and the good. They say 'stop', and are tied to a desire to control, prevent or punish.[9]

One of the virtues of Sumner's position is that it keeps in view the relation between particular instances of censuring or blaming and the general realm of culture. What is at stake is the competitive exchange of meanings – the problem of trying to make your interpretation count (to climb up the hierarchy of credibility). Thus in Sumner's view the possession of social power and the capacity to censure successfully tend to go together, while conversely the struggles of subordinate groups almost inevitably include an attempt at redefinition (at counter-censuring). Censures are thus not something apart:

> Social censures have a profound existence: at the heart of intense
> emotional patterns, in the centre of politically and economically sig-
> nificant moral–ideological formations, and in the struggles and
> self-justifications that make history ... As such, they are vital forces
> in the constitution of societies.[10]

I take the view that television is implicated in the circulation of social
censures in at least two ways. First, television narratives themselves
propose and prefer categories of virtue, vice and threat. The ratified use
of violence is only the most evident of the means used to resolve crises
in the equilibrium of the world which the narrative projects. We might
call this censure *by* television. Second, television's moral tales, and its
use of 'violence' in telling them, can also be taken as reprehensible in
themselves. Hence the medium and its messages are in turn prone to
being considered as social problems. This leads to censure *of* television,
and is among the grounds for calls for its more stringent regulation. At
the same time the content of television is used to warrant further
arguments about the existence of a crisis of social 'law and order'. To
this extent television content can be called upon as evidence in support
of a censorious outlook on more general aspects of modern life.

The television medium thus gathers and provokes public languages
of response. Academic research (especially to the extent that 'effects'
research has been stimulated and sponsored either by government
agencies or by lobbying organisations: see Rowland[11]) is one such. An
interplay between textual commentary and social comment is an
entrenched feature of journalism and punditry and of political polemics.
If we define 'moral enterprise' as the attempt to secure acceptance for
particular categories of censure and their attendant regimes of regulation
– what Becker[12] calls 'the creation of a new fragment of the moral con-
stitution of society' – then we can see that television has provided scope
for morally enterprising activities of various kinds. Either it is called to
account as being responsible for a postulated 'crisis', or it is called upon
to provide evidence of the existence of the 'crisis', or both together.

This generation of talk signals an alteration in the place of popular
culture in relation to the public sphere. It is an inherent, perhaps the
only truly demonstrable, 'effect' of broadcasting. The two registers of
response which I have isolated are illustrative of my concerns in the
following ways. First, the pessimistic testimony of literate observers,
loosely styled the 'theory of mass society', corresponds for present
purposes to the longue duree of the development of modern media. It
encodes a deep and lasting tendency to censure forms of popular
diversion.[13] Second, the populist inflection of a related pessimism as it

has occurred in the campaigning activities, since 1964, of Mary Whitehouse is more conjunctural and pressing: it recalls the connection to which Mills alerts us between personal 'troubles' and public 'issues'.[14] It has set out to define the 'problem' of television as a distinct political issue, but it has also set this argument in a wider antimodernist perspective which has much in common with the 'mass society' position. Each of these constituencies has registered the rise of television in terms of deep shock: it has been taken to signify the drift of history beyond willed control or direction. The censure of television bears witness to the fear of the future. It is here, in the questions of censure and the sense of crisis, that the problems of the critical apprehension of television drama and the immediate issues of the politics of crime and justice rejoin. In seeking to identify some connections between the priorities of film and television studies and central criminological concerns: do the prevailing modes of response to television actively impede the rational public discussion of crime and punishment?

Television and the theory of 'mass society'

As Seneca's fears suggest, the rhetoric of apocalypse is by no means new or confined to our period. None the less it has been argued that motifs of chaos and crisis have been particularly characteristic of the intellectual production of our own century. Kermode states this view:

> The critical issue, given the perpetual assumption of crisis, is no less than the justification of ideas of order ... in terms of what survives, and of what we can accept as valid, in a world different from that out of which we came.[15]

I take the view that the medium of television, particularly its violent fictions and the 'ideas of order' which they both express and seek to justify, is necessarily involved in the 'assumption of crisis'. If the politics of television 'violence' are indeed articulated with particular allegations of political 'crisis' (of the order which Hall et al. claim to identify[16]) this is perhaps because both are predicated on a prior, more general and diffuse set of domain assumptions about a crisis of social regulation in modern society.

The expression of anxiety about the effects of television incorporates responses which have been grafted on to some durable and entrenched pessimistic and censorious style of thought. The latter pre-exist the advent of the medium, but the arrival and growth of the television industries have been received as providing corroboration for, indeed as intensifying, such existing anxieties. The development of television has provided this body of opinion with fuel and energy. In particular, inasmuch as commentators have been preoccupied with 'ideas of order' and have assumed the existence of crisis, a popular, technological medium which devotes a significant proportion of its attention to the representation of 'violence' offers an especially clear opportunity for social criticism and complaint. The medium's perceived attentiveness to violence readily suggests a set of terms in which to criticise it, and by extension the society of which it is taken to be indicative. As Barthes notes, the term violence 'lends itself to dissertation', not least because 'Mass culture itself has provided us with all sorts of ways of looking at this world.'[17]

Discovering what these ways are thus becomes very much part and parcel of the enterprise of studying the culture industry and its role in the invocation of societal understandings of crime, law and order. It is perhaps no longer enough to 'read' or 'decode' media texts themselves: it is also illuminating to consider the discourses which they in turn prompt. One of the most characteristic of these is to take television as emblematic of the travails and problems of consumer societies, and hence to hold it responsible for having spoiled a culture that would otherwise have remained pristine. Indeed, as Cohen remarks, 'Nostalgia does not depend on intellectual rigour: what matters is the symbolic evocation of a lost world.'[18]

Mass society and moral panics

These reflections, however, suggest a degree of inadequacy in certain terms claiming to describe relevant rhetorics. Principal among these in recent social science is the notion of 'moral panic', which is intended to designate a periodic tendency towards the identification and scape-goating of 'folk devils' whose activities are regarded as indicative of imminent moral breakdown.[19] Such moments are characterised by the disproportionate demand for the punishment or disciplining of deviant subordinate groups. Cohen's original formulation of the term was a modest and descriptive one, beginning by simply noting an observed tendency: 'Societies appear to be subject every now and then to periods of moral panic.'[20] One danger in attaching too much weight to this idea would be that, while usefully drawing attention to the recurrence of themes of social anxiety and their association with rhetorics of crisis, it elides all such 'panics' under a single heading, representing them as a consequence of some (hypothetically universal, endlessly cyclical) feature of social life, namely panickyness. The aim, then, is to counter or subvert the allegation of crisis by an account of its repetitious and historically relative character.[21] In such usages the notion of moral panic comes close to being 'obsessed with debunking' in the way that Cohen has since warned against:[22] it sets out with the formed intention of reaching an agnostic conclusion. This kind of argument sometimes fails to apprehend that the very fact of the recurrence of 'moral panics' might suggest not so much a persistent irrationality as the expression of fundamental contradictions in social relations, that is a 'crisis tendency' in something more akin to Habermas' sense. Why do some panic-prone themes crop up repeatedly? Conversely, in assigning each present 'crisis' to the inclusive category of moral panic it risks disregarding the particular features of the language and imagery, origins and implications of each: why for example do some 'panics' gain weight and momentum and others not? What is thus not given due weight by such analyses of these rhetorics is the depth and continuity of the fear and loathing of modernity which they represent, nor the specificity of the constituencies from which they emanate. What is at stake is not a series of discrete 'panics' about crime, or about television, or even about these two conjointly, but rather a continuing and intrinsic involvement between these terms and the impulse to refuse the present time.

More than this, the tendency within both the theory of mass society and what I shall call populist conservative fundamentalism to seek comparisons and justifications by reference to an ideal, organic past community, however vaguely specified, is not an arbitrary fiction. It is easy to establish that tradition can be invented and that, to be politically serviceable, the past is subject to acts of appropriation; but such appropriations are not always merely fanciful. As Cohen observes, the images of community which nostalgia generates are 'deep and historically resonant enough to have been genuinely believed as well as genuinely influential'.[23] In this sense nostalgia records, perhaps sentimentally, a variety of responses to the fact that the world does indeed change, and it can use an expression of commitment to the past as a way of rejecting the present. Karl Mannheim pertinently comments: 'Thus modern society is a world of rifts and dislocations, contradictory views and moral codes ... In a word, the modern world is beset by the contemporaneity of the non-contemporaneous.'[24]

The experience of dislocation may have distinct origins and inflections among different classes or 'taste cultures'.[25] Yet these may coalesce in taking popular media, whose predilection for violence is both the most evident and the most charged of their alleged misdeeds, as emblematic of and/or instrumental in bringing about the most shocking and frightful aspects of modernity. For the mass society perspective, given its intimate association with and constant appeal to a canonical tradition of literary texts as the embodiment, in Arnold's dictum, of 'the best that has been thought and said', one dimension of the experience of dislocation is the displacement of writing by other, and intrinsically inferior, technologies of inscription. Where the criterion of aesthetic value is given by the 'transcendent masterpieces of world literature'[26] television is automatically deprecated.[27] Within this perspective the growth of crime is explicable both in terms of the diminution of informal social controls (loyal loyalties, deference, respect for elders) and of the substitution for an educative discourse of mutual obligation and aesthetic value, of a schematic moral universe centring upon acquisitiveness and revenge. The fear of mass society and the fear of television go hand in hand. A particular sense of desertion attaches to the fear that the master institutions of cultural continuity and identity have, as it were, gone over to the side of modernity, of scepticism, of the heterogeneity of belief and experience. The discourse of Protestant moral conviction, whose legitimising principles include a certainty of centrality and orthodoxy, finds itself marginal and in dissent.

Television and permissiveness

This returns us to my opening point: that the strength of feeling which is generated within arguments about the regulation of television stems from an anxiety about the relations between the public and private spheres which the issue of 'television violence' is taken to encapsulate in a special way.[28] For Whitehouse and others such violences are specifically the outcome of 'permissiveness', construed not just as a general social trend but as the orthodox position of the state.

Although, as Hall[29] has argued, the 'first wave' of permissiveness (under R.A. Butler's Home Office) did little more than rationalise legal regulation in the direction of existing current practice, it nevertheless signified a drift which was unacceptable to Whitehouse.[30] The grounds for the beginnings of Whitehouse's interventions are thus provided by the conjunction of events of the turn of the decade, especially as they crystallised around the television medium: the beginning of officially sponsored liberalism, the arrival of ITV, the mass ownership of television sets. The 'second wave' of 'permissive' measures under Roy Jenkins' tenure at the Home Office (relating to abortion, divorce, homosexuality and capital punishment, and which were in any case more pronounced) provided further stimulus to a reaction which was already under way.

Insightful observers of Mrs Whitehouse and the National Viewers and Listeners Association have noted the inherent ironies of this position. As Wallis remarks: 'The members of moral crusades may feel that the very foundations of society are threatened by some form of behaviour, but they organise in defence of that view for the very reason that it lacks consensual acceptance.'[31]

Television in law and order mythology

The certainty with which both academic observers enquiring into television's effects and polemicists castigating the modern era by reference to television have claimed to know exactly what social influences television exerts have been delusive. As Cohen has observed:

> Any topic of interest in social science has a peculiarly amorphous quality. It looks distinct, tangible, separate – empirically or concep-tually – but the closer you examine it, the more it merges into the surrounding space ... We move into spaces which are not just amorphous but imagined and imaginary.[32]

One confronts a situation in which either the fixity of an excessively formal model or a rhetorically exaggerated account of television's implication in events risks doing violence to the fluid complexities of social process. Whitehouse's passion is itself an 'effect' of television, whether or not the claims she makes (which may in principle be empirically investigable) can be substantiated.

It is apparent that Whitehouse has a good deal in common with the critique of mass society, in the association which both forge between the historical trajectory of the modern era and the history of the mass media. Ironically, at the same time as the notion of television 'effects' enters the common currency of our everyday speech, the critic of television is forced to present herself as being always against the current.

The interest in recounting the history of Whitehouse's interventions lies not in their being dominant (they are rather the reverse, emanating from a growing sense of marginality) but from the fact that they never-theless indicate in a concentrated way some of the ideological weight which television and 'violence' have been called upon to bear. Albeit in more sporadic and attenuated ways elements of these anxieties also permeate more central debates about crime, law enforcement and moral regulation.

Hence, for example, the *Daily Mail* (13 November 1985), reporting on Mr Norman Tebbit's Disraeli Lecture the previous evening, asserted that:

> If a week's peak hour viewing could be retrieved from the archives of 1960 ... and compared to the diet of gratuitous violence, sex and swearing that in 1985 passes for family viewing we should all of us be able to see how far standards have plunged.

Even this language is insufficiently florid for some observers; witness *Cambridgeshire Pride Magazine* (August 1985):

> It was Winston Churchill who pointed out to the British people the need to stand up to an aggressor — or plunge forever into the abyss of a new dark age ... The good fight was fought and won, but the new dark age has nevertheless descended upon us with the grim inevitability of predetermined fate. Today on any television news bulletin ...

Television, therefore, occupies a special place in the demonology of populist conservative fundamentalism. Not only is it an evil influence in itself, but it also provides a token or symptom of modernity which seems to allow comparison with images of order and stability drawn from some indefinitely specified point in the past.

Both crime and television function as metaphors for contemporary troubles. Their intersection in television violence is thus doubly resonant. Television is both the bearer of bad news and bears responsibility for it. The constant reiteration of characteristic generic forms of television, within a relatively predicable schedule, lends credence to the ordinary critical stances built around it.[33] The fixity of these perspectives suggests the possibility of addressing concrete events and processes through television yet, in reality, displaces the discussion on to a plane whose purchase on actuality is ever more tenuous.

> Truly, though our element is time,
> we are not suited to the long perspectives
> Open at each instant of our lives.
> They link us to our losses.[34]

Myths of crime and punishment are very ancient. The particular features of their inflection through television are very recent, but none the less deeply entrenched. It is through the appeal that these tales make to the modern audience that the myth of crime and punishment infiltrates the fine grain of our cultural experience.[35] In particular we can see the vehement enthusiasm with which certain constituencies within the general population retell the narrative as though it showed the way the world is now.[36] This secondary narration, inherently moral and rhetorical, conservative and yet dissenting, adds a myth of television to the levels of myth which television itself propagates. In so doing it corresponds very closely to what Nisbet sees as the defining appeal of conservative popular belief:

> But when men become separated or feel themselves separated from traditional institutions, there arises, along with the spectre of the lost individual, the spectre of lost authority. Fears and anxieties run over the intellectual landscape like masterless dogs. Inevitably in such circumstances men's minds turn to the problem of authority.[37]

The rhetorical critique of violence on television is a 'story of change' about the loss of community.[38] The persistent force of the story which Whitehouse wishes to tell and the reason for its ultimate failure both derive from its 'demodernising' rhetoric.[39] Cohen asks how, if the ideal form of social control is always in the past, and has always been spoiled by modern trends (even where the vision has some claim to authenticity), one can 'recreate mimetically' something for which, on one's own account, the conditions no longer exist in industrial society? One is left retailing myths of purification and, as Sennet observes, the 'essence of the purification mechanism is a fear of losing control'.[40]

Implications for the study of 'violence' in the media

There seems little prospect of diminishing the rhetorical force which attaches to 'violence on television' simply by introducing a sceptical argument about alarmism and moral panic. The 'passions and social sentiments'[41] involved are deeply ingrained, and it is a measure of television's importance as a medium of exchange that people engage with and against it passionately. Never mind that professional social scientists sometimes sound pained at the impression with which 'their' topic is spoken about; they should first note that it is spoken about with feeling. There is an analogy here with the indeterminacy of crime statistics themselves.[42] Although it seems more oblique, we can actually study the record of what has been thought and said about television and violence with more certainty than we know its supposed 'direct' or 'objective' effects.

  There could be little scope therefore for a magisterial sociology of the mass media which, in attempting to ground its claim to 'know better',[43] sought to disregard the rhetorics in which its subject matter is 'always and already'[44] enmeshed. There are many empirical claims to be settled, but the politics of television violence are not reducible without remainder to these terms. Populist conservative fundamentalism poses in an acute form Kermode's problem of the 'justification of ideas of order': perhaps one can respond only by seeking to recover some criteria of reasonability for such justifications.

It seems that the channels whereby crime is introduced into everyday speech and belief are not conducive to the growth of such reasonability. The prevailing (and the marginal) understandings of crime and television in their relation to social change must be both accounted for and objected to as a precondition of an informed public discourse. The analysis of public representations of crime is not adequately treated either by content analyses which merely enumerate factual errors and distortions (as it often appears in Gerbner), nor is it properly understood as a technical operation in discourse analysis.[45] However, it is necessary to insist that media imagery and public vocabularies are part of the object domain of criminology, at least to the extent that these inform and drive public perceptions and define the position which 'law and order' occupies as a term in public debate.

On what then does a more reasonable discussion depend? As Arendt argues, following Chomsky, rationality is not the opposite of emotion.[46] Rather, the opposites of emotion are the 'detachment and equanimity' of a spurious objectivism and the 'sentimentality' of inauthentic responses. The positions which Mrs Whitehouse and the critics of mass society variously adopt are disreputable not because they are normative, or even rhetorical, but because their rhetoric is inadequate, inappropriate and therefore sentimentally irresponsible. As Arendt comments, 'Rage and violence turn irrational only when they are directed against substitutes.'[47]

Both television crime drama, as a schematic fable of purification, and the nostalgic critique of modernity through television are directed at substitutes in just this way. Schematic texts have permitted schematic criticism. Thus when Holbrook writes 'Our industrial–commercial culture is the culture of hate, and it is spoiling human society everywhere',[48] he counterposes a mythical past to a paranoid present and winds up talking nonsense in the way that Pearson identifies as characteristic of law and order mythology.[49] Holbrook's language is excessive and offers no cogent orientation to the future. Marcuse writes:

> The word becomes cliché, and as cliché governs the speech or the writing; the communication plus precludes genuine development of meaning ... the sentence becomes a declaration to be accepted – it repels demonstration, qualification, negation of its codified and

declared meaning ... This language, which constantly imposes images, militates against the development and expression of concepts. In its immediacy and directness, it impedes conceptual thinking; thus, it impedes thinking.[50]

It is an irony that the iconography of television violence and the critical vocabulary which opposes it speak, in a profound sense, the same language. They employ the same rhetorical figures of order and disorder, they appeal to the same anxieties. If we are to talk responsibly about crime and punishment then we must make the attempt to disentangle ourselves from this rhetoric, which we can only do by understanding and accounting for it. If, as Hall fears, we stand in danger of 'drifting into a law and order society,[51] the colonisation, in our society, of the main channels of communication (both fiction and reportage) by an imagery of order and symbolic threat may be one dimension of this movement. In resisting such tendencies the recovery of articulate discussion of social order and the cultivation of sophisticated critical responses to the mass media are necessarily related tasks. The responsibility of critical examination is that of 'finding and exposing things that otherwise lie hidden beneath piety, heedlessness or routing'.[52] Between the piety of Whitehouse and the heedless routine of everyday television a great deal is hidden which is dangerous. One point at issue is thus the way in which connections have been posited between the regulation of television and the overt politics of 'law and order' in such a way as to collapse any distinctness between these spheres. Another concerns the difficulty for analysis in describing this assimilation without sacrificing its own prerogative of critique. This poses questions for both the objectivist theory of media 'effects' and the relative notion of 'moral panic'. Is either of these capable of postulating a normative theory of 'television violence' which is both empirically grounded and morally persuasive?

Some questions, propositions and provisos

Why are 'cop shows' appealing, popular and widespread? Why are we 'fond' of heroes, anti-heroes, villains and others? How has it come about that we, the audience, know the contours of the projected world so well that we are able to move about in it as habitues? How do cop shows achieve 'followability'?[53] I propose that they achieve followability by fencing in a dominant representation of the city and of its sites and sources of danger. In so doing they stipulate courses of action and justified responses. They thereby also hedge away the constant possibilities of dissolution and chaos; but at the same time they sometimes act against complexity and heterogeneity. The 'violence' in 'television violence' cannot be isolated, from its perpetrators, from its victims, from its positions within 'codes of conduct in action',[54] from its metaphorical and allegorical resonance. To analyse 'violence on television' is thus to take issue with a whole rhetoric: what does it posit about the world? What does it want us to feel? What does it urge? Whom does it censure? Whom does it praise and reward? To look at the issue in this way qualifies both the happy empiricism of content analysis and the more grandiose pretensions of classical structuralism and formalism. It suggests instead a more sociologically concrete as well as a more critical enterprise. Is it the case that at the level of our daily pleasures some forms of narration act against lucidity by superimposing on the real sources of our needs and anxieties a simplistic, diverting closure?

I do not regard these as easy issues and I have discovered no definitive answers to my questions. Indeed I consider that the premature certainties of objectivist content analyses, and the presumed self-evidence of the category of 'violence', have muddied the waters around the difficult questions of representation and reception and have tended to foreclose more insightful approaches to the placing of crime and law enforcement in contemporary culture. It is worth stressing again therefore that I regard the interpretations offered here as being provisional and illustrative rather than exhaustive and final. They are undertaken from a particular point of view: they seek out the features of 'content' which I have identified as being of interest for present purposes and form a part of the larger argument I have been developing. That is, I believe that crime fiction presupposes an inherent tension between anxiety and reassurance and that constitutes a significant source of its appeal to the viewer.

Furthermore, it is in the dialectical play between these terms that anything resembling a specific ideology of law and its enforcement is to be found in crime fiction. More particularly, it is in the satisfaction which comes from seeing that 'play' enacted and resolved that such importance as these fictions may hold in the lives of their viewers should be sought. As I have already suggested these satisfactions may have to do with the displacement of an indefinitely large range of anxieties, which in turn may be either manifestly or obscurely related to crime and law enforcement and the personal, moral and social significances they carry. Fabular and allegorical stories often begin from a premise of anxiety, though many of them go on to impose a pleasing order and coherence on a shifting and troubling world. It would be an easy matter to show that this imposition of order is false, or simplistic or unreal. What is more interesting is to ask why we should find it pleasing, and how our finding it so stands in relation to our everyday conditions of life.

It is imprudent to lay claim to conclusive answers to questions of this kind. This is all the more obviously so here since the interpretations I am undertaking effectively deal with only one 'moment' (namely the formal or discursive analysis of media content) in a complex and ramified chain of connections between conditions of production, distribution and reception.[55] To claim to know all the ideological consequences of a discourse on this basis would be, as Thompson puts it, to 'take for granted what needs to be shown',[56] while paying insufficient attention to the specific social and institutional conditions within which, and by virtue of which, media messages may be ideological.[57] In so far as what I am attempting here is, properly speaking, an effort of interpretation, it is at once more limited (in forgoing the claim to enumerate the 'objective' features of a message system) and more ambitious than is content analysis as classically conceived and practised. As Thompson comments:

> However rigorous and systematic the methods of formal or discursive analysis may be, they can never abolish the need for a creative construction of meaning, that is, for an interpretative explication of what is represented or said. In explicating what is represented or said, the process of interpretation transcends the closure of the symbolic construction, puts forward an account which is risky and open to dispute.[58]

It is important to be perfectly plain about this. Not only is the kind of interpretation at issue here necessarily caught up in a realm of 'claim and counter-claim'[59] but neither can the 'actual communicative effectiveness'[60] of a particular mode of representation ever be treated as given. Neither of these recognitions undermines the importance of attempting the interpretation of cultural forms and associated practices. If, as Unger has it, society is both 'made and imagined'[61] we are able to chart some features of these particular kinds of 'making' and 'imagining' and thereby to unfold some of the connections between 'formative frameworks' and the ordering of 'formed routines'[62] in everyday life, so as to lay them more open to discussion, evaluation and revision. The critical analysis of television and other media is not an arcane or unusual activity. It is not radically different in kind from what individuals allude to in any case in everyday life, but it seeks to extend ordinary processes of interpretation in more than usually concerted, systematic and self-conscious ways. In so doing it seeks to deepen and refine the activities of interpretation and evaluation in order that we may engage in group life without becoming the victims of compulsions we do not master and hardly understand.[63]

The depiction of crime and law enforcement in television drama remains amongst the most fertile resources out of which the culture industry spins its tales, in order variously to distract, move, frighten and reassure us. At one level the crime drama remains what it always was – a repertoire of imagery of social order, of the threats it undergoes and the means of its restoration and repair. But the stories that emerge are not fixed or invariant. They are inflected by the successive moods, themes and stylistic variations of their surrounding cultural movements. Thus in recent times we have seen on the one hand a move towards a more rounded depiction of the police officer as troubled ordinary citizen, confronting the difficulties and challenges of the job and of social and personal relations in a way that emphasises a more mundane and fallible (yet stoical) sense of their lot (*The Bill*, perhaps *NYPD Blue*). But on the other hand we also have images of a more troubling variety, pitting heroic individuals against an establishment that is not merely cumbersome but a compromised and no longer trustworthy arm of an increasingly secret state (*Between The Lines*). And against this we have still other kinds of police officer, some imbued with a certain nostalgia not just for the redemptive hero but also for the certainties of the classic detective narrative and the world of its settings, in which crime emerged from the passions rather than the dark heart of the dispossessed and alien city (*Inspector Morse* [64]). The police story is no longer one thing, if it ever was. It has become in multiform and various ways a screen on which the point of contact between our personal and social anxieties is enacted.

Notes and references

1. Cohen, S., *Visions of Social Control* (Cambridge: Polity Press, 1985), p. 115.
2. Winn, M., *The Plug-in Drive* (New York: Viking Press, 1977).
3. Postman, N., *Amusing Ourselves to Death* (London: Heinemann, 1986).
4. Berger, A., *Television as an Instrument of Terror* (New Brunswick, NJ: Transaction Inc., 1982).
5. Gitlin, T., *Inside Prime Time* (New York: Pantheon, 1985) p. 16.
6. Gerbner, G. et al., 'Political correlates of television viewing', *Public Opinion Quarterly*, 48, 1984.
7. Keane, J., *Public Life and Late Capitalism* (Cambridge: Cambridge University Press, 1984) and also Ericson, R., 'Mass media, crime, law and justice: An institutional approach', *British Journal of Criminology*, 31, 1991, p. 234.

8. Sumner, C.S., 'Rethinking deviance: Towards a sociology of censures', in Sumner, C.S., (ed.), *Censure, Politics and Criminal Justice* (Buckingham: Open University Press, 1990) p. 25.

9. Sumner, C.S., 'Rethinking deviance', pp. 26–7.

10. Sumner, C.S., 'Rethinking deviance', pp. 28–9.

11. Rowland, W., *The Politics of TV Violence*, (London: Sage, 1983).

12. Becker, H., *Outsiders* (New York: Basic Books, 1963) p. 45.

13. Hirsch, P., 'The role of television and popular culture in contemporary society', in Newcomb, H. (ed.), *Television: The Critical View* (Oxford: Oxford University Press, 1976). See also Pearson, G., *Hooligan: A History of Respectable Fears* (London: Macmillan, 1983) and Carey, J., 'Revolted by the masses', *Times Literary Supplement*, 12–18 January 1990.

14. Mills, C.W., *The Sociological Imagination* (Harmondsworth: Penguin, 1959), pp. 9–32.

15. Kermode, F., *The Sense of an Ending* (Oxford: Oxford University Press, 1967), p. 124.

16. Hall, S., Critcher, C., Jefferson, T., Clarke, J. and Roberts, B., *Policing the Crisis: Mugging, the State and Law and Order* (London: Macmillan, 1978).

17. Barthes, R., 'On the subject of violence', in *The Grain of the Voice* (London: Jonathan Cape, 1985), p. 307.

18. Cohen, S., *Visions of Social Control*, p. 118.

19. Cohen, S., *Folk Devils and Moral Panics: The Creation of the Mods and Rockers* (London: MacGibbon & Kee, 1972).

20. Cohen, S., *Folk Devils*, p. 9.

21. Barker, M., *A Haunt of Fears* (London: Pluto Press, 1984) and *The Video Nasties: Freedom and Censorship in the Media* (London: Pluto Press, 1984).

22. Cohen, S., *Visions of Social Control*, p. 156.

23. Cohen, S., *Visions of Social Control*, p. 121.

24. Mannheim, K., *Man and Society in the Age of Reconstruction* (London: Routledge & Kegan Paul, 1940), p. 41.

25. Shils, E., 'Mass society and its culture', in Davison, P. et al. (eds), *Literary Taste, Culture and Mass Communications* (Cambridge: Chadwick-Healey, 1978).

26. Shils, E., 'Mass society', p. 207.

27. Schiach, M., *Discourse on Popular Culture* (Cambridge: Polity Press, 1988).

28. Ericson, R., 'Mass media', pp. 283–9.

29. Hall, S., 'Reformism and the legislation of consent', in National Deviancy Conference (eds), *Permissiveness and Control* (London: Macmillan, 1980).

30. Whitehouse, M., 'The corruption of culture', *Books and Bookmen*, May 1978, p. 15.

31. Wallis, R., 'Moral indignation and the media: an analysis of the NVALA', *Sociology*, 10, 1976, p. 272.

32. Cohen, S., *Visions of Social Control*, p. 197.

33. Garnham, N., *Structures of Television* (London: British Film Institute, 1973). See also Gitlin, T., *Inside Prime Time*.

34. Larkin, P., *The Whitsun Weddings: Poems* (London: Faber, 1964), p. 40.

35. Scheingold, S.A., *The Politics of Law and Order* (New York: Longman, 1984), p. 64.

36. Hall, S. et al., *Policing the Crisis*, p. 158.
37. Nisbet, R., *The Sociological Tradition* (London: Heinemann, 1970), p. 108.
38. Cohen, S., *Visions of Social Control*, p. 115.
39. Cohen, S., *Visions of Social Control*, p. 122.
40. Sennet, R., *The Uses of Disorder: Personal Identity and City Life* (New York: Alfred Knopf, 1970), p. 98.
41. Garland, D., 'Frameworks of inquiry into the sociology of punishment', *British Journal of Sociology*, 14, 1, 1990, pp. 1–15, esp. p. 8.
42. Pearson, G., *Hooligan*, p. 218.
43. Dunn, J.M., 'Identity, modernity and the claim to know better', in *Rethinking Modern Political Theory* (Cambridge: Cambridge University Press, 1985), p. 142.
44. Keane, J., *Public Life*, p. 176.
45. Pecheux, M., *Language, Semantics and Ideology* (London: Macmillan, 1982).
46. Arendt, H., *On Violence* (London: Allen Lane, 1970), p. 64.
47. Arendt, H., *On Violence*, p. 64.
48. Holbrook, D., 'Television and the new brutality', the *Listener*, 16 October 1976.
49. Pearson, G., *Hooligan*, p. 212.
50. Marcuse, H., *One Dimensional Man* (London: Routledge & Kegan Paul, 1964), p. 79.
51. Hall, S., *Drifting into a Law and Order Society* (London: Cobden Trust, 1980).
52. Said, E.W., 'The text, the world and the critic', in Harari, J.V. (ed.), *Textual Strategies* (London: Macmillan, 1980) p. 188.
53. Kermode, F., *The Genesis of Secrecy* (Cambridge, MA.: Harvard University, 1979), p. 117.
54. Hall, S., 'Encoding and decoding in the television discourse', Occasional Paper, Birmingham Centre for Contemporary Cultural Studies, 1975. See also Ericson, R., 'Mass media', p. 235.
55. Thompson, J.B., 'Mass communication and modern culture: Contribution to a critical theory of ideology', *Sociology*, 22, 3, 1988, pp. 359–83, esp. pp. 377–8.
56. Thompson, J.B., 'Mass communication', p. 360.
57. Thompson, J.B., 'Mass communication', p. 376.
58. Thompson, J.B., 'Mass communication', p. 369.
59. Thompson, J.B., 'Mass communication', p. 373.
60. Eco, U., 'Towards a semiotic enquiry into the television message', Working Papers in Cultural Studies 3, Birmingham Centre for Contemporary Cultural Studies, 1972.
61. Unger, R.M., *Social Theory: Its Situation and its Task* (Cambridge: Cambridge University Press, 1987), p. 1 ff.
62. Unger, R.M., *Social Theory*, p. 4.
63. Unger, R.M., *Social Theory*, p. 5.
64. Sparks, R., 'Inspector Morse', in Brandt, G. (ed.), *British Television Drama in the 1980s* (Cambridge: Cambridge University Press, 1993).

4 Black Cops and Black Villains in Film and TV Crime Fiction

Jim Pines

The detective story is generally an urban drama. As such, one might have expected blacks to have been integral to the genre since the beginning of television. Such was not the case. Not until the mid-1960s did Afro-Americans appear as regulars in detective programs. Invariably, however, they were never the heroes of such shows. And this pattern persisted throughout the 1970s when blacks were quantitatively more obvious, but qualitatively still unfulfilled.[1]

The vicious beating of Rodney King by white LA police officers in 1992 – perversely (but fortunately) videotaped by a distant white onlooker – and the subsequent acquittal of the officers by a white jury, qualifies as one of the most extraordinary examples of racialised crime represented as a 'post-modern spectacle'. The documentary (videotape) 'evidence' seemed to reverse all the popular expectations and conventions of race crime drama – the perpetrators of the offence were white law enforcement agents, while the 'victim' was a black man. Yet, like a piece of narrative crime fiction, these documentary images were somehow re-presented in such a way as to lend themselves to a wide, even perverse, range of polysemic readings including ones which, extraordinarily, placed King in the role of aggressor and the police officers in that of victims defending themselves. If images are so completely unreliable, as these readings suggest, then what does it say about the codes and conventions which are deployed to give structure and form to narrativised imagery? Are they, in the end, just a sleight of hand designed to further disguise rather than reveal?

The combination of crime and the representation of race and race relations is a highly sensitive topic which can easily spill over into controversy. The criminalisation of black subjects is, of course, a well-established convention both in popular narrative fiction and in everyday life. One of the effects of this, in terms of representation, is that the repertoire of cultural themes and images which circumscribes black-related subjects is very narrow indeed. A great deal of this media cultural imagery, moreover, effectively (and stereotypically) also marks black subjects as 'deviant' in some way. It is in that sense that the representation of blacks within the crime genre is already a highly problematic issue, even before one begins to consider for example the impact of generic conventions on racial representation. Hence the appropriateness of Brunsdon's observation that:

> the crime series offers particular problems for the representation of race if the production company wishes to move away from the stereotypical presentation of black villains. *The problem lies in the way in which the effect of realism is created in a genre.*[2]

This reality effect, according to genre theory, has more to do with the 'reality' constructed in other crime series than with the 'real' world or concrete social reality as such, however. Analytical stress is thus placed on the aesthetic (iconographic) elements which define the crime genre – that is its internal dynamic, its 'recognisable repertoire of conventions' – rather than focusing on sociological readings of the genre's 'realistic' tendencies or verisimilitude.[3] This critical framework would seem to suggest that it is primarily the generic codes and conventions which circumscribe black-related themes and images in crime fiction. It might also partly explain why it is extremely difficult to find black-related themes and characterisations within the crime genre which function outside the exigencies of 'race relations' discourses and so-called negative stereotyping (that is typical criminalisation). If that is the dominant tendency, the obvious question arises: is the crime genre therefore inherently racist?

Some crime stories consciously set out to create 'positive' black characters. However, these liberalised black characters often appear alongside a preponderance of 'negative' black villainous types in the story. This tendency is particularly evident in the controversial and short-lived British cop series *Wolcott* (1980–81), where the construction of the eponymous black cop 'hero' depends almost entirely on the wholesale criminalisation of 'the black community' in the story. A similar binary opposition is brought into play in relation to the Pakistani detective 'hero' Ahmed Khalil in the British regional (Birmingham) crime series *Gangsters* (1970s).

It is worth noting in passing that this image of the black policeman as 'hero', which many socially concerned liberals at the time considered a worthy concept, was nevertheless regarded by many black viewers as flagrantly contradictory in essence, since for them (understandably) a police figure could not be identified with as a hero, whatever his or her race or ethnicity. Another problem in connection with so-called positive representation is highlighted in Caesar et al. and their observation that the 'Americanisation' of the black British socio-cultural milieu in *Wolcott* not only misrepresents the character of the British black experience but also grossly exaggerates the contemporary moral panic surrounding 'muggings' (street crimes which had become racially coded as specifically Afro-Caribbean youth).[4]

Wolcott has a lot in common both in content and style with the 1970s' Hollywood 'blaxploitation' cop/gangster film; it also displays many of the excesses which typify the less polished examples from that exploitative cycle of popular black-oriented film. The difference here, of course, is that *Wolcott* is situated in Britain, it deploys only a small number of generic elements of the classic detective/crime drama, and it was made for television. However, it does illustrate fairly well the kind of slippage that often occurs when 'race relations' is placed at the centre of narrative attention in genre films and TV drama.

The 'realism' that is invoked in these narrativisations of the black criminal milieu is constructed largely on the basis of popular racist imagery connected with the reporting of 'black crime' and the socio-cultural perception of (ethnically demarcated) neighbourhoods. This imagery is re-presented in much crime drama, more often than not, in an unquestioned manner for dramatic effect. Thus, extrageneric elements do come into play in the structuring of (racial) representation; or, to put it in other terms, the so-called reality effect articulated within the crime genre is to a large extent built on the effluence of 'tabloid realism'. Consequently race-related crime narratives can easily be dismissed as populist and deeply reactionary in form and content.

In certain respects *The Bill* conforms to this pattern of racial representation, though this highly popular British series has been somewhat unpredictable in its approach since it started over ten years ago. Some early episodes in the series, for example, feature the arrival of a new black officer at Sun Hill Police Station. This inevitably provides an interesting focus of attention which might run for a number of weeks. Occasionally, the crime that frames a particular episode might be located within a 'black community' as well. These two race-related narrative elements – the black police officer and the black-related crime in the story – often play against each other in the episode whereby, for instance, the presence of the black officer provokes a certain amount of anxiety (and occasionally explicit racist reactions) among some of the white officers, while the simultaneous police handling of the black-related crime in the story brings into focus the uneasy relationship between police and black communities.

This construction does not mark 'a shift in the moral basis of the series and the genre', but instead represents what Clarke has called 'an inflection of the moral domain of the hero' (the 'hero' in this case might be represented collectively by the more liberal minded officers involved in the police drama). Clarke mentions an early use of this ethically framed 'race relations' motif in the seminal British police series *Z Cars*, where the racial encounter appears primarily as a moral issue with individual white cops, rather than suggesting a more substantive, structural or political critique which explores (say) the relationship between the state and the so-called newly emerging 'immigrant' communities in Britain at the time.[5]

The appearance of a black police officer in British cop shows such as *The Bill* is often welcomed as an important breakthrough, both in terms of developing interesting storylines and of integrated casting. However, the introduction of the black police figure into the narrative also introduces a new set of tensions as well as an ethical dimension which is not always present, and which potentially threatens the credibility of the black police officer character. Indeed these racially motivated tensions are not always easily contained within the narrative. This is particularly striking during dramatic moments when the black police officer has to function as the mediator of tensions between the police and black communities. This is clearly evident in episodes of *The Bill* which feature black woman Detective Sergeant Johnson (1994–95), the superior officer in the small, all-white, predominantly male CID team stationed at Sun Hill. Both gender and race are sharply articulated in this construction, although the series tends to leave it slightly ambiguous as to which of the two 'identities', in the final instance, is the most critical in terms of Johnson's survival in the job.

However, in episodes which involve black villains, there is a sense in which Johnson's vulnerability as both law enforcer and mediator is undercut by the way in which the narrative stresses the idea of the police as institution, and the way in which the police are represented in these situations as successfully 'managing' the potentially explosive (racial) crisis. Perhaps more disturbing is the way in which the series occasionally reverted to more conventional racist imagery relating to black crime and villainy, especially during Johnson's tenure (she left the series in early 1995, having been 'promoted' to a desk job), and the greater stress put on racial caricature rather than 'realism'.

Despite these deficencies, however, there does seem to be a development in racial representation in *The Bill*, from simplistic motifs seen in early episodes to relatively more sophisticated articulations of black/police interactions evidenced in some more recent ones. The arrival at Sun Hill of PC Lyttleton (mid-1980s), for example, is constructed almost entirely around a series of racist encounters with fellow white officer, PC Muswell, who is portrayed as an objectionable character who makes bigoted remarks about the Welsh as well. A somewhat different approach is introduced later in the series with the arrival of another black police officer, PC Haynes. His appearance initially provokes the usual stereotypical reactions from white officers, but he quickly becomes integrated into the police team. Indeed, Haynes never becomes a serious 'problem' issue or an ongoing bone of (racial) contention; in fact, perhaps surprisingly, there is relatively little direct reference to his race or colour as a 'problem' or as a target of racial abuse as such.

In one particularly notable episode – 'Duty Somewhere' (31 January 1989) – Haynes is seconded to a South London police station where he is given the task of infiltrating a local black gang. His 'ethnic' identity is obviously relevant to the task in hand, but it is presented both to him and to the audience as being a 'normal' part of his duties as a police officer, merely an additional and convenient asset. The important point about this contrived 'integration' of the Haynes character is that it works so as not to undermine the overriding demands of the half-hour police series; it is structured so as to maintain the overall consistency and identity of *The Bill* (that is its recognisable features). This construction also ties in with what Hurd has said about the typical police series, that it 'does not simply reflect the social world of policing but must actively construct a coherent version of social reality within which the playing out of the nightly drama of law and order can be contained'.[6] Thus the deracialisation of the black policeman serves as a cue for PC Haynes to do what all TV cops are supposed to do, catch criminals.

The representation of black villains in the same episode of *The Bill* is also very interesting and can be read as part of a similar ideological process at work. These characters are clearly marked as 'black' and 'criminal' but, significantly, they are also constructed as an isolated, indeed highly marginalised section within *both* the black community and the wider society. In other words they are constructed as social deviants of an extreme nature. This imagery could be read as a particularly extreme instance of racist representation; or it could be viewed as a generic convention which conforms more to typical screen villainy and to the representation of the criminal milieu seen in numerous other crime dramas, than to anything that is specifically racial or ethnic. Racial representation is obviously an important framing device in the episode; but, again, what is interesting is the way in which it is neutralised or assimilated into the exigencies of generic conventions (for example the representation of the Haynes figure), while at the same time being overexaggerated in relation to the construction of the villains.

American gangster films and TV crime series tend to be more sophisticated than their British counterparts in their handling of race relations
themes and imagery. The reasons for this mainly have to do with the
different trajectories of race/cultural politics in the respective countries.
Since the Second World War, for example, liberal Hollywood movies
have played an influential part in actively promoting social integrationist
themes (the early films of Sidney Poitier being prime examples of this
initial impetus). American commercial television, on the other hand,
has tended to take a lot longer to respond to social change with similar
'progressive' texts. As Stanley Robertson, a black producer with
Universal Television remarked in the late 1970s, 'because of the preponderance of comedy, the American people have the idea that black
people are funny ... except for *Roots* we haven't had the opportunity
to see blacks get emotionally involved'.[7]

American cinema therefore provides some of the more interesting
examples of the way generic conventions can be inflected in order to
incorporate otherwise untypical 'race relations' themes. In *Odds Against
Tomorrow* (1959), to take an early example — which McArthur has
described as part of the cycle of American gangster films made during
the fifties 'in which a group of men from various backgrounds ... come
together for the purposes of the robbery, the rewards of which they are
kept from enjoying by internal tensions and, sometimes, malicious
fate'[8] — the 'race relations' element, that is the presence of the black
member of the small group that is about to embark on the bank
robbery, represents only one of a number of tensions which threaten
group cohesion. In other words, racial tension is integrated into the
narrative and is made to work more or less strictly within the conventions of the genre.

However, by the end of the film, 'race relations' emerges as the
privileged discourse around which the narrative closure is constructed.
But while the black character in the narrative tends to have an
emblematic function, which is typical of liberal Hollywood films of the
period, his presence is nevertheless not a stereotypical plot device
aimed merely at eliciting an exaggerated racial effect such as comic relief
— a tendency that is particularly evident in many British (crime) dramas
which involve black characters and situations. In *Widows*, for example,
which in most other respects can be regarded as a relatively sophisticated crime series featuring (working-class) women in the principal roles,
the presence of the black member in the group of women (who are also
embarking on a robbery) was marked pejoratively, by the use of such
parochial devices as racial badgering. This device appears to be intended
to signal 'white working-class racial prejudice' (not surprisingly, it is

mirrored in the men's/husbands' gang behaviour), but it actually serves no dramatically important purpose other than to provide incidental moments of light relief. As such it has has no *ethical* value within the narrative. Scenes such as these, in which a black figure beomes the target of racial insult, can in fact be traced directly to the earlier British sitcom tradition, which historically has been the primary site of this kind of racist humour, mockery and insult.

Racial badgering is not a tendency which is deployed in contemporary American (urban) crime drama. If anything, 'race' tends to be mobilised in somewhat more complex, sometimes subtle and often oblique ways. A typical example of this is the dramatic tension between Sipowicz and his superior Fancy in *NYPD Blue* (1994–95). There are clearly racial undertones here, but they are never allowed to develop into full-blown conflict (as this would undermine the overall thrust of the cop drama). Even more significant, however, is the way in which this interpersonal (or racially understated) tension is eventually 'resolved' or, rather, held in check – not on the basis of interracial accommodation but through the exigencies of male bonding. This resolution gives overriding importance to the corporate identity and effectiveness of the law enforcement institution which, of course, is quintessentially patriarchal.

There no longer seems to be a particular stigma attached to the representation of black (or, indeed, of broadly ethnic) villains in popular crime drama. Nor are 'ethnic' villains expected to invoke racist caricature in order to get across a dramatic sense of villainy or social deviancy. The development towards relatively complex 'ethnic' characterisation seems to have started in the late 1970s (probably influenced greatly by the huge success of the African–American historical family epic *Roots*); and it is strongly evident in the popular police series *Hill Street Blues*, where the whole panoply of multiethnic urban American/New York society is mobilised in support of the series' innovative representation of the urban social context and the 'modern' police precinct. Ideologically this construct gives the appearance of naturalising (neutralising?) numerous social and ethnic divisions within the general flow of the narrative.

Many of the dramatic 'situations' represented in *Hill Street Blues* centre on some kind of interethnic interaction, though they are generally not presented merely in those narrow terms (that is 'race' does not occupy a privileged space within the narrative). The exception to this is perhaps episodes which revolve around a riot situation that threatens to erupt in a non-white community/ghetto and possibly spill over into the wider 'community'. But these incidents – along with others such as the one in which Lt Howard accidently shot a 14-year-old black boy, or the episodes which centred around the controversial promotion of a black officer as a result of an institution-wide positive discrimination drive – are usually introduced and developed in the series in terms of individual or personal and professional angst rather than in terms of socially and politically explosive issues which the series sets out seriously to explore.

Indeed, the celebrated 'open' narrative structure that characterises *Hill Street Blues* enables the drama cleverly to elide moral issues and to play down racial conflict (which is always present just beneath the surface) and other important social concerns. On the other hand, the way in which the series has succeeded in extending the boundaries of (racial) characterisation is worth highlighting. For example what would have come across as racial caricatures (say) 20 years ago, particularly in relation to some of the ghetto 'types' that come into contact with the Hill Street precinct, are read today as 'characters' in the old-fashioned, quaint sense of the term. It could thus be argued that this apparent shift in (racial) representation illustrates the extent to which it is now possible to incorporate erstwhile sensitive racial themes and imagery into the popular TV crime series, without necessarily having to resort to more obvious racial or 'race relations' motifs.

And yet the fact remains, if we look closely at any number of TV police/crime shows, both British and to a lesser extent American, that black characters and black-related dramatic situations tend to be constructed within fairly narrow parameters. Black villains are stereotypically linked to drug dealing, violent street crime (for example mugging) and prostitution; while black cop 'heroes' tend to be characterised as noble figures whose mission is to clean up the criminalised black neighbourhoods. In other words there are no flawed black cop 'heroes', notable white-collar black villains, 'sophisticated' black corporate gangsters and raiders or computer-based defrauders in the urban crime drama. There are no complexly drawn villains and heroes, only emblematic figures.

This seems to be in sharp contrast to the white police–gangster setting, where a much broader range of character types and situations are drawn upon. Black-related motifs, in contrast, tend to be rigidly defined according to popular images which are already in circulation in (white) society. The repertoire of television screen villainy (and heroics, for that matter) for black performers is highly restricted. But this is not a problem unique to the crime genre as such; I would suggest that it is largely one of the consequences of 'race relations' conventions and motifs which have permeated mainstream cultural media representation. The problem is further compounded by the fact that most (white) writers and producers of these programmes seem unable (or unwilling) to approach black subjects imaginatively, going beyond the narrow confines of tabloid race imagery. However, as I have tried to suggest, especially in relation to *The Bill*, there are notable instances where British TV crime dramas have attempted small gestures of experimentation, even if it has been mainly in terms of constructing 'deracialised' black imagery in a style that is indicative of some American cop shows. More cynical critics might suggest that these minor shifts in content are intended primarily to meet certain socio-cultural requirements of the American market-place, where programmes need to be sold and where the audience has different expectations regarding images of black people.

Wolcott attempted to mimic the American urban crime drama and failed. *Gangsters*, on the other hand, was clearly located in an English regional city and this was reflected in its style and imagery. Indeed, it was the first British TV crime drama that self-consciously invoked a sense of the multicultural urban setting as a strange and exotic milieu, and did so in a particularly stylised and seductive manner. The only comparable example might be the later and more polished American *Miami Vice*. It is as if the 'otherness' of the black subject, and its socially marginalised location, have been thoroughly exoticised and pushed to extremes both visually and narratively. No one said it then, but there is something slightly 'post-modern' about this.

What I am suggesting here is that there is a sense in which the crime genre represents the most intriguing (dare I say it, potentially exciting) form of race-related imagery in both American and British television; certainly more so than sitcoms and soaps, which are fixed in relatively static, formulaic conventions and which endlessly regurgitate the same old jokes and dramatic situations. The majority of crime dramas eschew the excesses of *Gangsters*, of course, but *King of the Ghetto*, despite its serious flaws, does show the facility with which the crime genre is able to incorporate 'experimental' or idiosyncratic styles of (racial) representation while at the same time raising (if not fully addressing) politically relevant themes, notwithstanding the sort of issues raised by Salaria in her critique of the series.[9]

The sense of immediacy is obviously an important element in the efficacy of TV crime fiction – the (racial) topicality of many of its themes and imagery have clearly been drawn from what I have described as 'tabloid reality'. This particular style of 'reality', with its populist underpinnings, is what gives the stories their particular energy. British crime drama, and particularly representations of blacks within that genre, often evokes a form of vulgarity that goes straight to the heart of social anxieties, something which other genres of television (including race relations documentaries) are unable to achieve. However, the question remains whether TV police/crime drama opens up new possibilities in representing blacks within mainstream generic conventions, or whether it can only simply reinforce existing racist imagery, only now in a strikingly stylish and seductive manner.

I am inclined towards the latter, not because I think the crime genre is ipso facto racist (there is much evidence to suggest otherwise), but because most writers and producers of these programmes have rarely attempted to incorporate black imagery *within* the conventions of the genre, experimentally or otherwise. What they have conventionally done in the past is simply graft black-related situations on to storylines, rather than engaging 'experimentally' with the possibilities that generic conventions offer. This, of course, makes it difficult to criticise black representation in crime drama without making constant reference to the exigencies of 'race relations' representation. The temptation to engage in sociological analyses around, say, the problem of racial stereotypes is thus hard to resist. My own sense at this juncture is to treat the majority of black-related police–crime drama as primarily 'race relations' narratives, then to examine to what extent the narratives have attempted to incorporate generic conventions and finally examine the tension between the two elements (crime genre and racial representation).

One of the complaints about recent television has been that while blacks are quantitatively more visible (particularly in the US) the quality of their roles still leaves much to be desired. Although the presence of blacks in serious drama is often seen as an important break with the sitcom tradition the conventions (and I mean this in the old-fashioned, pejorative sense) used to structure black imagery in the narratives of various kinds have tended to revert to more popular (and often reactionary) racial and social stereotypes. My argument is that this common tendency should be challenged and its relevance questioned, both critically and industrially (that is within production practices). The possibility of articulating more interesting uses of the crime genre needs to be examined a lot further, especially in relation to the wider diversity of black and white experiences, expectations, desires and fantasies.

However, to return to where this paper started, one of the corrosive effects of the so-called post-modern condition is that very particular aspects of black experience have now become part of a widely consumed but none the less grotesque spectacle. And it is in that sense that *The Trial of O.J. Simpson* (1995) signals yet another critical turning-point in representations of race and racism vis-a-vis representations of crime – with the hero/villain dichotomy turning upside down; the public and the private merging to become part of an entertainment driven box-office spectacle; with the binary opposition of 'positive' and 'negative' imagery finally being buried.

Notes and references

An earlier version of this article was published in Therese Daniels and Jane Gerson (eds.) *The Colour Black: Black Images in British Television* (London: British Film Institute, 1989).

1. MacDonald, J. Fred, *Blacks and White TV: Afro-Americans in Television since 1948* (Chicago: Nelson-Hall, 1983), p. 200.
2. Brunsdon, Charlotte, 'Men's genres for women', in Baehr, Helen and Dyer, Gillian (eds), *Boxed In: Women and Television* (London: Pandora, 1987), p. 192. My italics.
3. For an overview of genre theories see Pam Cook (ed.), *The Cinema Book* (London: British Film Institute, 1985).
4. Caesar, Imruh; Martin, Henry; Prescod, Colin and Shabaz, Menelik, 'Wolcott', in Cohen, Phil and Gardner, Carl (eds), *It Ain't Half Racist, Mum: Fighting Racism in the Media* (London: Comedia, 1982), pp. 34–8. This originally appeared in *Grassroots* magazine (March 1981). See also an interview with the series producer Jacky Stoller which appeared in the *Guardian*, 13 January 1981 and is reprinted in Cohen and Gardner, pp. 39–41.
5. Clarke Alan, '"You're nicked!" Television police series and the fictional representation of law and order', in D. Strinati and S. Wagg (eds.), *Come On Down? Popular Media Culture in Post-war Britain* (London: Routledge, 1992), p. 240. In a particularly harrowing episode, of *Z Cars*, 'A place of safety' (1964), this moral angst is triggered by a somewhat racially understated encounter which is driven primarily by humanism rather than relatively narrow 'race relations'. See an interview with the writer of the episode, John Hopkins, in Pines, Jim (ed.), *Black and White in Colour: Black People in British Television since 1936* (London: British Film Institute, 1992), pp. 92–7.
6. Hurd Geoffrey, 'The television presentation of the police', in *Popular Television and Film*, Bennett, Tony; Boyd-Bowman, Susan; Mercer, Colin and Woollacott, Janet (eds) (London: British Film Institute/Buckingham: Open University Press 1981), p. 56. This analytical point is developed in greater detail in Sparks, Richard, *Television and the Drama of Crime: Moral Tales and the Place of Crime in Public Life* (Buckingham: Open University Press, 1992).
7. Quoted in MacDonald, J. Fred, *Blacks and White TV*, p. 223.
8. McArthur, Colin, *Underworld USA* (London: Secker & Warburg, 1972) p. 53.
9. Salaria, Faima, *Artrage*, 17, 1987.

5 Telling Tales: Media Power, Ideology and the Reporting of Child Sexual Abuse in Britain

Paula Skidmore

Like fables, news stories contain hidden morals.[1]

Child sexual abuse became a key 'media issue' in the late 1980s and early 1990s, predominantly in Britain and America but also elsewhere. This chapter will examine to what extent previously suggested concepts within media theories such as primary definers, agenda setting and news management are appropriate to an understanding of how this has happened. It will outline the degree to which 'official' versus 'unofficial' voices are heard in child sexual abuse debates and examine the various points at which 'alternative voices' such as feminist and survivors' groups get heard. The research which informs the following analysis is based on work completed as part of the Child Sexual Abuse and the Media Project based at the Glasgow University Media Group (GUMG). The research project was set up to explore the significance of such reporting, both in relation to public beliefs about child sexual abuse (CSA) and in terms of examining the shifts in types of news coverage about the subject since the mid-1980s, when there was the launch of Childwatch as well as the impact of the Cleveland case on the reporting of the existence of CSA. The media *production* process is being examined through interviews with journalists, newspaper and television editors and source agencies; the *content* of the mass media coverage is being documented through a detailed analysis of the national British press and TV news reports and the *effect* of the coverage is being explored through focus group discussions with 'the public'.

First I will overview developments in media research which are of significance in understanding the 'power' of the media. This will then be connected to the issue of ideology and news production processes, in particular highlighting the concept of source–media strategies. The findings from the Child Sexual Abuse Project will be evaluated in relation to this and conclusions drawn about the applicability of current theoretical trends within media studies to an understanding of the reporting of sexual assaults against children. The chapter will explore what this means for the public's wider understanding of what to do about CSA and how to do it, as well as what is indicated for theories of media power and ideological control. Are the media 'telling tales' about the abuse of children that are to be believed?

Reflecting reality? Problems in understanding the power of the media

The British road to revelation in the tradition of media sociology has been rocky but paved with good intentions. It is important to examine some of the key suggestions that have been made with respect to understanding the power of the media. I will concentrate on what Fejes[2] has termed critical research which examines the role the media play in maintaining and changing the structures of power in society. This tradition encompasses three distinct but interconnected trends: examining the content of media messages with particular reference to the selection and presentation of information;[3,4] analysing the process of media production to explain selection and presentation[5] and finally assessing the ideological significance of media messages through an examination of the social context of production.[6] Such approaches encompassed the belief that: 'The media do not merely "reflect" social reality, they increasingly help to make it'.[7] These early developments came on apace in the late 1980s and more recent critical media research is addressed below.

Critical media research was born out of a tradition which believed that the ideological role of the media was important.[8] Based on original Marxist theories which proposed that the existence of a dominant ideology favoured ruling-class interests and therefore perpetuated the class system, it was seen as a significant area for sociological inquiry. Quite simply it was believed to be crucial in an understanding of how the powerful retain power. If, as Schlesinger and Tumber[9] suggest, media systems tend to privilege in particular 'the holders of state power, exponents of establishment politics and representatives of major capitalist economic interests', it is important to examine the specifics of such in relation to key social problems. As Schlesinger and Tumber neatly summarise:

> Arguments about media and democracy are at root about the relative openness and closure of communicative processes, both nationally and internationally, and the broader implications that these have for the conduct of political life. To the extent that media systems in a

variety of ways limit access to the production, distribution and consumption of information they affect the capacity of the wider public
to deliberate and determine decision-making processes in the state
and in wider society. The workings of the media and the capacities
of citizens as participants in public life are therefore connected:
openness and publicity are means of making political life transparent
and accountable.[10]

In a straightforward way then, as sociologists we are 'bothered about
the media' in relation to its apparent power, either to inform or censor
information and knowledge about our society. At a theoretical level such
work is having an impact on understanding the 'public sphere' in a
Habermasian sense[11,12] as well as on Gramscian notions of hegemonic
ideological domination.[13,14]

Developments in critical media research have begun to recognise the
complexity and sophistication of this process at three connected levels;
production, content and effect.[15] Equally it has been recognised that
previous research approaches to examining the media have increasingly
fallen into either political–economic models, organisational or culturalist approaches.[16]

For our purposes here the most useful studies have been within the
culturalist arena (or 'culturological'[17]) which, it has been suggested, have
the potential to incorporate the best aspects of the other two
approaches.[18] Culturalist approaches cut across numerous theoretical
analyses of the state and civil society as Curran[19] points out. However
a common aspect of such research is the finding that there is a 'relative
autonomy' of media personnel from their respective organisations. As
Curran concludes:

> the culturalist thesis assumes that authority within media organisations
> is devolved to relatively autonomous journalists. Their reporting is
> structured by cultural and ideological influences – whether inscribed
> in news routines, relayed through sources, mediated through market
> influences, or simply absorbed from the dominant climate of opinion
> – rather than by hierarchical supervision and control. This view is
> apparently substantiated by ethnographic research into media organi-
> sations, and supported by critical studies of broadcasting content.[20]

So how do we perceive power in this model? The most influential thesis
in Britain has been termed the 'structural culturalist' model and the key
exponent of it Hall et al.[21] in *Policing the Crisis*. This analyses the
hegemonic elements of media systems through the concepts of primary
definers, structured access and moral panics. Hall et al.'s[22] work grew

from the sociology of deviance and labelling theory and in as much is specifically focused on crime as a social problem. However, both they and Cohen and Young[23] examine the role of the media in terms of an 'amplification spiral' or 'signification spiral'. In this way they seek to explain how individual incidents and events, such as 'mugging', become associated with a general notion of 'social crisis' through the application of a 'moral panic'.[24] A key aspect of this work was the social production of news and the structured relationship between institutions of the state and the media. This has become known as the *primary definition model* which argues that journalists are dependent on 'official sources' – those who are powerful and enjoy 'privileged access' as special status of source. This structural relation

> permits the institutional definers to establish the initial definition or *primary interpretation* of the topic in question. This interpretation then 'commands the field' in all subsequent treatment and sets the terms of reference within which all further coverage of debate takes place.[25]

In this way the authors argue that a reciprocal relationship between the media and powerful state institutions produces clear definitions of what is acceptable or deviant behaviour and therefore creates a 'consensus' over social problems. Related to this is a key concept of the moral panic as originally devised by Young[26] and Cohen.[27] The notion of moral panics as presented by Hall et al.[28] fits within a theoretical framework which seeks to analyse the extension or continuation of *social control* in society. The authors' thesis seeks to explain the perpetuation of institutional mechanisms for controlling deviance, as 'labelled' by those with social, political and economic power. As others have pointed out it is a seductive thesis which contains strong arguments about the power of the media, but aspects of the analysis are now being criticised conceptually.[29]

The structural–culturalist model sees power as a subtle and complex field in the media system, as McNair summarises:

> journalists are not *necessarily* biased towards the powerful – but their bureaucratic organisation and cultural assumptions make them conduits of that power ... journalistic output is shaped primarily by a combination of ideological, economic and cultural influences acting on the news organisation from without. Journalists themselves are relatively autonomous from direct proprietorial and editorial control but nevertheless reproduce preferred accounts and interpretations of social reality by internalising the dominant value structure of their society.[30]

There have been key criticisms of this hegemonic dominant ideology thesis from Schlesinger[31] and Schlesinger and Tumber.[32] The overall problem highlighted has been that of 'source–media relations' and the underdeveloped analysis of primary definition. Based on numerous empirical studies Schlesinger, amongst others, has concluded that the model is 'blind to the question of source competition' and 'closes off any engagement with the dynamic processes of contestation in a given field of discourse ... it offers no sociological account of how [definitional power] is achieved as the outcome of strategies pursued by political actors'.[33] The specifics of such a research strategy, described as 'rethinking the sociology of journalism' will be elaborated in the next section.

Finally there has been an appeal to reassert the 'cultural' in media sociology.[34] Schudson argues that the 'cultural givens' in our society should be of key concern methodologically:

> while they may be uncovered by detailed historical analysis, they cannot be linked to social organisation at the moment of study. They are part of culture – a given symbolic system, within which and in relation to which reporters and officials go about their duties.[35]

As the author states the 'cultural air that we breathe' is an aspect of news generation beyond what political, economic and sociological analyses can explore, and it has 'both form and content' (p. 278). By content Schudson describes 'unquestioned and generally unnoticed background assumptions through which the news is gathered and within which it is framed'; what could be termed the *common-sense paradigm*.[36] It is therefore important to remind ourselves that both media personnel and sources do work within cultural givens – the gritty question has to be, how do we identify the power dynamics of the 'cultural air we breathe'?

A key point should be emphasised here – times have changed. This is not an ideological cop out but recognises that, as Curran[37] says, 'there have been profound changes in the British media since the more sophisticated culturalist perspectives were first proposed in the early 1970s'. Not only that but it could be argued that contemporary media sociologists have relied too heavily on the 'founding fathers' yet again, without rigorously evaluating this specific intertwining of theory and method for its present application.

In order to examine the current applicability of some of these traditional media concepts it is necessary to apply them to specific contexts. By examining the research on news production around child sexual abuse issues it will be suggested that some serious theoretical holes have been knitted into the critical media research jumper.

'Constructing the news': analyses of production processes

Before examining the specific findings of the Child Sexual Abuse Project it is important briefly to overview concepts of news values, news management, agenda setting and source–media strategies as suggested by previous research work on news production.

Journalists and newsroom culture

There is now a reasonable body of work within media research which pays attention to what goes on in media organisations which might affect their output. Traditionally much of this has been in the North American context. White,[38] Tuchman[39] and Cohen and Young[40] are the earlier studies which recognised that newsrooms and their journalists were important to news production. Interestingly Chibnall[41] and Ericson et al.,[42] although separated by ten years, show marked similarities in their analysis of crime reporting. Both suggest that the newsworthiness of any event is based around 'news values', that is the criteria which journalists use to select certain events as news over others. Chibnall suggests that news values are a product of newsroom culture – journalists learn the tricks of the trade literally on the job.

Obviously many journalists have completed courses of training and this is increasingly necessary in a competitive climate.[43] Individually however a lot of them still suggest you need a 'sixth sense' or 'nose for the job' as well[44] and in my own research confessed that they learnt more from a week in the job than several years at college. Barrat[45] talks about novice journalists writing 'for the waste-paper basket' under the supervision and guidance of colleagues. So, as Ericson[46] confirms, journalism becomes a self-perpetuating profession in respect of accepted work practices. From my own past research journalists have suggested that the profession is a 'closed shop' with out-of-favour journalists restricted in career opportunities. This is confirmed by Hollingsworth[47] who points out that non-conformity can have serious personal repercussions, as does Soloski.[48]

What all the above means is that journalists are generally guided in their work by professional news imperatives[49] or what Ericson[50] calls a 'vocabulary of precedents'. In other words, not laid-down rules as such but 'what previous exemplars tell them should be done in the present instance'.[51] It is important to note how this is flexible and complex – a kind of 'game model' for the production of news. In this way Ericson[52] suggests that there is not 'normative consensus' in the newsroom, but an arena of *negotiation* and *conflict* over values and practices.

This view is in contrast to Whitaker,[53] who suggests that news criteria can easily be seen as based around either tradition, precedent and experience; expectations of superiors; or judgement of colleagues. He suggests that these are the three points of reference against which journalists check their news judgement of a particular event.[54] In this sense Whitaker[55] suggests that journalists are unlikely to venture outside the realms of news-making conventions. Rather than an approach of negotiation and conflict over practices Whitaker suggests the majority of journalists fit into well-established routines and regulated practices which inform their news-gathering procedures.

The differences between these two conclusions can, to some extent, be accommodated by recognising the relevance of different news mediums. In other words the end product, the newspaper or broadcast, can be seen as a result of a range of interconnecting pressures, constraints and demands on, and expectations of individual journalists. The 'function' of news gathering is to produce a 'product', and this varies, from tabloids to qualities, from the six o'clock news to *Newsnight*. Therefore the function varies, and directs journalists to different ends in different news organisations, resulting in the spectrum of news 'products'. In a simple way what is being suggested here is that newsrooms vary and are different entities within each organisation and this therefore has an impact on the newsroom culture of each.

The above arguments are most recently verified by Soloski[56] in his discussion of news and professionalism. Soloski argues that news organisations need to be fluid and allow journalists some discretion, but that they also seek to keep this within their control by the call to 'professionalism' and by the related 'news policies' they develop (p. 207). He argues that news organisations rely on the interplay between the two to control journalists' behaviour. He argues that news professionalism is a 'transorganisational' entity which both sets standards for journalists' behaviour and offers a 'professional reward system' (p. 212). He supports Roscho's[57] point over the standard of 'objectivity' for example when he says that for journalists this means to 'seek out the facts and report them as fairly and in as balanced a way as possible'.[58] This is problematic, because in reality it means to rely on sources to provide 'the facts'. Secondly he discusses 'intra-organisational control' of news policies that direct journalists, which he analysed through a participant observation case study at a medium-sized daily newspaper (in North America). Although journalists may sometimes disagree with a news policy of their organisation, in his study Soloski found they nevertheless all followed it, thus proving his point that their discretionary behaviour was in the main controlled in this way by the news organisation. He concludes that in these two ways, professionalism and news policy, the news organisation creates 'boundaries' which do not dictate '*specific* action' but 'provide a *framework* for action'.[59]

Lastly, it is important to pick up on a point made by Schudson[60] over newsrooms. He comments on the importance of the news editor in the production process and how many studies have noted the effect of the editor but 'rarely look at the social relations of newswork from an editor's view'.[61] Soloski[62] also refers to the significance of the role of the editor, and in fact is participating as an editor in his newsroom study. He raises questions about the editor as a mediator between the news organisation's management and the journalists, particularly over disputes around news policy.

Having raised the issue above about variation between working practices in different newsrooms, there is one factor which is constant across different papers/channels and news mediums – the issue of news sources.

News sources and production processes

Traditionally media studies have emphasised how the overwhelming majority of the news has its origin in officialdom. The police, courts and government officials have been seen in past studies as providing much of the raw material for news, particularly crime news.[63,64,65] In this research we see how most journalists rely on original information sent to newsrooms rather than going 'out and about' to find out what's happening. As detailed above, Hall et al.[66] present official sources as having unfettered access to the news media and as such they can be seen as primary definers of social issues and problems.

However, more recent work has begun to emphasise the process of *negotiation* which often occurrs between journalists and their sources and in addition raises the 'question of how sources organise *media strategies* and compete with one another'.[67] This is the area addressed by Ericson et al.,[68] Schudson,[69] Schlesinger,[70] Miller and Williams[71] and Schlesinger and Tumber.[72]

As mentioned previously, Schlesinger[73] offers a strong critique of the concept of primary definers, particularly around the issue of inequalities of access within the 'privileged' groups themselves and disagreements over policy. A particularly pertinent issue is that of 'longer-term shifts in the structure of access' (p. 66). As Schlesinger concludes, it is important to analyse 'the degree of potential openness available in different media sites or through different forms of output and the scope that these might offer for alternative views' (p. 68). Schlesinger importantly concludes that such previous work has not addressed the issue of 'forms of action adopted by non-official sources' (p. 76). In this way he suggests it is important to recognise that we are raising 'broader questions about the nature of information management in society by a variety of groups in conditions of unequal power and therefore unequal access to systems of information production and distribution' (p. 82).

As work from the Glasgow University Media Group on the reporting of HIV/AIDS confirms, media strategies of official sources or powerful groups do not always succeed, and those of the less powerful pressure and activist groups do not necessarily fail.[74] Equally, work by Deacon and Golding[75] on the introduction of the Poll Tax/Community Charge by the Thatcher administration in Britain revealed the 'ideological failure' of the attempt. It is within this spirit that the Child Sexual Abuse Project has sought to examine news production. A key addition to the critical media research tradition is being emphasised by the work based at GUMG – that of audience understandings about the social world.[76]

Demons and dawn raids: issues in the reporting of CSA in Britain

The issue of CSA has been a persistent theme in news coverage throughout the 1990s. Specific cases of alleged organised sexual abuse in the Orkney Islands (Scotland) and Rochdale (Greater Manchester), to name only two, became major 'scandals' where the actions of social services were questioned. The other extreme has been the coverage of allegations against Woody Allen and Michael Jackson, where the celebrity personalisation of news stories has been paramount. There has also been the 'latest craze' approach, with the reporting of women abusers, 'False Memory Syndrome' and false allegations against teachers all occurring in quick succession between 1993 and 1994 – in many instances these too were calling into question social work practice around intervention in CSA.

This section will address the preliminary findings from the project by summarising the findings from the *content analysis*; outlining the structure for the *production* of CSA news in relation to journalists and source organisations; highlighting the key *issues* raised in the coverage of CSA; and summarising the main problems over *source–media relations* in this field of news production.

The content sample

The content analysis of all press and TV news coverage of CSA which appeared during 1991 resulted in a comprehensive archive of 1,668 press items and 149 TV news bulletins which covered this topic during that year.[77] Initial findings from the content analysis reveal that 71 per cent of all the press coverage, and 83 per cent of all the TV news coverage was case based. In other words most reports focused on describing events around one particular incident or set of allegations, rather than discussing areas of general concern.[78] The biggest single category of coverage (27 per cent for the press) was of the alleged organised sexual abuse in the Orkney Islands where several children were taken into care but later returned to their parents with no charges ever brought (see Asquith 1993 for a discussion of the case). The one exception to the case domination of reporting was that a significant proportion of the coverage, approximately 9 per cent for both TV and press, concerned the general question about how best to intervene when abuse was suspected (what we termed the 'diagnosis and intervention' category).

By contrast other general issues, such as the causes of CSA, or how it could be prevented from happening in the first place, received very little coverage. For instance there were only four items in the press, and none on TV news which focused on the possible causes of abuse.[79] There were only 68 items in the entire press archive (4 per cent) and only 12 items in the TV news coverage focusing on prevention.[80] The category of consequences of abuse, or help for survivors, was only 1 per cent of press coverage and there were no TV items. Similar emphases are emerging from the ongoing analysis of the 1986 coverage – a concentration on the coverage of cases/events. We can also tell from an analysis of the format of 1991 press items that most were news reports (n=1,307), rather than longer articles (n=162), or editorials (n=39) and column pieces (n=29).

Particularly due to the case-based coverage the issue of 'ritual' or 'satanic' abuse featured repeatedly in news reports.[81] There were several key cases in 1991 of alleged organised abuse of children which had ritual overtones: Orkney, Rochdale and Epping Forest. A related issue here was the representation of the social work profession. Approximately 15 per cent of press sample and 25 per cent of TV was coded as having an 'image of social work' – this was not necessarily negative, for example 17 out of 78 press items included 'sympathetic' (or neutral) statements. However, positive representations are rare and often undermined by negative comments elsewhere (such as in editorials), as other media research has shown.[82] Examples of headlines with negative coverage of social work are given below.

'THE BABY SNATCHERS: A MOTHER'S PROTESTS ARE SILENCED AS SOCIAL WORKERS TAKE AWAY HER CHILD'
(*Mail on Sunday*, 18 August 1991)

'THROW THE BOOKS AT CHILD STEALERS'
(*Today* 29 March 1991)

'IN THE DOCK AGAIN: THE CARE STAFF WHO GO TOO FAR'
(*Daily Mail*, 5 April 1991)

'BAN THESE BLUNDERERS'
(*Daily Mirror*, 14 March 1991)

'SACK THE LOT AND START AGAIN'
(*Daily Mail*, 5 April 1991)

'MINISTER SCORNS ABUSE "GHOSTIES"'
(*Guardian*, 11 April 1991)

A closer qualitative examination of the category 'diagnosis and intervention' revealed a reinforcement of the negative portrayal of social work. The sample (nearly 10 per cent of total press and TV coverage) excluded much discussion of how to diagnose and intervene in alleged abuse *outside* the social work profession. In other words the responsibility of 'doing something about' CSA was placed at the door of social services. The actions of social workers were focused on to the exclusion of other parties, such as the police or the medical profession.[83]

To summarise, then, the reporting of CSA in 1991 was about cases and intervention and rarely about the underlying causes of abuse, how to prevent it or the help that survivors may need or get.

The structure for the production of CSA news

JOURNALISTS[84]

Given the case-based nature of the content analysis it is not surprising to find that a high percentage of the news coverage of CSA is done by general reporters – people working on shifts whose job it is to report a whole range of news stories.[85] Journalists with a specialist knowledge of some sort only deal with a minority of the coverage, in other words those who are crime, social services or education correspondents, or those who through prolonged involvement in one case have gained specialist knowledge of CSA. In fact there is no such thing as a 'child sexual abuse specialist', only those journalists whose ongoing work has enabled them to develop a more detailed understanding of the often very complex issues involved – for example by attending conferences and scrutinising academic research. Thus the majority of reports concerning CSA are informed by general news values associated with the news of the day such as immediacy, drama and often sensationalism.[86]

From interviews with both press and television journalists there was confirmation of the reliance on case-based stories, but often emphasising the necessity of taking a sensationalist angle. Several identified the increasing trend of only covering a case in the first place when it has an '*angle*', often related to a scandal of some sort (see 'child abuse fatigue', p. 94). When covering cases there is often the issue of geography and the '*pack mentality*' of such coverage to consider – a newsline emerges which is very '*seductive,*' as one specialist put it. The emergence of a 'pack' of predominantly general news reporters in one locale can lead to a significant lack of context to case coverage, a point emphasised particularly in the coverage of dramatic cases such as Orkney.

All interviewees talked of a '*formula*' or similar to CSA stories, or '*phases*' of a story, and suggested it was usually through local interest in a case that the nationals picked it up. If sensationalist, unusual or a scandal of some sort, it will carry into national coverage, otherwise not. A major or dramatic case could result in replacement of a social services specialist by the chief or senior reporter.[87] Such placement of a CSA story in the hard news arena can also lead to a lack of wider context due to the absence of detailed knowledge over related issues. It was described by one specialist as '*send the boys to war*' journalism.

Many journalists recognised the lack of wider context in news coverage of CSA – several identified the competition between papers and channels as responsible. As one broadsheet specialist described it: '*news reporters tend to focus on the stereotype "social workers have made a mess of it again".*' In addition the very structure of news worked against contextualisation; there has to be a '*news peg*' for a CSA story – usually connected to a case. One senior BBC news editor emphasised this and said they were not very good at covering wider social issues, what he described as reporting '*child abuse as a constant social problem*'.

To some extent what the above adds up to is the impact of journalistic culture, described below by one specialist:

journalists are terribly incestuous if I can use that term when we're talking about this but they mix together, they drink together, they all [call] each other up ... and I mean, I like them, but they have a different view of life from the general public.

As well as the impact of journalistic or newsroom culture, pack mentality and the dominance of the newsline on a story there is the issue of what I have termed 'history repeats itself'. Past cases clearly had an impact on new ones in terms of specific understandings, practical routines and general ideology. For instance one BBC specialist described the '*frisson of fear*' passed on from Cleveland about the wrongful removal of children. General reporters in particular rely heavily on 'going through the cuttings', that is looking at past coverage to build up their stories. Ironically, however, no one currently interviewed had any knowledge that post-case revision of journalistic or editorial practice occurred following the Cleveland, Orkney or Rochdale stories.

On the whole the picture from the media side is of a fairly smooth-running system with accepted ways of working and an established routine for case coverage. However, the process does emerge as conflictual at two key levels; first around the dominance of what I have termed 'male news' and secondly over source–journalist relationships, both of which will be addressed below.

SOURCES[88]

It is also necessary to look at sources of information for CSA stories. Because of the emphasis on cases and the use of general news reporters, stories are often produced within the framework of newsworthiness associated with the coverage of crime and deviance, an area of news gathering which relies heavily on official sources such as the police, court reports and the Home Office/Scottish Office.[89,90] An important difference from other crime stories, however, is that they fall into the realm of personal social services and child protection work, so sources will be statutory social services and voluntary organisations (for example, National Society for the Protection of Children, National Children's Bureau etc.). Once a story is 'running', usually a case-based one, there are other sources such as academic researchers and other 'experts', pressure groups including trade unions and community organisations (for example, Parents Against Injustice (PAIN), rape crisis services).

In terms of dealing with the media all organisations have well-developed PR systems which are quite sophisticated and complex, usually following a 'pyramid' structure (management at the top down to local officers). Some voluntary groups have a 'simple' version due to lack of resources, but they all recognised the importance of having a system to respond to press inquiries. All highlighted the same problem of resources as a restriction on developing their work. What also emerged was how the organisational priorities were not necessarily in line with those surrounding the subject of CSA, a particular problem for local authority press work.

All sources highlighted their work as overwhelmingly reactive on CSA. The criteria associated was emphasised, for example the speed and efficiency necessary, accessibility and using 'off the record' (OTR) briefings to give background information, particularly when there were issues of confidentiality (for example during the process of a case). All emphasised the crucial importance of this for CSA and social work-related PR generally. As the General Secretary of the British Association of Social Workers (BASW) put it:

> *a lot of the calls are for background briefing which absorb a phenomenal amount of time but don't lead to quotes and recognition, I mean for example we get phoned up sometimes, I don't wish to exaggerate it, but we do get phoned up sometimes by leader writers in papers wanting to check out thinking or by columnists, who write under their own name an opinion piece, but like to check things out with us in advance. So we're an important resource there and it's very frustrating that it doesn't ever show in any sort of public way – although of course it is about ensuring that we maintain our influence and often, you know, things that we say are then translated into the opinion of the journalist who's writing the piece.*

The most effective use of OTR was through utilising contacts sources had with known and trusted specialists, or trusted local journalists. Another aspect emphasised was 'seeking editorials' through contact between top management of an organisation and key editors. In the voluntary sector key management individuals would cultivate contacts with editors or use them to 'correct' mistakes if published.[91]

The main problems with journalists mentioned by sources were to do with the number of general reporters covering CSA, resulting in a high rotation of individuals on any story. A Royal Scottish Society for the Prevention of Cruelty to Children (RSSPCC) representative summarised this:

> *you'll get a story handled one day by one journalist and the same story carried on because of change of shift the next day by someone else, and quite often you feel you're running to stand still to keep them up to date ... you do sometimes wonder that they never look at the previous person's input to see*

what line they'd gone through ... A broad issue like trying to further the under-
standing of child sexual abuse is one that's very difficult to make sure that,
you know, consistent lines are taken by more than one or two or three indi-
viduals.

This was exacerbated by competition and tabloid imperatives. One local
authority press officer in Scotland described the problems dealing with
general reporters:

yeah you do get people apologising for coming back to you. That's quite common
... they don't know the kind of ways we work you know so they tend to just
sit with directories and ring up everybody and we've had a few — they'll come
on and they're very into finding victims, they're always looking for victims,
people who're in terrible situations ... eventually you kind of point out to them
how unrealistic they're being and they'll say 'Och, I know' and off they'll
go and then ten minutes later they'll be back on saying 'Oh, I'm sorry, I've
still to get this' [laughs] — 'cause they're basically out the door if they can't.

The impact on individuals was high: extra time spent repeating the same
information, having to 'stonewall' or refuse as a result of this lack of basic
understanding by journalists. Another emergent trend which was
detected was described as the 'wilful neglect' to check with sources, so
that a story would fit into a certain newsline. One PR manager for a
children's charity stated:

journalists have a hard time in pushing away from the editorial line particu-
larly if the editor or sub-editors have a vested interest, or have taken a specific
line on it themselves. They do not like to be backed into a corner and then
have to paint their way out of it.

On the whole most sources felt they had been able to build up good
relations with key journalists and sometimes editors and producers.
However, there is still an ongoing struggle over definitions around CSA
issues. An RSSPCC spokesperson described his experience in this
respect:

you can get newspapers who have journalists who're allowed to specialise in
the sort of spectrum of social services issues and, you know, health. Journal-
ists like that can be identified and they can actually be informed — and I don't
mean that to sound patronising. They want to be informed, they actually make
efforts themselves to make sure of that, at their own level. They do have an
ongoing battle within their own organisation as to how they portray what it
is they know. The other problem is one that not many newspapers allow people
to specialise in such a way as we can inform their knowledge.

An extra element here, which was emphasised particularly over the Orkney case, was the issue of geography and the sudden national (English) attention to a local issue. Many organisations felt fairly happy and confident about their PR systems in the local context but realised the problems of '*the troops from the London broadsheets*' as one press officer described them.

Issues in the production of CSA news

The above illustrates from both the journalists' side and that of sources what kind of structures they have to work within to produce CSA news. More importantly it highlights the problems experienced and the possible reasons for these. I now wish to turn to a discussion of the key issues perceived by these individuals which cut across these structural difficulties. Common to journalism and source organisations has been the impact of the Orkney case as well as the general issue of the existence, or not, of 'ritual' abuse. There is insufficient space to go into detail about these two issues. What is key, however, is that both journalists and source organisations agreed that the subsequent reporting of CSA has been significantly affected by them.

In particular what emerges as important here is the 'credibility of sources' and who is regarded as 'expert' in the debate around CSA. Given the predominance of general reporters many specialists felt that simplistic and uninformed responses to allegations of abuse, particularly those with ritualistic elements, were made. From the source side as well the significance was highlighted. One local authority press officer commented:

> *I think the problem with the kind of ritual abuse thing ... there is definitely a pack instinct there. You know, once a story is up and running and everybody's out looking for their own angle on it and ... there's an awful lot of tactics that are used, you know ... There's all this kind of conspiracy theory operating among the press that they try then to pin on to the social workers.*

Similarly the head of press at the RSSPCC stated:

> *I say that the minute you give the journalist or the media the opportunity to sensationalise the issue, it then moves into the realms, further into the realms of disbelief and incredulity for the public ... so that creates a climate whereby the public find it very hard to believe and that makes the whole issue of informing the debate very difficult. It certainly makes the whole issue of protecting children or leading prosecutions much more difficult.*

The Orkney case has had a major impact on some of the source organisations contacted so far. Two were heavily involved in the case and had to deal with criticism of their actions but felt quite positive that they had done so without too much negative impact for the organisations as a whole. Major reviews of organisational procedures had resulted and decisions made to adopt proactive campaigns/PR strategies. However, on the journalists' side, the case had not led to any revisions in practice and at the ideological level appears to have had a significantly negative impact on the acceptance of the existence of organised CSA.

As mentioned above, a related issue to that of 'ritual' abuse was the negative portrayal of social work actions over CSA, especially the idea of deciding if 'ritual' abuse existed or not. Journalists with good social work contacts and more specialist knowledge felt that there was general 'disbelief' among journalists about organised ritualistic abuse in the Rochdale and Orkney cases. One social services specialist stated:

> there were some reporters desperately trying to prove that satanic abuse didn't exist, it was a figment of social workers' imaginations and I was seen, falsely, as somebody that was completely arguing the opposite of that ... so I was basically seen as a believer, she [another journalist] was a non-believer, I was a social work ally, I believed everything social workers said.

Two key issues which emerge distinctly in the news coverage of CSA are 'child abuse fatigue' and 'male news'. More than once it has been suggested that the impact of the dramatic major cases of recent years has resulted in a reluctance by newsdesks to carry too many CSA stories – what has been described as 'child abuse fatigue' by interviewees. One journalist summarised this as:

> there was an overkill on child abuse, I mean I was going to my editor with another story on child sexual abuse and he'd say 'Oh, for God's sake', so you were always trying to think of how can I still report on an issue that's incredibly important without it being 'boring'.

The *Guardian* Social Services Editor estimated that he still has brought to his attention approximately two to three cases a week which do not get used as stories. There has to be a scandal, institutional errors, inquiry or similar angle for a case to get picked up. This is significant in the understanding of the emergence of 'new' topics such as woman abusers and False Memory Syndrome. The *Guardian* Women's Editor phrased this in relation to her understanding of the 'public':

> what the readership can cope with, what the people in charge are going to let you get through. If we keep coming again and again ... you know you could take it right to the line and you'd lose your job really – and I don't think

> *that you would have been a martyr to a great cause, because you would have lost a lot of readers as well. There's a limit to what people can take.*

Several individuals, not all women, commented on the imperatives of 'hard news' as being male dominated – what has previously been termed '*male news*' by one senior BBC radio journalist. They felt this influenced the decision making process around past CSA news stories and continued to influence news values, for example the desire to cover the 'False Memory Syndrome' debate in 1993. One senior press officer for social services suggested:

> *I think the press generally are fairly sceptical about it, particularly organised abuse, even though there have been cases of paedophile networks. So you might, if you wish to, see it as a male power sort of thing, that the media is largely controlled by men and people are feeling uncomfortable about it and I don't know, that's a value judgement, but there may be some of that in it, certainly in the tabloids.*

A picture of the different conflicts over case coverage emerges – difference of opinion between journalists, the newsdesk and the editor which were often divided according to gender. One female social services journalist from a broadsheet said:

> *I would have constant arguments in the office with reporters that just think basically – well male reporters probably don't want* [to think about the existence of] *child sex abuse ... I would sit in the office and come out with these arguments in a very matter of fact way, because I was always desperately trying not to get angry – there was one particular occasion where I was saying all of this and the chief reporter was being hysterical about it all and I was told that I was probably too involved with the case! So there was always, there was always a feeling of extreme* frustration *about it.*

Another freelance journalist on the same newspaper described the situation over the Orkney case in similar terms: '*I have never known the whole office to be so divided along gender lines as over that issue – it was so totally, you know* [makes parting motion with hands] *men* and *women*.' This journalist confirmed that the gender division included the women support workers at the newspaper – such as secretaries and cleaners. In other words the possibility of abuse having happened was more readily accepted by women working at this particular news organisation, whether or not they had a feminist perspective.

Other, male specialists who had similar disagreements with their newsdesks felt that the negative image of social work was 'used' in order to underpin this reluctance to believe in widespread *familial* child sexual abuse. In other words the belief that social workers could make mistakes was used in preference to 'explain' allegations in particular cases – rather than the adoption of a middle ground which most specialists thought to be more appropriate (in other words, not 'deciding' if abuse had or hadn't happened).

Another issue about ideology can be detected in the widespread use by journalists in interviews of the term 'common sense'. This particularly applied in descriptions of cases when it was suggested that it was common sense that certain individuals could not have abused their children, and it was therefore acceptable to use them as sources in stories.

Source–journalist relationships

Up to this point in the research the key area of source–journalist relationships has primarily been examined outside of the category of 'official' sources, such as the police, judiciary and government. However, it is clear that the sources cited here are crucial to an understanding of news production.

On the whole the most significant issue for both journalists and sources was the negative image of social work. This was expressed in slightly different ways – journalists primarily described it as a *'trench mentality'* between the two professions. It was often suggested, particularly by sources, that the general imperatives of 'hard news' went against the contextualisation of individual cases and ignored the complexities of CSA issues. One broadsheet journalist summarised:

> if you're the news editor, you're sitting with a story that one reporter's given you about parents saying 'Oh, it was awful, the social workers came at dawn and whipped the children from my arms and they were crying and the animals were all barking it was just the most awful moment of my life' and your social affairs correspondent is saying 'Yeah, but the social workers have got this great story about how they prepared everything and how they gave juice to the children and they gave them some toys.' It doesn't really sit.

However in both the voluntary and statutory sector this hostility was bemoaned by sources, with suggestions for improvements high on the agenda. Most source interviewees felt that the existence of specialists was crucial and helped to develop contacts into the social work world and child protection field. Related to this was a reliance on the use of OTR. Both the media and sources felt OTR was a successful way of contributing to an individual journalist's understanding of either a case or issue within CSA. A senior PR officer with BASW commented:

That is actually a real strategic problem for the social services, the lack of a clearly co-ordinated voice and sadly the fact is that, I mean I would say that, social workers and particularly social services managers don't really in my view understand how to use the sort of independent voice that we have to comment, not on the specifics of cases which in the end have to be handled locally, but on the general principles and to set it in the wider context ... When the chips are down, there is an instinctive and indeed planned way of working together but it's, it doesn't deal with you know residential care, the child abuse stuff, these things. We say similar things but it isn't co-ordinated and part of that is also the time the co-ordination requires.

Much time and effort was spent by source organisations minimising the impact of negative ideas about social work in relation to child protection and all wished they had the resources to do more proactive work in this respect.

A key development in relation to source–journalist relations is the organisation of 'parent pressure groups' – representing parents who allege they have been falsely accused of abusing their children – such as PAIN. Several specialist journalists saw this as a problem, particularly with the vast majority of journalists not having in–depth knowledge about the complexities of CSA. One broadsheet specialist commented: '*The problem with child sex abuse now is that parents and lawyers have started speaking to the media and it is much easier to carry an emotive story than just a hard straight-forward news story.*' The good co-ordination and efficient 'news management' of parents' groups has been mentioned widely by journalists, particularly those involved with the Orkney case. Most identify as important the issue of 'making up one's mind' about the parents – 'taking sides' definitely happened and was usually based on a combination of previous knowledge about CSA (and specifically 'ritual' abuse), identification with 'ordinary' articulate people and the well–organised parents' campaigns.

'Credibility' of the families was crucial but also combined with the lack of credibility of other sources, particularly social services. In such instances general reporters were battling with the '*trench mentality*' mentioned above whilst being offered unlimited access to parents' accounts of the removal of their children into care. As one specialist on a left–wing broadsheet paper summarised:

the paper also was much keener on the emotive stuff than everyone else was and I would argue this ... saying I just think this is a nonsense that we should be, as a radical paper, we should take a different stance. We should try and work out whether everything is going the way the families say it's going, we shouldn't just believe that the families are all innocent, that we shouldn't say they're guilty — that's the way this was interpreted in the office. I was saying they were guilty.

A clear difficulty in source–journalist relations in CSA cases was that of ascertaining 'hard news' facts. This was mentioned across reporting of many different types of cases. The specialist journalists used OTR as a device for understanding complexities in diagnosis of and intervention in the sexual abuse of children. As one broadsheet social services journalist who covered an alleged 'ritual' abuse case commented: *'I think the key formative experience of my view was talking to foster parents ... these were women who were very practical, they didn't seem imbued with — they hadn't been reading books from America.'*

One social services specialist with a Sunday broadsheet summarised it thus:

> *I mean for me the problems before were to do with an emotive situation, the people didn't know, you couldn't write a balanced news story, that was the problem and maybe that's the problem with child sex abuse cases or with social work issues — you can never write a balanced story 'cause we're never given the full story ... If we were given confidential information, off the record, not to use, it would help us write a balanced story.*

It was at these points that the personal ideologies of journalists and editors were crucial in informing the news production process. Pushing away from the general reporters' 'common-sense paradigm' for many specialists was a process informed by their specific contacts with sources in the child protection world. 'Setting it in context', as many journalists mentioned, was ultimately part of this process of accepting, or not, that the abuse of children exists, that it can be organised, with ritualistic elements — and crucially it can be *familial* abuse. One specialist commented on her battles with the news editor and senior journalists:

> *I mean it could happen on any other story, but child sex abuse causes so many emotions for everybody ... they would always try to pin me down on whether I believed abuse had happened and I kept saying it's just not my job, you wouldn't ask me this about any other story, we would just go on the information I was bringing in.*

This has been summarised by one social work source as the media not being able to *'handle the potential of conflicting interests and conflicting human rights'* in the reporting of specific cases.

Another significant element is clear here. Most interviewees were keen to explore suggested improvements around news reporting in relation to case coverage and child protection work. There was a great reluctance or expressed difficulty in discussing the issue of prevention and long-term strategies to eradicate the sexual abuse of children. This has been commented on by one press officer from the children's charity Kidscape, involved with prevention work, who revealed:

> *We have found that one of the difficulties about getting across messages about children abused by people they know is that very often it's not a message people want to touch ... People don't want to be associated with child abuse as incest ... it's a message we try to get across to the press but they're very wary, I think, of going with it. It's not a fun subject, it's likely to put readers off, may upset readers, and it's easier and safer to concentrate on strangers and bullying.*

Most notable was the lack of engagement from journalism with any feminist analyses in this respect. Those feminist groups or individuals who do try to engage with such debates are significantly marginalised in two ways: either they are not contacted for information at all, and are therefore absent from a specific discussion, or when they are contacted the specifics of a feminist analysis they raise are later 'edited out' or not engaged with. One source from a key feminist research organisation summarised this:

> *There are some cases where our input has actually fundamentally changed the tone or the content or the line that a piece has taken and that feels very rewarding and exciting and there are other times when you feel it's shifted something a little bit but not really. And there are other times when you think why did you bother because there are none of the qualifications or the complexity that you wanted them to think about actually there, and I think we've got ... times when we talk to journalists and it's very clear they haven't liked what we said so they've ignored it totally, so we don't even appear in the piece at all.*

This 'lack of credibility' attributed to feminist perspectives and source agencies was emphasised by sources, who are rarely contacted unless the press want to do a 'victim story'. They are not asked to contribute to debates or provide expert testimony.

Telling tales? Media power and audience beliefs about CSA

I want to try and conclude what these preliminary findings on news production tell us about ideology and the power of the media. It is instructive to reflect on what sources themselves see as key issues in the media reporting of CSA. One press officer from a major children's charity put it this way:

*if you look at the media role within the development of understanding of child
sexual abuse and the scale of the problem, it's really quite critical. It has on
the positive side given a tremendous amount of exposure and publicity to a
taboo which people were not prepared to accept could happen and did happen
and certainly not to the extent that we believed that it does. On the other hand,
it has trivialised and simplified and sensationalised stories which are a highly
complex pattern, you know, to understand. The media still tend to look at
it in many instances as the acts of a pathological individual rather than accepting
that there's a complex set of psychological and other dynamics involved in this.
So their understanding of, the purist understanding of child sexual abuse, other
than within the academic field, is still at a relatively low ebb. Now the media
have at least performed the service of bringing it into the open. They have not
yet properly, in many instances, although I would say there are some very
honourable exceptions, they have not yet learned to handle the debate
completely responsibly.*

The research so far has identified key aspects of organisational practices
for media and source personnel which explain the types of stories
produced about CSA. Specifically from the sources we have dealt with
several key things are apparent. All are acutely aware of the necessity
to operate efficient and manageable PR systems related to their work,
from the smallest feminist group to the largest children's charity. In this
sense political and social activism has become very 'media literate'. Interestingly they are not only aware of their own limitations regarding their
PR work, but also of those of the media organisations – particularly the
individual pressures on journalists.[92] However, as well as recognising
both structural and organisational factors which can inhibit or facilitate
their work, most sources realised the particular problems around the
coverage of CSA – the debates about definition, identification and intervention are very complex and difficult to translate into a news format.

There is no co-ordinated voice to represent CSA issues, but there
are a plethora of individuals and groups who at any given time may be
used as sources. The issue of media strategies outlined previously is very
important to the development of a more co-ordinated approach. Many
journalists, particularly those with a social services specialism, did not
take unquestioningly the definitions and accounts of 'officials' but
sought to develop known and trusted sources for information, many
of whom are used in an OTR capacity. For the main block of 'general'
reporters, what seemed to be crucial was the measuring of the competing
sources against 'common sense' as they defined it. Journalist culture in
relation to negative ideas about social work and scepticism about the
existence of 'ritual' abuse is clearly pertinent in understanding the

struggle to define the 'boundaries' of covering CSA, to use Soloski's terminology.[93]

There is not much to support a straightforward 'dominant ideology' thesis from our findings. Although there is evidence of structured access to journalists from officials such as the Department of Health, police and judiciary this does not support a 'primary definition' model. Rather there is a significant *field of contestation* in the attempt to 'define' issues around sexual assaults on children. Journalists acknowledge a much wider range of potential sources and specialists, in particular, are acutely aware of the 'competition' between them. They are constantly 'balancing' the information they get with their newsdesk and the editorial constraints they perceive, illustrated, for example, by the '*I wouldn't get it through my newsdesk*' statements which many made to me. This also supports Schudson's[94] emphasis on the importance of examining the role of the news editor in the production process.

Organisational and structural constraints do therefore exist; particularly notable in its impact on CSA coverage is the erosion of specialist journalism, for instance. However, from this research it is important to stress that sources *are* significant in the struggle to define issues around the sexual abuse of children. Sources clearly approach media organisations as basically 'unequal' – that is certain if one compares the resources of, say, the Department of Health with those of an organisation like Rights of Women. However, increasingly, source–media strategies are developed to offset such inequalities, for instance in the use of editorial 'connections' to influence output. Equally, if resources were the only problem, how can the apparent 'success' of parents' pressure groups to get media coverage be explained? The 'credibility' of such sources can only be explained by an awareness of the ideological dimensions of news production.

This connects strongly to Aldridge's[95] findings over the coverage of social work generally. She asserts that one significant problem for social services in dealing with the media is that 'good news' is not necessarily news at all. Consequently social work achievements will be ignored whilst errors are highlighted. In contrast to Aldridge's final pessimism about coverage of social work in the national (English-based) media, research from the CSA Project reveals that from both the source and journalist positions considerable energy and innovation are used to combat this tendency.[96]

To return to the issues raised by the first section of this chapter, how can we 'place' the findings from the news coverage of CSA? As well as the political–economic factors and organisational comments summarised above, the research is revealing some aspects of the 'cultural air' discussed previously, which informs the news production. This leads to the significant area of 'male ideology' as already mentioned. One of the real problems with applying the critical media research tradition to this area of analysis is the lack of connection to patriarchy.[97] I want to suggest that this operates in two, interconnected ways.

First, through *gendered news production* where women journalists often have a struggle to get social affairs issues recognised in the hard news arena in the first place, and find them frequently marginalised when they succeed. Similarly, the effectiveness of strategies by feminist source groups can be affected. Secondly it operates at the level of *patriarchal ideology* which persistently informs the news process, from journalists and newsrooms to sources and their management. This is particularly evident around the acceptance or rejection of the belief in widespread familial sexual abuse. It was often at this point, of naming the sexual abuse as predominantly by men, that 'negotiations', both between sources and the media and between journalists and editors, broke down. It significantly cuts across other ideological assumptions, such as the negative reputation of the social work profession.

Although critical media research has offered us significant concepts on which to form our methodological approach, we believe it needs to address more substantially these gender issues. As has occurred all too often in the social sciences field, the significance of gender has been sidestepped once again.[98] If, as the opening quote suggests, news stories can be understood as modern fables, we need to be concerned with the central elements of such moralising as it relates to gender.

As Eldridge[99] has commented, our research approach here is complex and more difficult, or as he puts it 'messy', in its theoretical exploration of the power dynamics of the media. It has to be so, in order not to resort to the simplistic pluralism or crude determinism of previous media theories. Of course the telling question we are left with is: how does the telling of tales relate to audience understanding of CSA? That is a question also often repeatedly absent from media research, but one which we hope to answer in our subsequent work.

Acknowledgements

The project acknowledges funding from the (British) Economic and Social Research Council (ESRC No R000233675). Thanks to all the interviewees who gave their time, in some cases a considerable amount. Grateful thanks to the following for their good-humoured assistance in compiling and coding a huge data base: Lesley Henderson, Rick

Holliman, Justine Rothwell, Dawn Rowley and Sarah Williams. Thanks are also due to Professor Eldridge and Jenny Kitzinger, both for comments on this chapter and continued hard work on the project as a whole. Always last but in no possible way least, Joanne Yuill, our resilient and cheerful project secretary, deserves special thanks and some kind of medal for putting up with us!

Notes and references

1. Soloski, J., 'News reporting and professionalism: some constraints on the reporting of the news', *Media Culture and Society*, 11, 2, April 1989, pp. 207–28.
2. Fejes, F., 'Critical mass communications research and media effects', *Media Culture and Society*, 6, 3, 1984.
3. Cohen, S. and Young, J. (eds), *The Manufacture of News: Deviance, Social Problems and the Mass Media* (London: Constable, 1973).
4. Glasgow University Media Group (GUMG) *Bad News* (London: Routledge & Kegan Paul, 1976); GUMG, *More Bad News* (London: Routledge & Kegan Paul, 1980); GUMG, *Really Bad News* (London: Writer and Readers, 1982); GUMG, *War and Peace News* (Buckingham; Open University Press, 1985).
5. Schlesinger, P., *Putting Reality Together* (London: Constable, 1978).
6. Hall, S., Critcher, C., Jefferson, T., Clarke, J., and Roberts, B., *Policing the Crisis: Mugging, the State and Law and Order* (London: Macmillan, 1978).
7. Curran, J. and Seaton, J., *Power Without Responsibility* (London: Methuen, 1981).
8. Althusser, L., 'Ideology and ideological state apparatuses', in Althusser, L., *Lenin and Philosophy and Other Essays* (London: NLB, 1971).
9. Schlesinger, P. and Tumber, H., *Reporting Crime: The Media Politics of Crime and Criminal Justice* (Oxford: Oxford University Press, 1994), p. 7.
10. Schlesinger, P. and Tumber, H., *Reporting Crime*.
11. Schlesinger, P. and Tumber, H., *Reporting Crime*.
12. McLaughlin, L., ('Feminism, the public sphere, media and democracy', *Media Culture and Society*, 15, 1993, pp. 599–620.
13. Schlesinger, P., 'Rethinking the sociology of journalism: Source strategies and the limits of media-centrism', in Ferguson, M. (ed.), *Public Communication: The New Imperatives* (London: Sage, 1989).
14. Zoonen, L.V., *Feminist Media Studies* (London: Sage, 1994).
15. Eldridge, J.E.T. (ed.)/GUMG, *Getting the Message: News, Truth and Power* (London: Routledge, 1993).
16. McNair, B., *News and Journalism in the UK* (London: Routledge, 1993).
17. Schudson, M., 'The sociology of news production', *Media Culture and Society*, 11, 3, 1989, p. 275.
18. McNair, B., *News and Journalism*.

19. Curran, J., 'Culturalist perspectives of news organisations: A reappraisal and a case study', in Ferguson, M. (ed), *Public Communication: The New Imperatives* (London: Sage, 1989).
20. Curran, J., 'Culturalist perspectives', p. 12.
21. Hall, S. et al., *Policing the Crisis*.
22. Hall, S. et al., *Policing the Crisis*.
23. Cohen, S. and Young, J. (eds), *The Manufacture of News*.
24. Hall, S. et al., *Policing the Crisis*.
25. Hall, S. et al., *Policing the Crisis*, p. 58. Italics in original.
26. Young, J., 'The role of the police as amplifiers of deviance', in Cohen, S. (ed.), *Images of Deviance* (Harmondsworth: Penguin, 1971).
27. Cohen, S., *Folk Devils and Moral Panics* (London: Granada Paladin, 1980).
28. Hall, S. et al., *Policing the Crisis*.
29. Schlesinger, P., 'Rethinking the sociology of journalism'.
30. McNair, B., *News and Journalism*, p. 48. Italics in original.
31. Schlesinger, P., 'Rethinking the sociology of journalism'.
32. Schlesinger, P. and Tumber, H., *Reporting Crime*.
33. Schlesinger, P., 'Rethinking the sociology of journalism', p. 69.
34. Schudson, M., 'The sociology of news production'.
35. Schudson, M., 'The sociology of news production', p. 275.
36. Obviously the 'common sense' appealed to varies over time and geographic place. See Gans, H.J., *Deciding What's News* (New York: Pantheon, 1979), for a description of what he terms the 'para-ideology' of American journalism. For a discussion in relation to gender discourse, see Zoonen, L.V., *Feminist Media Studies*.
37. Curran, J., 'Culturalist perspectives', p. 120.
38. White, D.M., 'The gatekeeper: A case study in the selection of news', *Journalism Quarterly*, 27, 1950, pp. 383–90.
39. Tuchman, G., *Making News: A Study in the Construction of Reality* (New York: Free Press, 1978).
40. Cohen, S. and Young, J. (eds), *The Manufacture of News*.
41. Chibnall, S., *Law and Order News* (London: Tavistock, 1977).
42. Ericson, R.V., Baranek, P.M. and Chan, J.B.L., *Visualising Deviance* (Buckingham: Open University Press, 1987).
43. To my knowledge there has never been any systematic analysis of journalists' training courses in Britain. Melin, M., 'Can women become cowboys?' John Logie Baird Seminar, University of Glasgow 1994, has studied the training of journalists in Sweden.
44. Ericson, R.V. et al., *Visualising Deviance*.
45. Barrat, D., *Media Sociology* (London: Tavistock, 1986), p. 94.
46. Ericson, R.V. et al., *Visualising Deviance*.
47. Hollingsworth, M., *The Press and Political Dissent* (London: Pluto Press, 1986).
48. Soloski, J., 'News reporting'.
49. Chibnall, S., *Law and Order News*.
50. Ericson, R.V. et al., *Visualising Deviance*, p. 348.
51. Ericson, R.V. et al., *Visualising Deviance*.
52. Ericson, R.V. et al., *Visualising Deviance*.

53. Whitaker, B., *News Ltd: Why You Can't Read All About It* (London: Minority Press Group, 1981).

54. This is interesting because it can explain certain 'anomalies' which occur in individual journalists' work. I am drawn to the example given by Miller and Williams (1993, p. 20) of the journalist who saw the 'amazing story' potential in a 'whole family with AIDS' even though this ran counter to what she knew was '100 per cent the truth'.

55. Whitaker, B., *News Ltd*.

56. Soloski, J., 'News reporting'.

57. Roshco, B., *Newsmaking* (Chicago: University of Chicago Press, 1975).

58. Soloski, J., 'News reporting', p. 213.

59. Soloski, J., 'News reporting', p. 226. My emphasis.

60. Schudson, M., 'The sociology of news production'.

61. Schudson, M., 'The sociology of news production', p. 272.

62. Soloski, J., 'News reporting'.

63. Chibnall, S., *Law and Order News*.

64. Schlesinger, P., Murdock, G. and Elliot, P., *Televising Terrorism* (London: Comedia, 1983).

65. Ericson, R.V. et al., *Visualising Defence*.

66. Hall, S. et al., *Policing the Crisis*.

67. Schlesinger, P. 'From production to propaganda?' *Media Culture and Society*, 11, 3, 1989, pp. 283–306.

68. Ericson, R.V., Baranek, P.M. and Chan, J.B.L., *Negotiating Control: A Study of News Sources* (Toronto: University of Toronto Press, 1989).

69. Schudson, M., 'The sociology of news production'.

70. Schlesinger, P., 'Rethinking the sociology of journalism'.

71. Miller, D. and Williams, K., 'Negotiating HIV/AIDS information; Agendas, media strategies and the news', in Eldridge, J. (ed.)/GUMG, *Getting the Message: News, Truth and Power* (London: Routledge, 1993).

72. Schlesinger, P. and Tumber, H., *Reporting Crime*.

73. Schlesinger, P., 'Rethinking the sociology of journalism'.

74. Miller, D. and Williams, K., 'Negotiating HIV/AIDS information'.

75. Deacon, D. and Golding, P., 'When ideology fails; The flagship of Thatcherism and the British local and national media', *European Journal of Communication*, 6, 1991, pp. 291–313.

76. Eldridge, J.E.T. (ed.)/GUMG, *Getting the Message*.

77. Each report was coded on to a specially developed software package, enabling us to search by headline, date, origin (for example which newspaper), name of journalist and format (for example an editorial versus a column). Additional details, such as the main topic of the item, how people were described and who was interviewed, were also recorded.

78. The key cases were: Orkney (445 press items); Frank Beck (140 items); Rochdale (61 items); Epping Forest (41 items). In addition to these there were numerous abduction/sex murders (120 items) and other miscellaneous cases (329 items). For a discussion of the Orkney case see Asquith, S., *Protecting Children: Cleveland to Orkney – More Lessons to Learn* (Edinburgh: Children in Scotland/HMSO, 1993).

79. Reports of cases did sometimes include *implicit* causal explanation – usually located in individual pathology of the abuser.

80. When the press did cover 'prevention' it often did so outside straightforward news-of-the-day reports. For a further discussion of prevention coverage see Kitzinger, J. and Skidmore, P., 'Playing safe: Media coverage of child sexual abuse prevention strategies', in *Child Abuse Review*, 3, 1994.

81. The description of 'ritual' and 'satanic' abuse will use inverted commas throughout as an indication of the disputed nature surrounding the meanings of such terms, *not* as indicating disbelief in the existence of such abuse.

82. Franklin, B. and Parton, N., (1991) *Social Work, the Media and Public Relations* (London: Routledge, 1991).

83. In terms of the specific diagnosis and intervention coverage, 81 per cent focused on the actions of social workers, 19 per cent on legal and/or medical or other professions.

84. All quotations in italics below are from interviews with press and broadcast journalists and editors, unless otherwise acknowledged. I have spoken to individuals from the broadsheet and tabloid press, and a range of television and radio news programmes throughout England and Scotland.

85. In the press coverage for 1991 78 per cent of journalists were unnamed or 'generals' who had produced three to four items in the year. Only 9 per cent wrote more than 10 items.

86. Chibnall, S., *Law and Order News*.

87. This happened to the social services correspondent for *Scotland on Sunday*.

88. All quotes in italics below are from individuals working within sources organisations such as the social services, children's charities and feminist groups.

89. Ericson, R.V. et al., *Visualising Deviance*.

90. Chibnall, S., *Law and Order News*.

91. An example from *Childline* was Esther Rantzen 'bending the ear' of a national editor at a social event over mistakes published in a press article on the organisation.

92. It will be important to contrast these findings with those from subsequent research on 'officials' such as those from the Department of Health.

93. Soloski, J., 'News reporting', p. 226.

94. Schudson, M., 'The sociology of news production'.

95. Aldridge, M., 'Social work and the news media: A hopeless case?' *British Journal of Social Work*, 20, 6, 1990.

96. This should be consolidated in respect of the reporting of CSA when the National Commission for the Prevention of Child Abuse assesses the importance of media coverage to long-term prevention strategies.

97. The only significant attempt to look at these issues is by Zoonen, L.V., *Feminist Media Studies*.

98. Smith, D.E., *The Everyday World As Problematic: A Feminist Sociology* (Buckingham: Open University Press, 1987).

99. Eldridge, J.E.T., 'Risk, media and society', University of Glasgow Lecture Series, 18 October 1994.

6 Media Reporting of Rape: The 1993 British 'Date Rape' Controversy

Sue Lees

Rape has received unprecedented press coverage over the past five years in the US and Britain. In this chapter I discuss the publicity given to British rape cases referred to as 'date rapes' (of Donnellan, Kydd and Diggle) which received much publicity in 1993 within the context of the falling conviction rate for reported acquaintance rapes. This can be seen as indicative of a moral backlash amid the rising concern about male violence. 'Date rape' is a term used loosely to differentiate it from 'real' rape, and is often used synonymously with acquaintance rape. The linking of the term 'date', which should be pleasurable, with 'rape' is subtly used to imply that the assault was not really rape.[1] (See Estrich 1987.) Press coverage of these trials gave the impression that men were being unfairly accused of rape and led to a backlash of adverse comment. It was argued that the pendulum had swung too far in favour of women's rights and that such cases should never have reached trial, let alone led to convictions. Others argued that bringing up rape exacerbated a 'victim mentality'. This chapter unveils a very different reality.

By sitting in on British trials and monitoring the results, I found the facts very different from those reflected in the volatile press, where women are alleged increasingly to be dragging men into court for pushing things a little too far, in retaliation for 'bad' sex or being rejected. During a four-month period in the summer of 1993[2] I monitored all rape trials where the victim was over 16 years old at the Old Bailey, the Central Criminal Court in London and ten trials at two other courts. I also examined transcripts of 31 trials. Only 32 per cent of cases which came to trial at the Old Bailey where 'consent' (rather than identification) was at issue resulted in a conviction. Evidence suggests that a number of men are acquitted over and over again.[3]

In order to understand press bias in reporting it is important to understand how few cases of reported rape lead to a conviction. The high attrition rate in rape and sexual assault cases was well documented in studies, mainly conducted by the Home Office and Scottish Office, undertaken in the early and mid-1980s (see Chambers and Millar 1983, Wright 1984, Smith 1989, Grace et al. 1992). These studies found that a high proportion of reported cases were categorised by the police as 'no crimes' and so were not recorded as offences, and cases were frequently dropped between report and committal (Chambers and Millar 1983). Of those cases which did proceed to court, several resulted in a conviction for a less serious offence and many more resulted in acquittals (Wright 1984, Chambers and Millar 1986, Smith 1989, Grace et al. 1992). At each stage in the criminal justice process, cases in which there was some prior acquaintance between the complainant and the suspect were more likely to be dropped or downgraded to a less serious offence than cases of 'stranger' attacks (Smith 1989, Grace et al. 1992).

Moreover, contrary to the picture painted by both the quality and 'gutter' press, the conviction rate for rape and attempted rape is decreasing year by year. The overall conviction rate decreased progressively between 1985 and 1993 from 24 per cent to 10 per cent.[4] (Home Office Statistics 1993.) In other words, in spite of the number of women reporting rape trebling since 1983, the same number of men were convicted in 1993 as in 1985. Additionally, according to research carried out by Temkin (1993), there is some evidence that a significant proportion of these convictions were reversed on appeal. It appears that women are being encouraged to report rape, often intimidated by their assailants, only to be denied justice and humiliated by the press.

There is also evidence that a lower proportion of cases are reaching the Crown Court for jury trial. In 1986 the Crown Prosecution Service (CPS) was created and took over responsibility for the prosecution of criminal cases, a task formerly undertaken by the police. It is the CPS which decides whether a case should have a jury trial. (All cases of rape and attempted rape have a first hearing in the magistrates court.) We do know, however, that between 1985 and 1993 the proportion of cases not proceeded with after an appearance at the magistrates court increased threefold from 10 per cent in 1985 to 30 per cent in 1993 (Home Office Statistics 1993). The CPS is under pressure to keep costs down and its performance is judged partly by the conviction rate of cases it recommends for trial. The complainant has no right of appeal against the decision if the CPS decides the case should not go forward. The difficulty of gaining convictions percolates through the system so that only very few cases go to trial. This means that many women who report rape and want to give evidence are denied the right to do so.

I found that acquittals appeared to result from serious imbalances in the trial procedures. For example, the defendant meets with his defence counsel beforehand to prepare the case and can converse with him during the trial but the complainant, as first witness for the prosecution in the

British adversarial system of justice, is not even allowed to meet the prosecution beforehand. This often results in a highly disinterested presentation of her case. More important still is the sexism embedded in judges' directions to the jury regarding the criteria of judging the respective credibility of the complainant and defendant. This is rooted in the different meanings of 'reputation' and 'credibility' when applied to men as opposed to women in society at large. Reputation when applied to women refers to her assumed sexuality, whereas for a man it usually refers to his general social standing in the public world (see Lees 1993). Sexual exploits for a man enhance his reputation but destroys it for a woman. It is for this reason that a woman's sexual character (as judged by such criteria as her marital status, whether her children were born in or out of wedlock, and even such factors as whether or not she has ever had an abortion or the race or social standing of her husband or lover) and her past sexual history are considered relevant.

It is often argued that rape cases are problematic because the jury has to judge one person's word against another, since the offence occurs in private with rarely any witnesses. There is some truth in this although corroboration (evidence from another source) to back one version rather than another is often present. It is not however generally recognised that the jury are instructed to judge one person's word rather than another's according to quite different criteria. In the defendant's case his 'good' character or reputation depends on his lack of previous convictions and his occupation. In the woman complainant's case her lack of previous convictions are not referred to as enhancing her reputation. Instead it is her sexual character and past sexual history that are considered crucial.

Public concern regarding the relevance of the woman's past sexual history and sexual character to verdicts led to the passing of the Sexual Offences (Amendment) Act in 1976. This was aimed at restricting the circumstances in which defence lawyers could refer to past sexual history and sexual character evidence to where such evidence was strictly relevant. This was only to be allowed at the discretion of the judge, to be decided 'in camera' on application by the defence counsel. Although this change had been introduced in the wake of public concern and in response to the findings of the Heilbron Committee (1975), the introduction of such evidence did nothing to advance the cause of justice while effectively putting the woman on trial; in a high proportion of cases judges continued to allow sexual history evidence. (See Adler 1987 and Brown et al. 1992 for an account of a similar fate that befell the amendment on sexual history evidence made to the

Scottish law in 1986.) Additionally, in my analysis of trial transcripts, I found that cross examination of the complainant relating to such evidence was frequently slipped in by the defence counsel, and rarely challenged by the prosecution or censored by the judge. For example, in one case a young woman was asked whether she had had an abortion three years previously, a question which was totally unrelated to the rape allegation.

The few judges who did attempt to implement the new rules in the spirit of Heilbron were soon stopped in their tracks by the Court of Appeal, who proceeded to quash a number of convictions on the grounds that defence lawyers had been refused permission to introduce 'relevant' sexual history evidence. (See for example R v. Viola (1982) 75 Cr App. R 125. This and other cases with disturbing implications for the case law on rape are discussed by Temkin 1993.) Inevitably judicial sabotage of this kind has an immobilising effect on reform initiatives at earlier points in the criminal justice process.

The press, rather than expressing concern at the failure of the Sexual Offences Act to limit the introduction of sexual history and sexual character evidence, have instead given wide publicity to such evidence and added further to the distress of complainants and their stereotyping as hysterical, vindictive or promiscuous.

In this chapter, I critically examine the various ways in which the press distort rape trials in order to give the impression that more 'flimsy' cases are now going to court and more men are being accused of rape. While it is true that the number of women reporting rape to the police has trebled, it appears that a lower proportion of cases are going to trial. This distortion is achieved through feeding off all kinds of myths about the nature of rape, the nature of rapists and of rape complainants. Such myths include: that rape is an expression of sexual desire[5] rather than of sexual power and violence; that rape is due to an irresistible urge of male sexuality, or a question of men 'misreading signals' in a sexual negotiation rather than a violent sexual assault; that women frequently make 'false allegations' of rape, or that the typical rapist is a stranger or black rather than an acquaintance, a relative or a past or present lover.

First I shall consider the way the press interpret rape allegations in purely sexual terms, playing down, if not leaving out, descriptions of coercion or violence. Such reports give prominence to the defendant's claim that he 'misread the signals' and often entirely exclude the complainant's version, which often rests on the coercion and violence or threat of violence involved. By only presenting the defence barrister's arguments (usually that the alleged rape was misunderstood seduction), the violence of the assault is left out or, if mentioned, is interpreted as what the victim wanted.

In this way press reports of rape mirror the judicial process in stereotyping the complainant as the precipitator of sexual misunderstanding rather than the victim of a brutal and violent attack.

Secondly, the press stereotype complainants as hysterical, promiscuous (sluts) or manipulative (or all three), where all kinds of reasons are presented as to why women should make false allegations or naively 'precipitate' rape. The press pick up on the defence barrister's tactics of destroying the victim's credibility by scapegoating her where possible as a 'slut' or as unreliable. In this way there is often a tendency to depict men rather than women as the true victims, which involves presenting the defendant as not the kind of man who could possibly be a rapist. Austen Donnellan, the student whose case is discussed below, was presented as 'the perfect gentleman' and in far more sympathetic a light than the complainant. In the case of Angus Diggle, a solicitor convicted of attempting to rape a woman solicitor after taking her to a ball, he was described as sexually naive ('not good at picking up social signals from women') rather than coercive; a depiction which contrasted with how he had behaved as revealed in the transcripts of the trial. It was reported that Judge David Williams in sentencing him said that his naivete in sexual matters had contributed considerably to the offence. As a result occasionally the press go so far as to report acquittals as 'victories' and rape convictions as 'miscarriages of justice'.

Thirdly, the placing of particular news items in the press is also crucial to the impression given. Reports of acquittals where a trial is being followed are front-page news, whereas reports of convictions tend to be given far less prominence, and then only if the suspect fits the stereotype of the psychopathic stranger. Similarly, serious analytical articles, if published at all, are placed on the women's page or given low prominence.

According to Barak (1994), an American researcher, the portrayals of sex, crime and rape both in myth and in the news media construction serve to reinforce negative images of women and of social justice. My own research suggests that this leads to a denial that rape actually occurs or a total absence of discussion of the reasons why men rape. Instead all the emphasis is placed on the woman's alleged provocation to sexual attack. Benedict (1992), another American researcher, who studied the portrayal of four well-publicised rape cases in the US[6] emphasises the print media's distorted portrayal of victims of rape as follows:

> Pushed into subordinate roles of sex objects, wives, mothers or crime victims, they have little opportunity to be portrayed as self-determining

individuals. When a reporter sits down to write a story about any woman, therefore, let alone a woman who has been victimised in a sex crime, he or she has an enormous burden of assumptions, habits, and cliches to carry to the story. Not only are conventional images of women limited, but our very language promotes those images. It is not surprising, therefore, that the public and the press tend to combine the bias in our language, the images of women and rape myths into a shared narrative about sex crimes that goes like this:

The 'Vamp' version: The woman, by her looks, behaviour or generally loose morality, drove the man to such extremes of lust that he was compelled to commit the crime. The 'Virgin' version: The man, a depraved and perverted monster, sullied the innocent victim, who is not a martyr to the flaws of society (1992: 23).

Sex crime victims tend to be squeezed into one or two of these images, either a wanton female who provoked the assailant with her sexuality or a pure and innocent victim attacked by monsters. Benedict (1992: 24) explains:

Both of these narratives are destructive to the victims of rape and to public understanding of the subject. The vamp version is destructive because it blames the victim of the crime instead of the perpetrator. The virgin version is destructive because it perpetuates the idea that women can only be madonnas or whores, paints women dishonestly and relies on portraying the suspects as inhuman monsters.

Images based on the vamp and virgin can appear simultaneously. An example of this bias was shown in the report of the British case of Michael Seear, involving the first woman police officer's allegation of rape against a colleague to go to trial in February 1995.[7] As a woman police officer who brought a case against a colleague explained, 'For the first day I was the poor weeping WPC, then I became this drunken temptress, covered in love bites, causing trouble.'[8] (There is another contradiction between the requirement that the complainant should appear upset as a victim but as a court witness should appear to be controlled and calm. If in court she appears lucid as a good witness, she is in danger of not coming across as a victim. If she appears too upset she runs the risk of being seen as hysterical and is therefore disbelieved.)

This case clearly illustrates that in focusing all the attention on the complainant and her assumed provocative and manipulative behaviour, the alternative possibility of rape by the defendant is not even seriously entertained, even when the complainant is a respectable serving woman police officer. Instead the defendant was acquitted and headline reports on the following day in the quality newspapers publicised the defendant's demands for complainants to lose their press anonymity in trials.

In this case, the WPC described her experience (in one of the few reports of her experience) in the following terms: 'Everything was put under a microscope. I have no sordid sexual past, nothing lurid to hide, thank God, because I felt as though my character, my whole soul, was being judged and found wanting.' Reports talked of how she had chatted with her boyfriend over drinks on the night although she did not in fact drink anything. She was also described as wearing a tight white blouse and a short skirt which was completely untrue. She described the effect: 'It's a classic thing of making me sound like I was asking for it, which is never justified in any case. Anyone who knows me could tell you the picture the papers painted wasn't me.'

Absent from the trial process and the press reports was any explanation of why the complainant might have been raped. All the focus was on the unlikely possibility that she might have made it up. Yet men rape often for reasons of competitiveness with other men, particularly close friends. In this case apparently the complainant, her boyfriend, another serving police officer and the defendant all used to go out together and were close friends. In court the argument was presented that she lied in order to explain her alleged 'infidelity'. Why she should need to do this is only explicable if she is seen as the property of her boyfriend. Yet the fact that men do rape the girlfriends of their best friends either as a result of competitiveness or jealousy is not even considered.

The scapegoating and the tendency to blame victims by scrutinising their past and their behaviour at the time, thereby subtly shifting the responsibility on to them, has also been previously highlighted by British research (see Soothill 1991, 1993). Both the prosecution and defence counsel submissions are used in such a way as to suggest damaging material in the way they present the case as though the victim is partly culpable for the rape (see Soothill and Walby 1991). For example in the 1985 Brixton gang rape, when two teenage girls were raped 45 times at knifepoint by six youths in a deserted garage after trying to return home by bus from a pop concert, the prosecution counsel was reported to have commented: 'It would have been much better if those girls had been tucked up in bed.' The detective inspector in charge of the case added: 'It was not wise for these two young girls to be out so late.' Anne Robinson, journalist for the *Daily Mirror* wrote:

I find these comments worrying. Because, whether intentional or not, both these men come close to implying the girls were partly to blame. And we are coming dangerously near to admitting total defeat if we lamely accept the solution to street violence is for women to forego their liberty and put *themselves under virtual night time house arrest*.[9]

Robinson puts her finger on another feature of both court trials and their depiction in the press, which is to *draw a line for legitimate behaviour by women*. One function of rape trials is to act as a form of control over autonomous female behaviour, particularly if it impinges on what is regarded as male territory. A classic example of this is the 1985 paratroopers' case where a 22-year-old woman, a member of the Women's Army Corps, got drunk with 13 paratroopers whom she said held her down, raped and assaulted her with a broom. All 13 were acquitted on the grounds that 'it would not have happened if the girl had not gone to the barracks for sex'.[10] A woman who ventures into the public sphere, the male sphere, whether it is the street, a public house or a male-dominated workplace such as an army barracks, is in danger of being seen as 'fair game'.

Background to the date rape debate

The Mike Tyson and William Kennedy Smith trials in the US, occurring at a time when more women students were demanding that universities develop sexual harassment policies in response to assaults on university campuses, led to an outburst of controversy in the US. The publication of Katie Roiphe's book, *The Morning After* (1993), in which she disputed the prevalence of rape in America and attacked feminists for exaggerating its incidence and heightening fears of violence, coincided in 1993 with the reporting of the three British 'date rape' cases under consideration and received much publicity in Britain. She poured scorn on the findings of recent American victimisation studies that one in four women reported being raped, suggesting this figure had come out of the 'addled brains of first-year students', and accused antirape activists of manipulating statistics to frighten students with a non-existent epidemic of rape and of encouraging them to view unsatisfactory or bad sex as rape and 'everyday experience' – sexist jokes, professorial leers, men's everyday straying hands and other body parts – as intolerable insults and assaults. Ignoring the evidence that most women fear to speak out about male violence Roiphe argued that feminists, by encouraging women to 'break the silence', had led them to view men as predators and to exaggerate fear of violence.[11]

Roiphe's book undoubtedly hit a nerve in the US and was greeted with jubilation by the press, being well reviewed in the *New York Times*. Roiphe was feted with interviews and meetings on both sides of the Atlantic. Unlike in the US, however, her book did not do well in Britain, where controversy over sexual harassment and rape at universities has not reached the same pitch as in the US. This may well change, as a study conducted by the Oxford University Student Union suggests that sexual harassment and rape are not uncommon and university administrations are being pressured to develop policies to address the issue.[12]

Changes in media reporting of sex crimes

According to an analysis of press reports of sex crime undertaken by Soothill (1991) and Soothill and Walby (1991), overall the press have taken an increasing interest in rape cases since the 1970s, coinciding with a higher level of women reporting rape to the police. They identified two main themes. The first, typical of the period prior to the 1980s, was characterised by a concentration on the stereotype of the stranger rapists or evil psychopathic fiend.[13] The emphasis on the psychopathological rapist or 'sex beast' is usually based on the selective reporting of specific facts and masks the reality of most sex crimes, which are by men who do not appear to be abnormal or psychologically disturbed. Often the sex beast of the media is linked to earlier fiends such as the Yorkshire Ripper or Dracula.

This stereotype was in contrast to the profile of reported rapes analysed by British Home Office researchers Lloyd and Walmsley (1989: 42), who compared all cases leading to convictions of rape in 1973 with 1985. They divided rapes into three groups dependent on the previous contact with the victim: strangers had had no contact, acquaintances who had some contact and intimates who were well known such as relatives, friends and partners. They found there had been a decrease in the number of gang rapes and of stranger[14] and acquaintance offences but *a significant increase in offences by intimates*.[15] Contrary to the statistical profile which showed an increase in reported rapes by intimates, such rapes were largely *absent from press reports*. Instead the media representation had depicted rape as primarily about sexual attacks in public places by strangers[16] and gangs in exactly the opposite direction to Lloyd and Walmsley's findings. This limited view of rape was exactly what the women's movement had campaigned against.

The second trend developing in the 1980s was an increase in dramatic coverage of a few selected cases. As Soothill (1991: 385) concludes: 'there have been some trials (usually those involving murder, sexual peccadilloes or a celebrity, and preferably all three) which attract so much publicity that they become like a national soap opera'. The 1993 Donnellan 'date' rape case had such ingredients: student sex at a prestigious university, 'false' allegations, drunkenness and a celebrity (Lord Russell).

Combined with two other cases, of Diggle and Kydd, this led to an outcry in the national press, where the underlying message appeared to be that allegations of 'date rape' were a threat to all men and every man's reputation was at risk. This indicates the ways that myths surrounding rape and the rhetoric are at odds with the reality, where only 10 per cent of men reported for rape are convicted, and where 'date rape' cases rarely reach court. In the Donnellan case it was the accused (backed by the CPS) not the complainant who insisted on the case going to trial. In my monitoring period only two out of 38 cases could be classified as 'date' rapes and the Diggle case was the only one which resulted in a conviction.

The context of 'date rape' cases

'Date rape', according to Mary Koss, the American psychologist who coined the term, refers rather to a *specific* form of acquaintance rape where the victim and perpetrator had some level of mutual romantic interest between them in which consensual sexual intercourse would be seen as entirely appropriate within the relationship (Koss 1988). Increasingly in the media the term 'date rape' is used to refer not merely to situations where the couple have made a date to go out together, but synonymously with 'acquaintance' rapes of all kinds. It is applied to situations where a woman chats to a man in a pub or accepts a lift from a party or is asked in for a coffee after a brief social encounter. It is misleading and dangerous to use the term 'date' rape in this way. If all acquaintance rapes are referred to as 'date' rapes the implication is that they are not only less serious but not 'real' rapes at all. Applying 'date' to a situation where a woman may ask someone in for coffee or be escorted home carries the message that she is inviting sexual intercourse, and is misleading and distorting. For these reasons the term 'date' rape should be abandoned as it carries connotations of casual consensual sex.

At the very least the term should be confined to situations where the couple had made a date or some *prior* commitment to meet socially or romantically. This would exclude using the term 'date' rape to apply to the student, Donnellan, who had met the complainant at a party but had not arranged to go out with her beforehand. 'Date' rape, therefore, would not refer to situations where the woman was offered a lift in a car or was invited to go somewhere under false pretences, and where the woman invited someone into her home who had accompanied her home. Such rapes are acquaintance rapes. 'Date' rape should be confined to describing cases where *there is a more defined relationship between the parties, from a first date to a more established romantic relationship* and this is the way the term will be used here.

In Britain two cases of 'date' rape occurring at two prestigious universities provided fodder for the press to celebrate the acquittals of both the accused by typecasting the complainants in exactly the way Benedict (1992) describes. First, the significance of the widespread reporting of these cases is to question whether 'date rape' was 'real' rape at all, again contributing to the myth that false allegations are the rule rather than the exception in rape cases. As the *Daily Express* argued: 'the word "rape" should not be used to describe these student couplings, often if not always lubricated with alcohol'.[17] Secondly, the women complainants in both these cases were mercilessly portrayed as false accusers and unreliable and thirdly, defendants are presented as the true victims of wicked false allegations so that rape acquittals are celebrated as victories for justice.

The Donnellan case

The quality and 'gutter' press unanimously celebrated the acquittal of Austen Donnellan, a History student from King's College, London, with headlines and prominent pictures over several days. Half-page size pictures of Donnellan kissing his supportive mother on his acquittal appeared on the front pages of the national newspapers on 20 October 1993. 'Told you so, Mummy: Joy as the "Cry Rape" Student is Freed', with a half-page picture of Donnellan kissing his mother, filled most of the front page of the *Daily Mirror*, while the *Daily Express*, after announcing 'A Model Student Forced to Fight for his Reputation', followed up on the day of Donnellan's acquittal with 'I Knew he was Innocent, My Brilliant Boy's Been So Strong: Mother's Joy as Student is Cleared of Rape'. The *Daily Star* headed the story 'The Gamble of the Perfect Gent: Brave Student took Big Risk to Fight Rape Slur'. The *Evening Standard* declared 'Hugs and Shrieks as Jury Clears Date Rape Case Student' and the *Daily Mirror* capped it by filling the whole front page with a 'world exclusive' on Donnellan's new relationship entitled 'Rape Trial Student's Own Story' headed 'Love That Saved My Life'.

'We made love passionately', Donnellan declared, 'but I always ask "Is this okay?"' Finally *The Times* confirmed this picture by heading the story 'Rape Trial Student A Perfect Gentleman, say Women Friends'.[18] The trial sparked a national debate about what the *Daily Mail* referred to as the rules of the mating game.

> We continue to excoriate the insensitivity that the male-dominated judiciary not infrequently still displays towards women who have suffered the outrage of rape, but in this date-rape age when common sense and the accepted decencies are being hijacked by the zealots of Political Correctness, is not the pendulum in danger of swinging too far?[19]

The case sparked widespread calls for restoring the law, abolished in 1988, under which rape defendants were unnamed unless convicted.[20] The *Sunday Mirror* declared: 'We agree with Austen that men cleared of rape are victims too. They should be anonymous until found guilty.' In an article hysterically headed 'Head-butting a Moving Train was an Easy Option ... In Prison they would have Murdered Me Anyway',[21] with the subheading 'Raped by the Law', Donnellan spoke of his anguish and his dread of being killed in prison. With a photograph of the victim with a strip across her eyes (which hardly protected her anonymity) the *Daily Mail* proclaimed 'Shouldn't she now be named?'[22] Janet Daley writing in *The Times* argued that definitions of rape had become so contentious that all concerned should remain anonymous.[23]

The *Mail* also carried two further articles, one an interview with the complainant and, below, a profile of Donnellan. No comment was made about the complainant but Donnellan was described as a sexual innocent, 'an awkward Catholic boy in a hedonist hotbed' who 'had no qualifications to prepare him for life in this sexual hunting ground, socially inadequate and romantically inexperienced he must have gawped at the hedonism that he saw all around him'. Donnellan's mother was quoted as saying 'his idea of a good time was to help her do the weekly shopping at Sainsbury'.[24] The complainant's Catholic background, on the other hand, of an 'ex-Convent schoolgirl' was given very different connotations, quite unreasonably since she was reported to have been a virgin on arrival at university, unlike Donnellan who had 'lost his virginity in the back of his Fiat at 16 and had had a sexual history'.[25] This was very similar to the description given in the American press of Kennedy Smith, who was described as 'quiet, different and somewhat aloof'[26], the implication being that he was not the kind of man who would rape. The complainant, on the other hand, was depicted as someone who liked 'to drive fast cars, go to parties and skip class'[27] who according to someone who claimed to have known her 'had a wild streak'. The *New York Times* broke anonymity by not only naming the rape victim but also printing details of her sexual past.[28] Similarly the complainant in the Donnellan case was referred to by the *Daily Mirror* as a 'campus wild child'.[29] As Lisa Longstaff of Women Against Rape commented: 'she had been painted as the venomous character seeking retribution. He had been called the perfect gentleman.'[30]

Had the pendulum swung too far in taking women's allegations of rape seriously? Are men routinely being falsely accused, charged or, even worse, unjustly convicted like the Guildford Four and Birmingham Six? As the *Daily Mail* leader of 19 October 1993 put it:

> In recent decades, women have won many rights – deservedly so. They now unequivocally have the right to say 'No'. But in return, they also have the duty to behave responsibly. If they swill alcohol and lurch around with naked abandon ... if they indulge in passionate and provocative foreplay ... they may still think the morning after that they had the right to say 'No'. What they should not have is the right to besmirch a man's reputation by dragging him through the courts and then themselves remain anonymous, even after such a man has been found innocent.

The bare facts of the case were as follows. The couple, both students on the same course, had been seen kissing at a Christmas party where they were both very drunk. According to Donnellan's evidence the complainant had taken him back to her room and had consented to sex. Donnellan claimed that their on–off non-sexual relationship (as she had refused to sleep with him), had fizzled out after five months. The alleged rape happened after this.[31] The complainant, on the other hand, could not remember what exactly had happened as she had passed out, but the next day had accused Donnellan of rape. She had first complained to the college authorities who had apparently asked Donnellan to apologise. According to informal sources the reason why she reported it was that she had wanted to be excused lectures as Donnellan had continued to harass her. The college did not have any parallel courses for her to attend and the tutor said this could only be arranged if she made a formal complaint, which she then did.

Some months later, when faced with the possibility of a disciplinary hearing, Donnellan (on the apparent advice of Lord Russell, his tutor), *contacted the police himself* and *demanded that he stand trial*. It is most unusual if not unique for an accused to demand a criminal trial. No woman complainant has such a right and, as we have seen, the proportion of cases not recommended by the CPS for trial has trebled since 1985.

In the Donnellan case neither the alleged victim nor the university wished for it to reach court.[32] As Donnellan, writing in the *Sunday Times* on 19 October, explained: 'I wasn't charged until March 20th. The main problem was that Miss X was desperate to avoid a court hearing. We later learned that she had been to the police station three times before agreeing to give a statement.'

It is not at all clear why the CPS, who decide whether to take cases to court, agreed to do so, but their reasons can hardly have been based on the expectation of a conviction. Crown Prosecutors are required to consider four main criteria in deciding whether a case should go to trial: whether there is sufficient evidence, whether there is a realistic prospect of a conviction, the credibility of the witness or victim and the public interest. Only about one in four of reported rape cases reach court and informally it is said that the CPS only take rape cases if they consider there is a 70 per cent chance of conviction. In this case the absence of corroboration and the inebriated state of the complainant can hardly have provided any chance of a criminal conviction, nor her evidence have led the CPS to regard her as a 'good' witness. Her failure to be able to remember what happened on the night in question raised a major problem. When drunk, people behave in ways they would not behave when sober and do not always remember exactly what happened.

Paradoxically in response to Donnellan's trial, which is quite atypical for the reasons I have already cited, some newspapers falsely argued that too many rapes cases were proceeding to trial. The *Sunday Mirror*, for example, argued: 'The Crown Prosecution Service MUST look again at how it brings cases to trial. The victims of rape are not served by cases which are brought to court which should never come before a jury.'[33]

The *Sun* was the only newspaper which asked the relevant question in its leader of 20 October:

> One question has yet to be answered in the rape charges against student Austen Donnellan. Why was the case brought in the first place? The evidence against Donnellan was thin to the point of near invisibility. Yet the Crown Prosecution Service insisted on mounting a lengthy and expensive trial which it must have known stood little chance of securing a conviction. Usually it's the other way round. The CPS is notorious for DROPPING cases unless the evidence is absolutely overwhelming. Maybe the real criminals are too tough a nut to crack. So the CPS goes after innocent students instead.[34]

Journalists on the whole, however, rallied to support Donnellan in protecting his reputation from the girl's allegation. The girl was labelled by sections of the press as his 'false accuser' although in terms of the criminal proceedings she was actually an unwilling witness as she did not even want the case to go to court. Lord Russell commented that his confidence in British justice had been renewed. A more enlightened press response was made by Matthew Parris,[35] who pointed out that reading the papers you could have been forgiven for thinking that rape had been shown to be a female plot against men. His trial raises another interesting possibility which is that the farce of rape trials is more about protecting male reputation than convicting rapists.

The Kydd case

'Student cleared of raping "slut of the year"'[36] claimed the *Guardian*'s heading to the report of the acquittal of Matthew Kydd,[37] a student at the University of East Anglia, which went on to explain how:

> the court heard that the girl '*was rumoured*'[38] to have slept with every boy in the residences. Mr Kydd told police he did not want to have sex with the girl because she *smelled* and because he was *scared he could catch Aids*. He said she agreed to all the sex acts that took place and had initiated some. Mr Kydd's solicitor said 'My client is just glad it is all over. He does not think it should ever have come this far.'

In this report an 18-year-old undergraduate is blatantly stigmatised as a 'slut' and, by implication, a 'false accuser'. Additionally she is presented as potentially polluted, contaminated, unclean, the source of germs and dirt, and finally the possible carrier of disease and death in the form of AIDS. The *Guardian*, a quality liberal newspaper which prides itself on its high standards of investigatory journalism, unreflectively repeats this slander and provides a totally one-sided report of the trial. No mention is made of the young woman's anger at the way she had been portrayed nor that another student had come forward detailing a vicious assault at Kydd's hands.[39]

Absent from the *Guardian* report is any mention of the woman's testimony. Similarly in court the woman's testimony is severely curtailed. There are parallels in the way the press and the judiciary treat rape complainants. The woman's voice, her standpoint and her story are only allowed within very defined boundaries. Her description of the experience of rape, her pain and her anguish are rarely considered relevant, are immaterial. Instead the defence focus on the intricacies of the actual assault in terms of body positioning, all centred round the penis.[40] We are told that Kydd said that 'the woman consented to all the acts and initiated some' and that he 'did not think it should have gone this far'. This is presented as Kydd's view but, since no other view is presented, it implies implicitly that it is the *Guardian's* view or the 'truth'. It implies that the woman is making a mountain out of a molehill, or perhaps is one of the band of evil or hysterical women who make false allegations. According to her account, she had accepted an invitation for coffee and once in his room Kydd had forced her to perform several sexual acts and then to have assaulted her with a truncheon. He had held her round her neck throttling her and had raped her. He told her that she 'liked pain as much as he did' and that she should return the next night 'in schoolgirl outfit'. When she was eventually allowed to leave he threatened that if she told anyone he would kill her. It is presentation such as this that challenges the whole idea of the 'objectivity' of the press. What is presented as objective, rational and factual is in effect objective, rational and factual only from the male standpoint. From the woman's point of view Kydd's statement is subjective, distorted, irrational and untrue.

The press concentrated on scapegoating the victim and vilifying her. It was *alleged* by Kydd that she had been named 'slut of the year' by students at a university ball. The complainant claimed this reputation was entirely false. Some years ago, after giving a paper at St John's College, Oxford, I was shown a college rag where on the front page was displayed a *league table* with girls' names and the number of assumed affairs they had had. The girl at the 'top' of the league was humiliated. In my research into adolescent girls I also found that a girl's reputation often bore no relation to her actual sexual activity (Lees 1993). Moreover all sorts of perfectly normal behaviour can open girls up to the 'slag' categorisation: appearance, independence, going around with a number of boys.

The question which should have been asked is why the judge considered that such allegations were relevant to whether or not she had been raped. If she had slept around so much why should she make a false allegation, and why should it have any bearing on her complaint of being kept a prisoner and forced to perform sexual acts for four hours? And why did the press report the assumed reputation of the young woman with such glee? Press reports were even more loaded than in the Donnellan case. The *Independent* headed their article 'rape case woman had sex two days later' with a subheading falsely claiming that 'student admits she was nominated as "slut" of the year at college' and *was said to have* 'slept with everyone in her hall'. In fact she had strongly objected to the label.[41] The tendency of newspapers to use defence allegations as statements of fact has already been mentioned (see Soothill 1988).

Also allowed was evidence that the complainant had taken part in a college rag dressed as a slave girl to raise money for charity, and had once appeared in a 'stripogram' (although the complainant said it was in fact a kissogram and she had been respectably dressed and had raised more money than any other student for rag week). The defendant did not enter the witness box but claimed his 'right to silence'. No evidence about his character, attitudes to women or past sexual history was therefore allowed. The jury took 35 minutes to return a verdict of 'not guilty'.

The 'Big Story', an ITV *Twenty Twenty* programme shown shortly afterwards based on interviews with other students at the University of East Anglia, provided other evidence of Kydd's violence. It transpired that Kate Brown,[42] a fellow student, had given evidence to the police that she had suffered a similar fate. She also swore an affidavit for the 'Big Story' detailing her treatment at Kydd's hands. She had been struck by the similarities in the way she had been treated by him: Kydd had pulled her hair and moved her head around and used her as a rag doll in exactly the same way as he had the complainant. He had spoken about his past to both of them, saying he had been involved in a lot of violent acts, but that if they told anyone he would 'rearrange their faces'. He had ordered her about and pushed her inside a wardrobe. A third student said that she had felt very threatened by him, and found him very unnerving. Norfolk police had given Kate Brown's evidence to the CPS but their lawyers had considered that it was 'not of a sufficiently similar nature' for the three cases to be dealt with together. This was in sharp contrast to the way the complainant's character was considered relevant and where the judge used his discretion for her past sexual history to be paraded before the court.

The Diggle case

The case of Angus Diggle,[43] a solicitor, heard in January 1993, occurred during my monitoring of trials at the Old Bailey. His conviction was primarily due to the respectability of the complainant, a lawyer herself, and therefore a woman of professional standing. The couple had met before but had not gone out together. Both lived in different parts of the country and had arranged to go to the solicitors' ball in London. At the ball they both drank a great deal and returned to a flat belonging to the woman's friends to sleep for a few hours before catching the train home. There, according to the complainant, she took off her dress and went to sleep on the sofa, to be awoken by Diggle attempting to rape her. Diggle, on the other hand, argued that the woman had sat facing him without her dress on with her legs open and he had 'misread' her signals. The press reports only presented his version and depicted him as 'sexually naive' rather than violent. According to his statement to the police he did not help his case by saying 'I spent £200 on her. Why can't I do what I did to her?' Even so it is unlikely that the case would have resulted in a conviction if the complainant had not been a professional woman with legal knowledge. This was one of the few trials I attended where no aspersions were placed on the complainant's past sexual history or character.

Some of the press, in spite of Diggle's conviction, persisted in seeing him as the true victim but were forced to be muted in their depiction of the complainant. *The Times*' headline to the third day they reported the case was: 'Lawyer mistook "sex invitation"' and reported only the case presented by the defence[44] which gave the impression, not that the woman had been fast asleep when attacked, but that she 'quickly took off her clothes ... then went to sit on the bed with her legs slightly apart in my [Diggle's] direction'. The *Daily Telegraph* was predictably incensed by Diggle's conviction, and announced: 'Victim's shock as lawyer Diggle gets three years',[45] reporting that the victim had said: 'I'm not saying it's too harsh but from my own experience of similar cases I did not expect it would be so long. I am quite shocked actually.' The defence barrister was reported to have said that 'the consequences of this conviction are catastrophic, they amount to a complete ruination of his character' and continued that 'it was inevitable, I expect, he will be struck off from the roll of solicitors and the loss of all he holds in high esteem'. In fact in January 1995 he was suspended for only a year. Such language is never used to refer to the effects of rape on a woman's reputation.

Another equally specious conclusion drawn from the case was that it represented a significant change in the implementation of the law on rape. In June 1994 the *Sunday Telegraph* devoted a whole page to the issue of how the failure of the Diggle case to be reversed by the Appeal Court 'throws light on new attitudes in the law'[46] in an article entitled 'When Sex is Crime', which bemoaned the 'miscarriage of justice' and the emphasis on what was referred to as Diggle's general wrong-thinkingness. He was described in the article as 'a man whose attitude to women left a lot to be desired, a man who had the arrogance to regard himself as the victim, a man who had failed to express remorse'. The *Daily Telegraph* fails to mention that just such a man is likely to rape women. The article continued, 'the conviction only makes sense on the basis that Diggle was being punished not for what he actually thought would be Ms X's attitude to his advances, but for what he ought to have thought'. Since the jury accepted the complainant was asleep when

Diggle assaulted her he certainly *ought to have considered whether she consented*. It is difficult to understand what the writer objects to here. He appears to be putting forward a justification for rape.

Conclusion

The argument that the 'date' rape controversy of 1993 was sparked by concerns about increasing numbers of rape convictions, whether founded or unfounded, and of women's greater proneness to making 'false allegations' is utterly false and represents highly irresponsible press coverage. I have shown how press reporting of rape is often biased, inaccurate and irresponsible and presents a totally distorted picture of the nature of the allegation, the victims, the perpetrators and the conduct of rape trials. It is deeply partisan, makes no attempt to put trials in any context and appears to be directed at discounting women's allegations of rape, and justifying the masquerading of rape as seduction. Its depiction of victims is scandalous.[47] This reflects the way the press, like the courts, often only present issues from the male and therefore the defendant's standpoint. This standpoint is presented as the only objective, rational position to hold.

The same processes identified in the above press reports are at work in the court room and lead to false acquittals. The complainants's voice, her experience and her account of what happened are from the start constricted and curtailed. In one rape trial I attended where the woman was explaining how she felt the defence counsel successfully intervened with the words: 'I sympathise your honour, but I fear this is becoming a speech.' Instead of hearing about the assault and the effect it has had on her life, the ground rules are laid by the defence barrister whose task is to use every trick available to discredit the complainant. That is his explicit role in the adversarial process of justice. The whole process is conducted from the male perspective, from the criteria used to establish credibility and the way rape is defined to the presentation in defence evidence of all the age-old myths about mendacious and promiscuous women who make false allegations.

In this way rape reporting gives a totally distorted picture of the inadequacies of the judicial system. It appears to be directed at discounting women's experiences, and presenting their allegations as false, or at best unreliable, and at clearing men's names of such unnecessary allegations. It is for this reason that the Donnellan case, where the woman had clearly drunk a great deal and could not remember exactly what had happened, fell like manna into the hands of those who present women's allegations as flimsy and unreliable.

What then can be learned from the outburst of press hysteria which I have documented? The only plausible explanation for the Donnellan case going to trial is that it was considered to be 'in the public interest' to prevent such allegations. At a time when student unions were (for the first time in Britain) taking sexual harassment seriously, and where women were coming forward to complain of sexism, the press appear to have found it necessary to label such women, who dare to speak out, as 'sluts', as fallen women, whose word cannot be relied on. Any woman who takes that road risks scapegoating of the most extreme kind.[48] Blaming women for speaking out about male violence is a subtle way the 'backlash' against feminism works. As Faludi (1991) pointed out, women are blamed for the very problems they face.

It appears that in 1993 the press coverage has shifted from a focus on the few stranger rapists who commit such atrocities to an attack on the women who make such allegations, and a depiction of the true victims of rape trials as men. This new development appears to have arisen in response to the fear that women are challenging taken-for-granted sexual practices and becoming too powerful. Contrary to the press outcry a far lower proportion of rapists are convicted than ten years ago and the courts, far from having been reformed, are just as prejudiced against complainants. The changes that the press are reacting to are not therefore changes occurring in the courts but in society at large, where for the first time women, and particularly young women, are challenging chauvinist behaviour.

The publicity around 'date rape' and political correctness can also be seen as a reaction to the greater recognition of the reality of male violence. Faludi (1992) argued that women's equality in America was more myth than reality, and that campaigns for equality had led to a virulent backlash emanating from conservative 'New Right's' hostility to feminism. In Britain, the moral crusade against single mothers and social security, which it was claimed encouraged single parenthood, coincided with an attack on women making allegations of 'date rape' and on political correctness in the early 1990s.[49] A backlash may arise in response to the fear of change rather than to change itself and may sometimes be an indication that women really have had an effect, but backlashes occur often when advances have been small. As the psychologist Jean Baker Miller (1976: 14) observed, it is almost as if the leaders of the backlash use the fear of change as *a threat* before major change has occurred.

The lack of responsible journalism in reporting miscarriages of justice requires explanation. Benedict, in her description of how the press reported US sex crimes (1992), pointed to the complete absence of any recognition or reference to misogyny in press reports and to the tendency of the press to prefer *individual to societal or cultural explanations* of rape. She concludes:

> These reporters and editors were willing to go to sociologists, psychologists, and community leaders to talk about class and race hatred but not about the hatred of women which revealed the extent to which they considered racism a subject of news stories, but saw sexism as fit only for columns and editorials. It also revealed that ... these reporters and editors seemed more able to admit to racism than their sexism – they were apparently more comfortable talking about the sick socialisation of blacks in urban ghettos than the sick socialisation everyone gets at schools, fraternities, and in society at large. (1992: 246)

Similarly for Britain I have shown how no attempt is made to put reports of trials into the context of the very low and falling conviction rate. Moreover much of the reporting even by the quality press is deeply misogynist. Acquittals often attract headline reports with reactionary publicity given to such defendants' demands for complainants to lose their press anonymity in trials.[50] It appears that reporters have a real blind spot over rape.

Notes and references

1. Yet paradoxically we know that some young women are murdered on dates. The media sometimes censor the fact that murdered women have been raped.
2. Acting as a consultant for a Channel 4 *Dispatches* documentary, 'Getting Away with Rape', which received the Royal Television Society award for the best home documentary of 1994.
3. See the *Dispatches* programme. See also Sue Lees, 'Getting Away with Rape', the *Guardian*, 16 February 1994.
4. According to the Home Office, statistics for 1985 (covering England and Wales) show that, of 1842 rapes reported to the police, 450 (24 per cent) resulted in convictions. By 1993 the numbers of rapes reported had increased to 4631 but the numbers convicted had dropped to 463 (10 per cent).
5. Mackinnon (1989) argued that feminism is a theory of how the erotisation of dominance and submission creates gender.
6. The 1979 Greta and John Rideout marital rape case in Oregon, the 1983 pool table gang rape of a woman in Massachusetts, the 1986 sex-related killing

of Jennifer Levin by Robert Chambers in New York and the 1989 gang rape and beating of a Central Park jogger.

7. See 'Rape case PC calls for law reform', the *Guardian*, 21 February 1995.
8. See 'WPC tells of ordeal by rape trial and media', the *Observer*, 26 February 1995.
9. See the *Daily Mirror*, 6 November 1985. Quoted in Soothill and Walby (1991: 70).
10. *Daily Mail*, 18 December 1985, quoted in Soothill and Walby, p. 70.
11. This is a classic example of how feminists are sometimes blamed for women's subordination (see Faludi 1991).
12. Oxford University Student Union Sexual Harassment study 1990.
13. Racism often enters into this depiction where a picture of the 'black rapist' who rapes a 'white' woman is given prominence although intraracial rape is far more common than interracial rape. See also 'I was raped by Aliens'. Headline, the *People*, 20 February 1994.
14. This fell from 47 per cent in 1973 to 39 per cent in 1985 (Lloyd and Walmsley 1989: 42).
15. There had been a steady but slow rise in the proportion reported where offenders and victims were known to each other prior to rape (15 per cent in 1961, 29 per cent in 1985).
16. For example the *Islington Gazette*'s headline of 14 January 1993, 'Sex Beast's Reign of Terror'; the report began 'A sex-crazed maniac tried to rape three Islington women three times in a day'.
17. 20 October 1993.
18. *The Times*, 19 October 1993.
19. The *Daily Mail*, 19 October 1993.
20. Rape complainants were given anonymity in the 1976 Sexual Offences (Amendment) Act.
21. The *Sunday Mirror*, 24 October 1994.
22. The *Daily Mail*, 20 October 1993.
23. *The Times*, 21 October 1993.
24. The *Daily Mail*, 20 October 1993.
25. 'Raped by the Law', an interview with Donnellan, The *Sunday Mirror*, 24 October 1993.
26. The *New York Times*, 11 May 1991.
27. The *New York Times*, 17 April 1991.
28. The *New York Times*, ibid.
29. The *Daily Mirror*, 20 October 1993.
30. The *Sunday Telegraph*, 24 October 1993, p. 18.
31. The timing of the rape lends weight to the complainant's allegation, as it is often after a relationship is over, whether sex has occurred or not, that rape occurs.
32. The *Daily Telegraph*, 20 October 1993.
33. The *Sunday Mirror*, 24 October 1993, p. 2.
34. The *Sun*, 20 October 1993.
35. *The Times*, 26 October 1993.
36. The *Guardian*, 2 November 1993.
37. See *The Times*, 27 October 1993, 'Alleged rape victim admits she was named college slut'.

38. My italics.
39. She was interviewed on ITV's *Twenty Twenty* documentary.
40. This is what is meant by the phallocentric focus of trials.
41. The *Independent*, 27 October 1993.
42. Not her real name.
43. I obtained an official transcript of this trial.
44. *The Times*, 20 August 1993.
45. The *Daily Telegraph*, 1 October 1993.
46. Martin Mears, 'When Sex is Crime', The *Sunday Telegraph*, 12 June 1994.
47. The *Guardian* women's page did publish three articles (7 June 1993, 16 February 1994 and 10 March 1995) I wrote on my research on attrition in rape cases but I was unable to place them in the main part of the paper.
48. The *Guardian* failed to publish a letter I wrote questioning the reasons for the case going to trial and their reporting of the trial was no better than that of the 'gutter press'. The lack of information about the very high attrition rate for rape was not considered relevant.
49. Mary Braid, 'Heretics of left point finger at feckless fathers', *Independent on Sunday*, 14 November 1993.
50. See 'Rape case PC calls for law reform', the *Guardian*, 21 February 1995 and *The Times* leader of the same date. This issue was taken up by two TV programmes and other newspapers.

Bibliography

Adler, Z. (1987) *Rape on Trial* (London: Routledge & Kegan Paul).

Barak, G. (1994) 'Media Process and Social Construction of Crime', *Current Issues in Criminal Justice*, vol. 10 (New York: Garland).

Benedict, H. (1992) *Virgin or Vamp: How the Press Report Sex Crimes* (New York: Oxford University Press).

Brown, B., Burman, M. and Jamieson, L. (1992) *Sexual History and Sexual Character Evidence in Scottish Sexual Offence Trials* (Edinburgh: Scottish Office Central Research Unit Papers).

Chambers, G. and Millar, A. (1983) *Investigating Sexual Assault* (Edinburgh: Scottish Office/HMSO).

Chambers, G. and Millar, A. (1986) *Prosecuting Sexual Assault* (Edinburgh: Scottish Office/HMSO).

Estrich, S. (1987) *Real Rape* (Cambridge, MA: Harvard University Press).

Faludi, S. (1991) *Backlash* (London: Chatto & Windus).

Grace, S., Lloyd, C. and Smith, L. (1992) *Rape: From Recording to Conviction* (London: Home Office Research Unit).

Home Office Statistics (1993) Available from Home Office Research and Statistics Department, London.

Heilbron Committee (1975) *Report on the Advisory Group on the Law on Rape*, Cmnd 6352 (London: HMSO).

Koss, M., Gidycz, A. and Wisniewski, N. (1987) 'The scope of rape: Incidence and prevalence of sexual aggression and victimization in a national sample of higher education students', *Journal of Consulting and Clinical Psychology*, 55, pp. 162–70.

Koss, M. (1988) 'Stranger and Acquaintance Rape', *Psychology of Women Quarterly*, 12, pp. 1–24.

Lees, S. (1993) *Sugar and Spice: Sexuality and Adolescent Girls* (Harmondsworth: Penguin).

Lloyd, C. and Walmsley, R. (1989) 'Changes in rape offences and sentencing', Home Office Research Study no. 105 (London: HMSO).

Mackinnon, C. (1989) *Towards a Feminist Theory of the State* (Cambridge, MA: Harvard University Press).

Miller, J. Baker (1976) *Towards a New Psychology of Women* (Harmondsworth: Penguin).

Roiphe, K. (1993) *The Morning After* (New York: Little, Brown).

Smith, L. (1989) 'Concerns about Rape', Home Office Research Study no. 106 (London: HMSO).

Soothill, K. (1991) 'The changing face of rape?' *British Journal of Criminology*, 31, 4, Autumn.

Soothill K. and Walby S. (1991) *Sex Crime in the News* (London: Routledge).

Soothill, K. and Soothill, D. (1993) 'Prosecuting the Victim? A study of the Reporting of Barristers' comments in Rape Cases', *Howard Journal*, vol. 32, no. 1.

Temkin, J. (1993) 'Sexual history evidence: The ravishment of section 2', *Criminal Law Review*, 1.

Wright, R. (1984) 'A note on attrition of rape cases', *British Journal of Criminology*, 254, 4, October.

7 Through the Looking Glass: Public Images of White Collar Crime

A.E. Stephenson-Burton

There is a comprehensive and contemporary corpus of writing on the media. Crime, specifically, is an expanding domain in terms of media reporting and media research, and in the United Kingdom (as in most places throughout the world) reports of rising crime rates abound. Whether resulting in, or being capitalised upon, the incumbent political parties and their competitors vie to be viewed as the toughest and most effective in handling the 'crime problem'. The politicisation of crime control therefore becomes a very public drama in which the media maintain virtually exclusive rights. 'Old' crimes with fresh twists as well as 'new' crimes rear their ugly heads and the media are on hand to take the picture, while articles on official and independent criminal justice research reports join those from purely academic sources, frequently gracing the pages of the press. Crime and control legislation have not always[1] been a substantial voting issue, but recently they appear to have attained the potential to become a major overriding concern which, according to the seemingly ever-increasing media library of crime news and programming, is in the process of altering British society.

Public perceptions of the incidence of crime, the types of crimes being committed and the frequency and distribution of these crimes, are the media's cross to bear. Market forces, organisational philosophies, insufficient and often misleading official statistics and the sheer depth and breadth of the reality of crime present grave difficulties for even the most conscientious of media agents. Although the fear of crime and the assessment of risk are not necessarily linked, associations between perceptions and degree of concern or fear do exist. Inflated perceptions, misrepresentation and exaggerated fears are all invoked in the name of media influence. To this end, within the academic and professional media discourse, questions such as how is crime represented? What types of crimes are being given air time/space? What is the essence of newsworthiness? Does ownership matter? are just the beginning. Specific crimes are studied, headlines measured, pictures and video clips analysed, words counted and thus the literature grows. Just as the realities of a united Europe take hold with the European and international segments altering the 'mix' of news, so too is news of crime dynamic, the dimensions highly susceptible to change. The answers to the above questions and others like it change over time and reveal untold avenues of inquiry.

Although white collar crime has been touted time and time again as 'the growth industry of our times' (often as part of a diatribe presented in the media) it has been essentially ignored[2] by academics and media cognoscenti with respect to its representation in content and form. This glaring oversight is not altogether surprising, taking into account the perpetual crisis of legitimacy surrounding white collar crime itself. This most perplexing of beasts has suffered from an identity crisis arising long before adolescence, and rumour has it this neurosis has decided to stay. Is it crime, is it not crime? If not crime, then what? What should the legislature do about it? Does the public care? Despite this barrage of essentially unanswered questions, astonishingly, research of white collar crime is characterised not by its powerful presence but by its flagrant absence. 'Throughout media history, it has been far easier to find critical statements than critical analysis concerning the news media' (Lemert 1989: 19).

What is known of the reporting of white collar crime in the media? Much amounts to little more than 'opinion and assertion'. White collar crime is not reported because big business takes care of its own. The public doesn't really care about white collar crime. Statements of this nature have been emphatically asserted for the last 50 years, with very little of the systematic study that media research demands. Not a complete anomaly, white collar crime being reported in the media shares this similarity with other areas within criminology such as the issue of female deviance and criminality before the 1970s; and was simply viewed as more or less a non-event. Information, statements and opinions pertaining to white collar crime are repeated at regular intervals with increasing frequency and, not unlike the common practice of journalists utilising colleagues' stories without checking the sources, as time passes the information more often becomes 'fact'. Very little effort is then expended on actively investigating whether or not the information was accurate before it became 'public knowledge' or indeed whether the reality changes over time. Much of the information commonly recycled as fact pertaining to white collar crime and media reporting has been gleaned from personal observation. Observation, though obviously relevant, has its limitations if not placed in relevant context and/or assisted by scientific rigour. If one is a reader of a popular newspaper, like the *Sun*, statements such as 'news of white collar crime rarely gets in newspapers' are hardly comprehensive as the balance of news stories in newspapers differs from tabloid to broadsheet as well as within the two categories.

The mainly qualitative studies of crime and the media conducted by Ericson et al. (1987, 1989, 1991) relied heavily on techniques of observation, supplementing those initial data by engaging in other relevant methodologies. Issues such as the relationships between reporters, sources and news organisations, organisational philosophy and ideological notions of deviance and social control were tackled. Getting beyond the 'what' questions into those of the 'how' and 'why' is crucial for the understanding of white collar crime in the media (Stephenson, 1992, Levi forthcoming). Historically most of the research which included information concerning media reporting of white collar crime did so as a sideline. Indeed it is important to acknowledge that much of the existing material on the subject was compiled using this secondary data. Therefore these examples, while acknowledging the undoubtedly important class and power differentials, failed either to tackle or recognise the practical dynamics surrounding white collar crime in the media in any systematic fashion. As their primary aims and objectives were rooted in other areas (mostly street crime, often emphasising violent and sexual offences) information pertaining to white collar crime remained cursory. Likewise a great many more of the studies dealing with crime and the media failed to include *any* information on white collar crime.[3] This paucity of research coupled with the perpetuation of outmoded, wholly or partially erroneous information deflects the convergence and thereby deters the growth of a constructive and perspicacious discourse.

The problem with white collar crime

Since the coinage of the term in 1939 by American sociologist and criminologist Edwin Sutherland, white collar crime has presented a dilemma for social scientists seeking to understand the deviant and criminal behaviour of human beings. White collar crime was the bastard son of criminology, grudgingly acknowledged and never fully understood. It is a well-known story. Sutherland placed the central tenets of white collar crime resoundingly at the door of the well-established theories of crime, rejecting the pathologising tradition of over a century. Early criminologists from Lombroso (1876) to Goring (1913) pinpointed biological pathologies of differing origins as the essential criminal criteria, while their positivistic descendants came to view crime in terms of the psychosocial. Poverty became a major focus of the sociology of crime. Deviant actions were seen to be brought about through necessity, isolation, despair and hopelessness, a material acknowledgment of the chasm between the haves and the have nots. In many of the ensuing theories crime was viewed as a bridge in the form of a slippery slope overhanging that chasm.

White collar crime was, and to a degree still remains, the proverbial square peg. Wrongs committed by the upper classes or the 'ruling elite' were just that, wrongs – not crimes – and were viewed in terms of politics. Crime as the ultimate social construction was characterised by specific offences and offenders. Subsequently, infractions of the law committed by the poor were viewed as criminal, those committed by their opulent cousins were merely immoral and not subjected to sanction. However, the rich v. poor argument appears to be entirely too simplistic to tackle the roots of the problem of why white collar crime has not been given a status similar to its underclass cousin. As poverty often precludes power wealth facilitates it, and certainly, then as now, the rich might be more likely to 'get away with murder', literally and figuratively. This, however, is precisely the dilemma. White collar crime does not usually refer to homicide.[4] White collar crime does not refer to rich men[5] deviating in a way that has been the proverbial precept of poor men. There are two important factors in this equation, first the status of the offender and secondly the type of offence committed.[6] White collar crime is not about the local insurance executive strangling the local insurance ombudsman and leaving him for dead (no matter how tempting he/she may find it). It is about the swindler, the con artist, the fraudulent business practitioner. White collar crime is about money and power, status and trust – and their abuse.

Prior to Sutherland of course, although the nomenclature did not exist the act certainly did, and in abundance (Robb, 1992). Sutherland defined white collar crime as 'a crime committed by a person of respectability and high social status in the course of his occupation' (1949: 9). This was a definition many would have loved to see expurgated as it was vague and did not strictly gel with the research findings to which Sutherland attached the phrase. In the decades that followed multiple attempts were made to expand and refine the definition of white collar crime. Well-known offspring of white collar crime are: occupational crime ('offences committed by individuals for themselves in the course of their occupations and the offences of employees against their employers' (Clinard and Quinney 1973: 188)), corporate crime ('an illegal act, punishable by a criminal sanction, which is committed by an individual or a corporation in the course of a legitimate occupation or pursuit in the industrial or commercial sector for the purpose of obtaining money or property, avoiding the payment of money or the loss of property, or obtaining business or personal advantage' (Clinard and Quinney 1973: 188)) and the newer terms economic and commercial crime, which are often utilised with general definitions such as 'crimes by or against business' or 'crimes with wide-scale economic consequences'.[7] These definitions are valuable as they not only illustrate the complexity, 'depth of field' and breadth of opportunity involved, but also serve to highlight the relative confusion over just what constitutes a white collar crime.

If we acknowledge the ideological confusion with which criminologists came to the study of white collar crime, perhaps it can help to illuminate the deficiencies within the study of the media. White collar crime is an area of deviance which has been underdeveloped, understudied and underexposed. While terms and definitions have been supplied, rejected, reformulated, established and discarded with alarming alacrity, rather than intellectual ardour, something altogether different was aroused – resignation. By the late 1980s, when the 'decade of greed' had thoroughly taken hold, white collar crime was given a great deal of media attention with cases such as Milken in the United States and Blue Arrow and Barlow Clowes in the United Kingdom. Perhaps understandably, as an unimaginable amount of money is estimated to be lost through white collar crime, academic interest took the form of a focus on crime control. In the late 1970s the American public had begun to 'warm' to the issue of white collar, especially corporate, crime (Conklin 1977, Clinard and Yeager 1978, 1980, Schrager and Short 1980) and a decade later Britain followed suit. Of course with former Prime Minister Thatcher at the helm crime, the inefficiency of businesses, the loss of funds and international confidence in the currency made the control of white collar crime an even more obviously attractive venture. Regulation and prosecution became the catchwords of the decade. The critical concern was no longer centred around the definitional nightmare which had never been resolved. Defining white collar crime was likened to 'the search for the Holy Grail' (Leigh (ed.) 1980: x) and the discourse moved on. Today an overwhelming portion of the research, articles and books from the UK's foremost experts in white collar crime have focused on control. It would be incorrect to imagine that white collar crime, once defined, would reveal itself as 'tamed' and roll over and play dead. In this case however the lack of a clearly defined framework both subtracts from the perhaps 'normality' of a particular kind of deviant activity and adds a completely non-deserved air of mystique to the phenomenon. While control is extremely relevant, and obviously one of the key aspects in 'the handling of white collar crime', or indeed any other type of crime,[8] the deficiencies in securing a definition or sets of definitions, and/or of challenging the assumptions relating to the subject before advancement to regulation and prosecution, appear to put the cart before the horse.

As the media provide the public with knowledge of crime (that which does not come from personal experience or word of mouth), the fact that prosecution and regulation are the current foci of the white collar crime debate has great importance. This affects the category of story reported and the way in which it is reported, or indeed if it is reported at all. News of white collar crime, not unlike news of street crime, is generally reported around particular points in the criminal justice process, with emphasis on the official sources such as the Department of Trade and Industry, Customs and Excise and the Serious Fraud Office (SFO), to name but a few, and appearances in court, committal proceedings and trials may be reported at crucial intervals. Editorial comment is often characterised by the acutely oversimplified 'rich beats poor, news at ten' perspective. The following commentary challenges some enduring assumptions while exploring the current picture of white collar crime reporting in the media and the major difficulties this genre provides, highlighting the grave demand for supplementary research.

The cyclical dilemma

Researchers studying crime in the media almost without exception were interested in conventional or 'street crime' in whatever particular form, and observations concerning white collar offences were more or less peripheral to the central issue. While reviewing crime news social scientists noticed the comparative lack of white collar crime stories. Various criteria of newsworthiness[9] (Wilkins 1964, Roshier 1973, Croll 1974, Chibnall 1977, Hall et al. 1978, Graber 1980, Cohen and Young (eds) 1982, Ericson et al. 1987, 1989, 1991) relating to conventional crime were seen to be strengthened by white collar crime news. Thus information regarding white collar crime in the media was often utilised to reflect upon reporting of street crime in the media, rather than as a subject of study in itself. Add this to the information mentioned previously regarding research of white collar crime as deviance, and a circular argument rivalling that of 'the chicken and the egg' becomes apparent. Crime is defined with specific characteristics, the criminal justice system does not deal strongly or efficiently with white collar crime, social scientists turn their minds to areas the law does tackle, the media covers stories from the police stations, courts and prisons, the public is concerned about what the media discusses and what the law is focused upon, the politicians are concerned with media stories and public opinion, policy is made, so the criminal justice system carries it out, and the social scientists study it, and the media report it, and the people read it and so on. White collar crime thereby appears to be left out of the loop – but to what extent?

Modernity may come and go but white collar crime endureth

Is news of white collar crime being reported in the media?

News of white collar crime is still being reported in the media, in a similar fashion to how it has always been reported: selectively. The myth of non-reporting of white collar crime remains just that, a myth. And should we imagine fraud, 'serious' or otherwise, started with landmark cases or the establishment of the Serious Fraud Office in 1985, Robb (1992: 1) states, 'the real origins of white collar crime ... lie almost two hundred years in the past, in the tremendous financial growth which accompanied the British Industrial Revolution'. While some could criticise this estimation as too conservative, Robb's comprehensive analysis of white collar crime in England in the nineteenth century helps to allay the claim of white collar crime going unreported in the media. Much of his source material is from print media as well as legal documents. His extensive bibliography and references are a clear reflection of the fact that white collar crime was indeed being 'discussed' in the media. A crucial component is that, then as now, much of the information concerning white collar crime comes from specialist media, professional and academic journals, occupational pamphlets and magazines and political paraphernalia. Robb's citations are heavily weighted in favour of specialist documents. Today there are several dozens of specialist journals and magazines in England which report information about white collar crime. Many of these documents have as their primary focus commercial law, insurance, banking, accounting, policing as well as other areas of finance and economics. Although specialist literary material is par for the course in our time, as there are journals for exclusive audiences in every imaginable field, exclusivity in this area provides consequences which may be deleterious if not unique. This emphasis on information for the exclusive or specialist audience aids many of the common assumptions of white collar crime which will be tackled in turn. Most of these assumptions converge upon the idea that white collar crime is a specialist issue, something Other than Regular crime, and that most of those involved, in whatever position, are also Other.

Although this idea of specialism is problematical, the most vociferous criticisms fall upon the at times deaf ears of the press and broadcasters – the media for the masses. Newspapers, television and radio are the main outlet for information on crime, with the potential for reaching well over 50 million people in the United Kingdom every day. Television and radio, although a huge part of the media pie, are more likely to produce special programmes. An occasional radio series, such as the offering from Radio 4 specifically on white collar offences, weekly television shows such as *The Money Programme* on BBC2 (as often covering some area of fraud as 'making your money work for you'), or one-offs like Channel 4's 'Greed and Glory' on specific cases, are the infrequent additions to the daily/nightly news and updates. Nightly news programmes do contain information of white collar crime and are very likely to cover the offences of fraud or corruption one reads of in the daily newspaper. Crime is an area which the electronic media favour (although perhaps not as much as one might think): on any given week there are probably no less than six regularly scheduled programmes dealing exclusively with crime between the four main channels.[10] These would mainly include serial 'cop shows' and 'legal dramas' as well as similar programmes of American origin, and regular crime exposé offerings. This number does not include the chat shows, soap operas, movies and exposé programmes of which crime is not the main focus but a very frequent one. It is a rare occasion when one of those programmes contains issues relating to white collar crime. Although the demands placed on the electronic media may affect output and be peculiar to that medium, (an issue that will be discussed in a later section) there does not appear to be a large selection of white collar crime on the menu.

News in the national daily and Sunday newspapers has a great deal more to offer the white collar crime enthusiast. The avid reader of *all* the 12 national dailies in England and Wales would not be surprised if he/she were presented with an average of seven articles per day[11] simply concerning[12] white collar crime, though much of the information would cover similar cases or information. This figure is no doubt much higher for street crime. Quantitative content analysis is the most obvious, and accurate, way of ascertaining whether or not white collar crime is indeed being reported in the media. It is a painstakingly slow and tedious process which gleans very limited results, necessitating precise disclaimers. The figures below are illustrative, albeit at a very small and limited level, of some of the quantitative components of the reporting of white collar crime in the press. The limitations of the following tables are such that the numbers are helpful *only* in illustrating the fact that indeed news of white collar crime is being covered in the media and that in this respect all newspapers are not created equally. Therefore the 'number of articles' listed should be taken as a legitimate approximation of the actual number of entries pertaining to white collar crime. These figures were tabulated with information assembled by a newspaper clipping agency for the Serious Fraud Office. The SFO press office boasts row upon row of Arch lever files lining several full-sized cabinets, each file is catalogued and contains photocopies of press and specialist journal clippings from the SFO's inception until the present. A small video collection adds television coverage of white collar crime to the library. This is certainly testimony to media–covered white collar crime, emphasising the fact that white collar crime can no longer be considered a strict media 'no–go' area.

Table 1 Monthly tabulation of articles in the national dailies pertaining to white collar crime,[13] July 1992

Name of national daily newspaper[14]	Number of articles on white collar crime
Financial Times	125[15]
Independent	108
Times	100
Daily Telegraph	98
Guardian	76
Daily Mail	37
Daily Express	31
Daily Mirror	31
Today	21
Sun	14
Daily Star	0·

Again, the benefits from tables such as these are limited, due to the purposes for which the primary information was compiled. Although it is likely that the true number of white collar crimes' representation in the press could be slightly higher for each paper, comparisons between papers may still be relevant. Nevertheless it is important to remember that many of the quality newspapers have many more pages than the tabloids and often include many more articles in general. It should also be noted that the SFO's instructions to the clippings agency may have left out smaller, non–SFO cases, or articles in which the key phrases were not utilised. These two limitations, added to the margin of human error, must be acknowledged when applying the data from these tables to explain the incidence of white collar crime news in the media.

Table 2 Monthly tabulation of articles in the national Sundays pertaining to white collar crime, July 1992

Name of national Sunday newspaper	Number of articles on white collar crime
Sunday Times	20
Sunday Telegraph	16
Observer	15
Independent on Sunday	14
Mail on Sunday	9
Sunday Mirror	5
Sunday Express	4
People	2
News of the World	1

Table 3 Monthly tabulation of articles in the national dailies pertaining to white collar crime, December 1992

Name of national daily newspaper	Number of articles on white collar crime
Financial Times	65
Independent	39
Guardian	33
Times	32
Daily Telegraph	29
Daily Mail	10
Daily Mirror	4
Daily Express	3
Daily Star	2
Today	2
Sun	1

Table 4 Monthly tabulation of articles in the national Sundays pertaining to white collar crime, December 1992

Name of national Sunday newspaper	Number of articles on white collar crime
Independent on Sunday	9
Sunday Telegraph	5
Mail on Sunday	4
Sunday Times	3
Observer	3
People	0
Sunday Mirror	0
Sunday Express	0
News of the World	0

You gotta know where to look

How and where is white collar crime news presented in the media?

Having established that white collar crime is indeed reported by the media, the manner in which this information is transmitted becomes an important area to explain. Finding news of white collar crime is not as easy as picking up your newspaper and carelessly perusing it as you go. Loyal readers of particular newspapers will immediately know where to look, should they want to find stories of crime. The 'Home', 'Home News' and 'News' sections of most quality and tabloid newspapers are the most likely sections, with the exclusion of 'information bullets' on the back pages of many of the qualities, or particularly newsworthy stories which make it to the front page. Quite deliberately and, many would argue, validly, the section entitled Home or News contains information concerning the British population. This section includes information of actions which have direct impact on the home team although some of the players may be international. This section informs 'you at home' not of global concerns but of personal concerns, and it very rarely includes news of white collar crime. Indeed, if the 'Home'/'News' sections can be viewed as the staple newspaper diet, usually beginning on the ever-important second or third page, white collar crime is certainly exotic fare, relegated to paradoxically 'exclusive' or 'specialist' latter pages. The exception to this rule occurs when the article contains information which may have political or large-scale economic repercussions, as well as if the status of the actor/offender is particularly high (which will be discussed in the following section). News of white collar crime most often falls under sections such as 'Law', 'Legal affairs', 'Business', 'City', 'Finance', 'Finance and Economics', and/or 'Government and Politics'. For the non-business person or the non-legally minded these sections may go completely unnoticed and/or unread. The implicit assumption is that most white collar crime will be of interest to a certain type of individual, in certain types of professions or with certain interests, whereas news of street crime is seen to be of interest to the collective. This adds not only to the myth of non-reporting of white collar crime in the media (for while it may be in the paper how many people are reading about it?) but expressly labels white collar crime as a special case, a specialist topic.

Quality v. tabloid?

The discrepancy between quality and tabloid representation of white collar crime is vast and would appear to have a directly proportional relationship with the number of stories covered, as the popular press relies to a much greater extent on the personal angle. The greater the opportunity for an article to be written on the personal life of anyone involved with the offence, the perpetrator or the victim, a member of their families or someone who 'knew them when', the more likely a case will make it into the tabloid press, especially if the story can be run with an accompanying picture. Headlines such as 'What Maxwell's milkman said after they questioned the bill'[16] appear in the popular press to the exclusion of any additional information about the progression of the case, while broadsheet contemporaries boast 'Natwest to release Maxwell shares'[17] as the leading Maxwell article. Tabloids may in certain cases keep white collar criminals in the spotlight long after the qualities have dropped the story. Three months after Roger Levitt had been sentenced for fraudulently misleading City regulators, interest lies in the fact that 'Levitt seat fuels row in synagogue'.[18] Choosing one or two headlines from a tabloid and quality out of many, however, is the sort of selective measure which has haunted the issue of white collar crime in the media. Selective descriptive accounts move the discussion no further than the 'sensationalism in the popular press' debate. While the tabloids, if viewed as an assemblage, undoubtedly engage in the exploitative personal angle and the qualities are expected to possess a higher standard of objectivity in reporting, it is nevertheless important to examine and acknowledge the similarities and discrepancies amongst the groups as a whole in an attempt to put the articles in context.

In a similar fashion to the *Sun*, the *Daily Express* opted for the 'light option' with 'And they didn't leave a tip', pertaining to brothers Kevin and Ian Maxwell's lunch at Bertorelli's Italian cafe and restaurant, complete with a picture of Kevin getting into his car and a copy of the lunch bill.[19] The *Daily Mail* carried a picture of Ian Maxwell on a moped, alerting the public to the Maxwell's scaled-down lifestyle with 'Economy drive and house wine only for the bailed Maxwell brothers'.[20] *Today*'s coverage of the same day brought the two together utilising a similar picture of Ian Maxwell on his moped, the caption below reading 'Ian Maxwell parks his moped after lunch with brother Kevin'. The most elementary of detective skill highlights the incestuous nature in the shared focus of the articles. On the quality side of the fence most of the press carried, among others, a story about a plan to liquidate the Bank of Credit and Commerce International (BCCI) after judgement by a Grand Cayman jurisdiction. 'Court backs BCCI payout plan',[21] 'BCCI plan approved in Caymans',[22] 'BCCI deal moves closer',[23] 'BCCI plan wins second approval'.[24] Not surprisingly, none of these particular stories ran with pictures.

As was spectacularly illustrated by 'Tabloid Express', an edition of BBC1's *Inside Story* exposé offering,[25] many tabloids receive photographs as well as entire articles from private firms who may or may not sell them exclusive use of the story. In the case of the Maxwell family, photographers would greet them in the morning as they left the house and follow them throughout the day, indefinitely, in the hope of a story. As is obvious in the 'lunch and moped' stories, either the story originated from a particular source and was sold indiscriminately, or a host of photographers were sharing the same vantage point. The quality newspapers as well suffered from non-exclusivity on the BCCI story, gathering their stories from Reuter, overseas correspondents or official sources. This aspect of reportage, the routinisation of stories and the emphasis of specific circumstances and peculiarities among them, highlights the variable news values and possible organisational practices between and amongst[26] the broadsheets and tabloids. If photographs and personal angles are in keeping with the philosophy or style of the news organisation, specific facets of information will be considered valid and therefore different practices will need to be employed in order to fulfil organisational demand. Clearly an argument can be made that 'news' is indeed a product, a commodity, of socially regulated and determined constructions of who and what are important (Janowitz 1975, Chibnall 1977, Graber 1980, Cohen and Young (eds) 1982, Terry 1984, Ericson et al. 1987). Herein lies the all-important issue of news sense, the journalist as gatekeeper.[27] This filtering of reality by reporters, excluding certain stories or events while shaping and promoting others, is inclusive not only of selection but of bias or slant. For news of white collar crime the areas requiring study must be expanded beyond the sensationalised rich v. poor stereotype into the analysis of content, form, organisational pressures and practices (as it has been achieved by Ericson et al. 1987, 1989, 1991 for street crime).

Lifestyles of the rich and infamous

What are the characteristics of the stories deemed 'newsworthy'?

'Degradation tales' among the elite have a high news value (Levi in Croall 1992) and thus news of white collar crime is often presented in a way that focuses not as much on the wrongdoing, the criminality of the act, as on the individual. It must be acknowledged, however, that the very definition of white collar crime emphasises the status of the offender, though it has been argued (Croall 1992) that white collar crime is not restricted to the upper echelons of society but exists throughout a wide range of positions and organisations. This is certainly not reflected in the media (Croall 1992, Stephenson 1992). Rather the emphasis is on the fact that a particular person in a particular position, known to the world or a particular community as a – sort of person (read 'whatever sort of person it would be damning for this activity to be associated with'), has been implicated in, alleged to have committed or found guilty of a specific act which happens to be white collar crime. It is not the heinous nature of the act which has the major impact in most cases, as often happens with articles on street crime. The 'blow by blow' of white collar crime speaks sternly of 'transactions', 'channels' and 'investments' while its working-class rival cries 'rob', 'home' and 'valuables' or, worse yet, in the case of a violent crime, 'assault', 'alley' and 'injury'. In fact the most important phrases in reporting white collar crime may be 'millions of pounds'. The usual profile of the street criminal and the gruesomeness of crime is easily converted to large amounts of money and the suspected greed of individuals involved.

Television news relies heavily on the existence of pictures rather than words alone, presenting a special dilemma for news of white collar crime. Camera crews must have the 'arrest or court shots' of the defendant for any substantial story to be run. The piece will be given even longer air time if stock or file footage exists on the individual in question prior to their criminal involvement. If the individual is or was a public figure it is very likely that a large part of the story will be comprised of past history, emphasising happier days when money flowed freely – in both directions. The composition of a news broadcast reflects the answers to such questions as: Who is this person? Who did we (the public) think he/she was? Why is this new information so damning/damaging? Television has been viewed as basically a domestic medium, the context within which the television 'makes contact' is in the home or in a domestic type of setting. Whereas game shows or situation comedies may make an effort at including 'you at home', the news plays a very different role. Ellis (1982: 166) argues that television 'confirms the domestic isolation of the viewer, and invites the viewer to regard the world from that position'. If one agrees with this notion of news as in some way exclusionary, news of white collar crime confirms it. Complete with existing file footage of 'fallen idols' before the fall and verbal emphasis on the past legitimate status in comparison with the recent il-legitimate status, white collar criminals are elevated (or lowered) to Other status. Television news, like newspapers, place the event in a particular context, their own. Media have found white collar crime's news value in characteristics other than its 'action', newsworthiness appears to lie in the image of the victim and the offender as well as the amount of money involved.[28]

Judging the quick and the dead

The importance of the victim in researching crime holistically, as well as being a crucial part of crime management, has become increasingly evident in the last two decades. The 1980s brought with it not only a lust for the expansion of capital markets but also the 'rapid increase in national and local victim surveys and in studies of the impact of crime, of victim needs and services' (Zedner 1994: 1207). This interest in vic-timisation, however, has not been forthcoming in either a systematic review or real acknowledgement of the victims of white collar crime.[29] In fact, although Mawby and Walklate (1994: 32) acknowledge the 'changing public perception of the broader crime equation' to include white collar crime and therefore victims of white collar crime,[30] they find themselves 'returning to [the discussion of] the crime problem as conventionally defined' a paragraph later. The persistence of the term 'victimless crime' in 1994 is an obvious disadvantage to the study of white collar crime as the two are often viewed by many to be opposite sides of the same coin, if not the same thing. When companies rather than individuals are involved the loss of the personal interest news value is felt by less or non-existent coverage (Grabosky and Wilson 1989). Clearly there are victims of white collar crime: individual victims, multiple victims, diffuse victims, corporate or organisational victims and often not easily identifiable victims. Who are these victims of white collar crime? What face represents victimisation to the media? 'When people scan the papers or catch the news on radio or television, they are particularly alert to stories about people like themselves' (Home Office 1989: 26).

Victims who are able to be identified and victims who the audience can identify with are crucial to news of white collar crime. Certain 'faces' of victimisation prevail in the media, faces such as the pensioners in the Maxwell case. Referred to as 'Dad's army',[31] 'Maxwell losers',[32] 'Maxwell pension victims'[33] and 'Maxwell pensioners' by just about every paper, here was a case with victims who were 'identifiable' on both counts. Although this case brought the notion of victimisation home to the punters, in the shape of their evening television news and morning papers, the victims were portrayed as weak and vulnerable, the quintessential picture of the helpless powerless against the almighty powerful. Interestingly a comparison of the case of BCCI illustrates a very different picture. Victimisation in BCCI was not as clear-cut as in the Maxwell case, as portrayed by the media. The real losers in the BCCI fraud were the many small investors from all over the world, the 'creditors' and the 'depositors' as they were frequently and efficiently christened by the print and broadcast media. In an official business capacity victims appear to lose individuality, the personal aspect forfeited for the professional. In BCCI, too many people looked like the 'baddies' and therefore the victims were seen as possibly greedy, as investors, readily taking a turn on the wheel of capitalism. White collar crime is often viewed as a by-product of a capitalist society, a possible risk and probable punishment for entrepreneurial risk. These individuals were often viewed as the high flyers who fell to a calculable danger. Undoubtedly the Maxwell and BCCI cases have limited similarities; while both are white collar offences − abuses of trust and finances, pensions are supposed to be secure, full stop − this aspect of the case made it different from many other frauds in the eyes of the public. The average member of the British population has a clear understanding of pensions; investments are not so applicable.

The underreporting of victimisation to the control agencies (by victims themselves) due to white collar crime is a grave problem. Lack of reporting on the part of the victims has been said to be due to:

1. The inability to assess that they had been treated wrongly.
2. The inability to assess that they had been treated criminally.
3. The fear that what happened was somehow their fault.

4. The feeling that their loss may have been too trivial (due to the diffusion in some crimes) (Levi 1987, Croall 1991, Bologna 1994).

Obviously this would also affect media reporting of victims – if they cannot identify them they cannot utilise them. The idea of exploitation rightly belongs within the constructs of white collar crime, however the victims need not be willing, unsuspecting or ignorant. Because the measure, in frequency and, more importantly, range of white collar offences reported in the media is limited the scope is even more restricted for news of its victimisation. With powerful images of the victims of white collar crime fitting neatly into categories of the needy, seedy or greedy, an opportunity is lost for a fuller picture of the reality of destruction it generates.

Clever dicks

The young child who decides that a playmate's property is worth having and who gets by inflicting physical injury is considered a bully. The same child, convincing another that the property is in some way either defective or useful in getting something much better, and thereby acquiring it, is considered devious, and very clever. There is often a similar grudging respect, or at the very least a lessening of antipathy, within media representations of the white collar criminal[34] (as well as amongst researchers). The language of white collar crime is steeped, if not in intellectualism, in legal or 'business–ese'. 'Assets' are 'plundered'[35] or 'lost', 'missing' or 'pillaged'[36] and only very occasionally are individuals 'robbed'.[37] The latter is usually found in the indignant tabloid press. One could argue that as white collar offences routinely develop as organisational or individual business dealings, terms other than financial ones would not be appropriate. It is important to note however that as the public's top-ranking crime 'informer' and utiliser of the language of crime, criminal conduct and crime control, words such as 'theft', 'robbed' and 'violated' in media reports may send a message that 'lost' and 'pillaged' do not. The plundering of assets may not mean 'crime' to the public or the news organisations and, as such, although this is an aspect of the 'white collar crime problem' in which responsibility certainly does not lie solely with the media, the situation must be acknowledged. This notion of seriousness, the severity of the action and the consequences of the crime, is central to this problem. Do media organisations feel that this type of activity is inherently deleterious? Does the public? Whereas words such as 'hoodwinked'[38] and 'rascality'[39] seem par for the course in articles of white collar crime, it might raise more than eyebrows if juvenile crime was referred to as 'shenanigans'.

'The subtlety of insider trading and and sharemarket manipulation is lost on most of the 95 per cent of Australians who do not own company shares' (Grabosky andWilson 1989: 93). This is a phenomenon which is true for many nations. A limited minority have a real conception of the nature of white collar crime, yet the effects of this activity diffuse exponentially. Though an earlier reference was made to the 'antics' of children, white collar crime is generally more complex than taking candy from a baby. Indeed the words 'complex' and 'white collar crime' are linked the way in which 'senseless killing' and 'random acts of violence' are linked with gang criminality. Certainly the notion of the clever criminal is not limited to white collar crime, especially in the media, however the scale of the 'booty' in reported white collar crime far outweighs that of the most ingenious street criminal. By the very nature of media reporting of crime, most of the information deals with either a reported street crime for whom no suspect has been apprehended or a 'solved' case wherein the offender has been charged, if not tried and/or sentenced. This leaves the 'clever argument' in one of two camps: the criminal was clever enough not to get caught or the actual crime was executed cleverly. News of white collar crime, due to the nature of the activity and the involvement of crime control agencies, does not usually occur unless someone or some organisation is in 'the hot seat'. The notion of the clever white collar criminal is born out of the idea that someone has been able to steal so much for so long without getting caught before now. The white collar offender becomes two parts shrewd and one part corrupt, shaken not stirred. The intelligence awarded to the business or legal–minded individual is amplified by behaviour which is reckless and pernicious and is somehow translated in the media as 'hoodwinking'. That many white collar crimes are a rather convoluted affair cannot be denied, making it difficult for journalist and audience to come to grips with the actual crime, much less the specifics of the case.[40] However the issues of complexity, severity and inherent deleteriousness necessitate careful disentangling by further research.

Suite crime v. street crime

Do the media treat white collar crime as somehow different from other types of crime?

It would be unrealistic to expect white collar crime to be treated in exactly the same fashion as street crime. Under the rubric of street crime, different offences and the diversity of behaviour and mitigating circumstances relating to those offences are reported in differing styles with varying frequency. Why should the reportage of white collar crime be any different? The importance of trying to uncover the way in which white collar crime is reported, or any other of the range of deviant and unlawful behaviours, lies not only in its description but in its proscription. Placing news of white collar crime in the wider context of easily accessible information concerning wrongdoing and the fate of wrongdoers serves to highlight the deleterious nature of this type of action to the public. The relative quarantine (rather than absence) of news of white collar crime as opposed to more conventional criminal activity forces the plaintive/anguished cry of '*why*?' What is so different about white collar crime? In reviewing the literature on street crime in the media the criteria of newsworthiness provides a helpful starting point. The previous section illustrated that in terms of newsworthy criteria white collar crime, although lacking, is not entirely without merit, and in many cases surpasses its impoverished relatives. One explanation might be that as crime in the suites has not enjoyed status as a major subject of research, as has crime in the streets, the latter has simply outdistanced the former in terms of newsworthiness. However as criminologists, journalists or for that matter an individual, we would be hard pressed to credibly peddle the notion that we stand unaffected by the social, political and/or cultural tone of the times, the reality may be more complex.

The power of fear

'White collar crime is not really the subject of public fear. Nobody ever felt threatened by embezzling from a bank. We will need to get the public mad about white collar crime as well' (Bauer 1989: 36). Perhaps this idea approaches a fuller truth: public fear in private lives. Fear is a very powerful tool, and fear of crime is an apparent national if not western pastime. Media utilise it well. Fear of crime has become an issue firmly enmeshed in the politics of crime control. Research studies are quoted, academics brought out and journalists and investigative teams produce articles and programmes specifically or tangentially about the fear of crime. White collar crime, however, does not fill the average heart with trepidation or the average mind with visions of dark corners and lurking strangers.[41] White collar crime is rarely viewed as part of the crime problem and therefore cannot represent more than a negligible part of the collective fear of the crime problem.[42] Although there may be some level of fear surrounding a wide range of crimes most of the academic literature linking fear with particular crimes focuses on violence (Gunter

1987, Bennett 1989, Hobdell and Stanko 1989, Last and Jackson, 1989). This is not dissimilar to the media, where an emphasis lies not only on violent acts but in targeting specific sites as more conducive to crime, certain types of individuals as more criminogenic and others (or in many cases the same individuals) as being prime candidates of victimisation. There is no identikit for white collar crime, and without a recognisable face and generalisable and identifiable villain it is difficult to conceptualise the object of fear. Because white collar crime begins as business, whether it is legitimate in reality or not, its point of origin is viewed as possessing prestige which may lessen the fear factor to some extent. While it could be argued that a certain amount of fear of personal safety and/or survival without handicap may be innate in the human species, fear of harm can be generated. Certainly research into particular 'crime waves' has proved the latter part of that thesis (Hall et al. 1978).

'A report on community safety in Brighton concluded that among elderly people: "Most fears stemmed not from direct or personal experience of crime but from mediated experiences received through the press"' (Home Office 1989: 25). Whether (or to what extent) the media aid the production of a fear of white collar crime, healthy or otherwise, is not known. As news of victimisation is not frequently forthcoming it may be the case that the restricted methods of reporting lessen the possibility of fear. However white collar crime may not be particularly fear invoking due to a view among the public that all politicians and/or businesspersons are corrupt anyway. This alleged impotence also corresponds with traditional Marxian philosophy of the lower-class sentiment toward the upper class (Pearce 1978). How widespread such a notion is, is not known.

The Avengers

Do news organisations have specialist white collar crime reporters? What special problems do reporters face in writing articles about white collar crime?

Reviewing the process by which journalists and news organisations come to write their stories is the next area of investigation. Although the word specialist has been repeatedly linked with white collar crime in this discussion there are very few reporters specialising in white collar crime. With the exception of national figures such as the late Barbara Conway and the flourishing Michael Gillard few media organisations boast white collar crime journalists. Just as articles of white collar crime are as likely to appear in the political pages as the financial, reporters who have written about white collar crime may be political or business or health correspondents. When trying to locate reporters who considered themselves fluent in reporting white collar crime it was interesting, though not altogether surprising, to find that very few would classify themselves or their peers as white collar crime experts. Many journalists had either no experience at all in writing about white collar crime or had 'fallen into' writing an article by having the crime touch an area in their forte or being in the wrong place at the right time, and they did not therefore feel 'competent' about discussing the area. As reportage of white collar crime tends to be irregular, but intense, few reporters would build up a portfolio of cases. Those who do, however, are viewed as an elite.

An editor of an Australian newspaper describes a 'good' street crime such as a 'rape, shooting or mugging' as 'a piece of cake' to write, but goes on to extol the virtues of the reporter capable enough to write an article on white collar crime as a highly 'skilled journalist' who understands accounting and law, and who has overall business acumen (Grabosky and Wilson, 1989). A seasoned English reporter echoed this sentiment when he stated that 'a lot of training and expertise' is what characterises any good reporter, and those who write about white collar crime have these attributes in abundance. 'Writing white collar crime stories demands the basic ability of business journalism. You have to know how to trace money, how to read assets and how financial systems work' (current affairs television producer and ex-print journalist). What makes these reporters different? Apart from a keen mind and diligent spirit, which many reporters could claim, the subject matter with which they deal is different. Interviewing techniques, while both are challenging, are quite different if one is interviewing a mugger or joy rider, or a market manipulator or fraudulent solicitor (if one can get an interview). Many journalists expressed the view that there are a 'very limited number of journalists who conduct investigative work' and often white collar crime stories necessitate a certain amount of investigation. While more half-hour to 90-minute special television programmes are devoted to 'candid and hard-edged' interviewing of street criminals, infrequent televised exposés on 'fallen idols' engaged in anything other than political corruption or deviance of a political, sexual or violent nature receive the accolades of 'critics choice'. The social status of the white collar criminal certainly can have a knock-on effect to those who research them, reporter and academic alike.

'White collar crime correspondents' do not exist in the way that 'crime correspondents' do. Several crime reporters still work on a particular 'beat', having established a solid working relationship with their sources. However, the persistent stereotypical court hack who knows every police officer, judge and bailiff of old, perpetually hanging around the Crown Court for his story, bears little resemblance to a reporter writing a story on white collar crime. While sources for news of street crime for the most part remain static, with the emphasis on the police, the Home Office, and the courts (Tuchman 1973, Chibnall 1977, Hall et al. 1978, Ericson et al. 1987, 1989, 1991), crime control mechanisms for white collar crime are characterised by their varied and complex nature (Clinard and Yeager 1980, McBarnett 1988, Stephenson 1992). This complexity of sources is aggravated by the fact that many regulatory agencies, departments and committees designed to combat white collar crime 'tend not to have developed the extensive public relations apparatus which characterises contemporary police forces' (Grabosky and Wilson, 1989: 90). There is no competing with the Scotland Yard Press Office, formed in the 1920s in response to the growing concern that crime reporting was becoming a specialised area.[43] Reporters covering news of street crime do so fairly confident in the belief that they will be able to interview the agents of the necessary and conventional institutions of crime control. However journalists' relationships to avenues of source material in white collar crime is not as systematic as it is in street crime. As much of the less 'hidden' white collar crime involves large companies, law firms, multinational corporations and organisations for whom 'no PR is better than bad PR', information from that direction may be slow in coming. Because the police are not always heavily involved with the control of white collar crime contacts must be made within the several regulatory agencies as well as possibly the SFO. Journalists also lose an important opportunity for comment as official statistics regarding the prevalence of white collar offences, as well as the presumed unimaginable loss they create, are not regularly tabulated (if at all) or made readily available if they are[44] (Croall 1987, Levi 1987, Clarke 1989, Naylor 1990).

Life after the SFO

An examination of the reality of media reporting of white collar crime would not be complete without acknowledging the very powerful (and public) presence of the Serious Fraud Office in Britain. Until the operationalisation of the SFO in April 1988[45] a publicly recognisable and official face of combating white collar crime did not exist in the UK.[46] The existence of SFO and the way it is seen to be handling white collar crime is crucial, especially as the SFO was formed from a perception of public malcontent. The Roskill Committee was set up in 1983 by the then Lord Chancellor and home secretary to examine the ways in which fraud trials could be improved, made more just and more expeditious. Lord Roskill's report in summary stated that a new system was needed as the public had lost faith in the criminal justice system's ability to successfully mete out justice to white collar criminals, specifically fraudsters, and that in light of the Committee's evidence the public was justified.[47] The SFO has altered the face of white collar crime in Britain and with it the reporting of white collar crime in respect to fraud. No research to date has been published specifically looking at the media reporting of white collar crime before and after the SFO. Should such a project be undertaken it would not be surprising to find that reporting has altered. The ease of availability and accessibility of an official 'line' from the SFO enables journalists to receive official information in a similar fashion to street crime. The SFO may have become akin to one of Hall et al.'s 'monopolies' of information (1978). That much of the reporting of white collar crime and the SFO is harshly critical, both in the print and electronic media, is hardly surprising, considering this fact. The media rarely take into account the many successes achieved by the SFO (interestingly enough, many of these are often in cases which were not covered in terms of widespread national attention in the first place). This is mostly due to the fact that political and, one might argue, public judgement of exactly what the office should achieve may be different from that of the SFO personnel themselves. Clearly it would be impossible to judge the efficacy of a system without first knowing what that system is set up to achieve and what its goals are, nevertheless this is what continues to occur. If the SFO is the main source of information for journalists, as well as the main focal point (the buck stops at the SFO) in the view of the public and the policy makers, scapegoating is inevitable. That the SFO has not been entirely successful in their mission to 'fight the decidedly bad fight' against fraudsters cannot be denied, that the SFO has not been consistent in their views concerning white collar offences should not be ignored. Both of these factors impact reporting and therefore the importance of the SFO in this context is its relationship to the reporting of white collar crime.

As the Serious Fraud Office handles cases of high levels of loss[48] it would not be too difficult to assume that it is the multimillion pound cases which are reported by the press. The importance to journalists of utilising official sources for crime stories has been expressed by numerous researchers (Tuchman 1973, Chibnall 1977, Hall et al. 1978, Ericson et al. 1987, 1989, 1991). The existence of the SFO as an official source handling white collar crime on a massive scale translates into the possibility of reportage of white collar crime skimming only the sensational. As this appeared to be one of the universal dilemmas of reporting white collar crime, 'do only the sensational stories get reported?', how does the SFO fit into the equation? High levels of money + an official source to set the action in context = newsworthiness. Information from the SFO would belie this. The SFO has a results sheet[49] of over 80 cases, and less than one-third have achieved news status in local or national media, a great deal fewer have received major nationwide coverage. The cases which are reported will have one or both of the other all-important criteria: an identifiable victim and a perpetrator, who may or may not be a public figure. Clearly there are a variety of critical elements which must be present in order for a particular case of white collar crime to be deemed newsworthy. Added to the practical barriers which must be overcome by journalist and news organisation alike, reporting white collar crime becomes a demanding task with questionable rewards in terms of public impact.

Capitalism incorporated

> The public agencies of communication do not express the organised moral sentiments of the community as to white collar crimes, in part because the crimes are complicated and not easily presented as news, but probably in greater part because these agencies of communication are owned or controlled by businessmen and because these agencies are themselves involved in the violations of many of these laws. Public opinion in regard to picking pockets would not be well organised if most of the information regarding this crime came to the public directly from the pickpockets themselves. (Sutherland, 1983: 59)

Does political affiliation/ownership of news organisations bias white collar crime reporting?

A persistent subject in white collar crime's tale of woe rests upon the idea that white collar crime is not passively overlooked but actively obscured. Exposing the crimes of the powerful are in the interest of neither the masses, who lose faith in the systems controlled by the powerful (Conklin 1977), nor the powerful, who undermine their position. As white collar offenders, by the nature of their position, are often 'connected' to a myriad of individuals and organisations who may be potentially useful in 'closing ranks' should they need it, this claim is a valid concern in the media debate. It is not however as simple as the rich protecting the crimes of the rich and focusing on those of the poor.

Reporting white collar crime presents specific problems for journalists and news organisations alike. Alistair Brett, solicitor for *The Times* and the *Sunday Times*, readily admits to long conversations with editorial teams during which complicated processes of weighing the pros and cons of printing an article are discussed. The issue of defamation in the case of a white collar offender is of the utmost importance, to both the news organisation as well as the alleged offender.[50] Libel, slander and malicious falsehood, components of the libel laws, are some of the white collar offender's most powerful and fear-provoking tools. 'Thinking long and hard' before publishing on white collar crime is not restricted to any one media organisation, it is a necessary precaution. News organisations cannot afford the drawn-out libel trials, fees or the exorbitant and seemingly arbitrary awarding of damages. Often the mere threat of writs is enough of an incentive for a news organisation to back down; the late Robert Maxwell and the Al Fayed brothers, current owners of Harrods, being two of the most high-profile examples in the United Kingdom. In both cases a diet of possible writs proved too rich for most news organisations. In the case of the Al Fayeds, intimidation and highly improper if not criminal action suppressed virtually every newspaper, with the exception of the *Observer*, whose owner, business tycoon 'Tiny' Rowland, had a vested interest in illuminating their nefarious leanings. That this group of offenders have at their disposal the money, prestige and contacts to stall or block a story cannot be denied. Articles go unwritten, at times temporarily, until perhaps an official source is ready to give a 'line' on the story or the case is firmly entrenched in the criminal justice system, or at times are scrapped altogether. The complete withdrawal of a story shatters the occasional incredulity with which the public, some journalists or industry externalise by asking the questions: Didn't anyone know? How could this go unnoticed? Why didn't someone do something? Journalists are viewed as being acutely aware of the potential interest of a story. Powerful commercial and political interests often direct crime news to particular issues while turning a blind eye to others. Cohen and Young (eds 1982) cite the incidence of widespread knowledge by journalists of suspicious financial transactions, or other illegality or scandal, by highly placed political figures which goes unreported for years (not unlike the rumours pertaining to BCCI several years before the scandal broke). This doctrine cites dangerousness to the status quo as its basis for selectivity. That criminal offences of a white collar nature exist without being recorded by the criminal justice system or reported by the media may cause less consternation and less distrust of the ruling elite[51] than the fact that they may be investigated or come to the attention of the media but not be reported upon.

The perils of the withdrawal of advertising has been less of a primary issue in the UK than in the US, where advertising plays a much greater role in television, radio and newspapers. Nevertheless, as most of the major news organisations are part of megabusiness conglomerates with strong arms in multiple arenas, conflicts of interest and business relationships are bound to interfere at some point. Indeed, extensive research has been devoted to the historical analysis of the newspaper as a business, highlighting advertising, proprietorship and economic power (Hoch 1974, Chibnall 1977, Curran et al. 1977, Schiller 1981, Curran and Seaton 1988, Parsons 1991). Hoch asserts that news is merely a commodity and is treated accordingly, as a 'slickly handled, brightly packaged' product in which advertisers must be 'deftly wooed [and not offended]' (1974: 17). Perhaps this exists as a greater problem for the press as editorials and political perspectives abound to an extent which does not exist in broadcasting due to the ruling that impartiality be preserved as of the Independent Broadcasting Act of 1973.

Due to the high-powered nature of many of the white collar criminals, organisational or political ties are a real concern rather than a liberal alarmist view. However the analysis, the search for information, must not terminated on that level. It is all too easy to blame the non-representativeness of white collar crime reportage, in form, content and number, on a governmental or industry related cover-up. The problems with reporting white collar crime are much more complex, and often rooted in practicality, marketability and perhaps nebulous personal or intrinsic properties of the particular case. While the media, and researchers, continue to view cases and players selectively, excluding both the normality of the crime and the practical bars of reporting, the myriad myths multiply exponentially.

Does white collar crime pay?

News organisations, above all, are businesses (but importantly, not *only* businesses). To this end ratings and circulation are all important. Market or commercial models in media theory view media selection and presentation as being determined by 'what the public wants' (Siebert et al. 1963). This has been characterised by 'what interests the public and what is in the public's interest' (Cohen and Young 1982). Theoretically, the finished product is a carefully balanced fare of 'all the news fit to print'.[52] Realistically news is a carefully balanced social construction, both reflecting and moulding 'what the public wants' in an effort to boost profitability, among other reasons. The checklist for a successful white collar crime story is long and convoluted, providing difficulties for a combination of individuals in their personal and professional capacities. Nevertheless, a 'good' white collar crime story can be a big and therefore lucrative story. During the week it was reported in the media that businessman Roger Levitt had been given 180 hours of community service[53] for making thirty-odd million pounds disappear, the newspapers and electronic media were filled with accounts of the Jamie Bulger case and no other. When the Levitt story was reported, it was often accompanied by a picture of Levitt and his handsome family in their party togs, after he had been sentenced, toasting the camera with champagne. How does white collar crime fit into the public perception of what is important?

> [White collar crime] sells papers if [the story] is easy [to understand] and the persons [involved] are easily identifiable. The more you can find a hero and a bad guy the more you can sell the paper. Again, in countries like Finland where the tax rate is 40–50 per cent, tax crime stories are more and more popular. (Finnish journalist)

The importance of this comment is that, because of the high tax rate in Finland, the public is concerned with tax crime. An English journalist echoed the same sentiment in stating that Britain is no longer a 'land of gardeners but of property owners'. Property ownership is no longer exclusively in the hands of the 'ruling elite', there is fairly widespread ownership and this position is one which, by its very nature and the juxtaposed responsibilities arising from it, is vulnerable to white collar crime in its many configurations. White collar crime, to all intents and purposes, should sell. It can affect the small business person, the executive, the consumer, the housebound, the student, the unemployed. While the sensational may sell because of its news value, it may be that news of white collar crime, based on less sensational events, but events which clearly affect Britons, may over time pervade the public consciousness as an activity that is not infrequent and is criminal. The issues tackled in this chapter have more to do with a preliminary exploration of the subject than the empirical components, and this is a question best tackled empirically. Clearly news of white collar crime *can* sell newspapers and leave remote controls untouched. What has become increasingly evident is that the important questions are not 'Does news of white collar crime sell?' or 'Does white collar crime make a good story?' but rather 'How do journalists and news organisations make white collar crime a good story, and hence a "best seller"?'

The media explores, explains and comments upon deviance and criminality in our society, and in doing so both reflects and distorts reality.

White collar crime as an ideological construct is full of contradictions and inconsistencies. It would seem difficult for the media adequately and efficiently to mirror that which is not more understood, much less accepted. The media cannot be held fully responsible for placing white collar crime in the 'correct' context (that is as a heinous and law-breaking act that is indeed damaging to society) as this context is rarely reflected anywhere else in society. News reporters, as well as the organisations which employ them, must triage a diverse set of variables such as marketing strategies, political sensitivities and organisational norms. The idea of what is news or newsworthy is wholly subjective and closely linked with the political, social, economic and historical context of the gatekeeper. Reporting news of white collar crime poses unique and often ill-understood difficulties. What must be researched is what the media is and is not doing in relation to white collar crime stories, and how, and why. Indeed, as the media is criticised for its selectivity, the facade of white collar crime remains. These infractions will be continued to be seen as those of the super rich and super powerful, while the victims are portrayed in the realm of the needy, seedy and greedy. It is far easier to caricature, as placing a human face on the body of white collar crime grows increasingly difficult for many media agents. White collar crime is rarely reduced to the lowest common denominator, theft and lying. Swathed in a cloak of Swiss bank accounts, off-shore tax havens, multiple transactions and high intrigue, it becomes a penumbra, of the law and the media.

Acknowledgements

The author wishes to thank the following people: Richard Osborne, Paul Rock and Robert Reiner for their commentary on earlier drafts; George Staple and Georgina Yates of the Serious Fraud Office for being as forthcoming with their ideas as with their resources; Michael Ricks, Alistair Brett and Harri Saukkoma for their invaluable insight; and the sundry journalists and members of news organisations in the text who remain unnamed.

Notes and references

1. See Downes, D. and Morgan, R., 'Hostages to fortune? The politics of law and order in post-war Britain', in Maguire, M., Morgan, R., and Reiner, R.

(eds), *The Oxford Handbook of Criminology* (Oxford: Oxford University Press, 1994).

2. With the general exception of certain 'white collar crime' or 'radical' academics who have acknowledged but not focused on it. Box, S., *Deviance, Reality and Society* (London: Holt, Rinehart and Winston, 1971); Croall, H., *White Collar Crime* (Buckingham: Open University Press, 1992); Levi, M., *The Investigation, Prosecution and Trial of Serious Fraud* (The Royal Commission on Criminal Justice: Research Study No. 14) (London: HMSO, 1993); Pearce, F., *Crime of the Powerful* (London: Pluto Press, 1978).

3. When reviewing the subject indices of enormous numbers of media texts dealing with crime, or crime texts dealing with media, a search for white collar, corporate, business, occupational, commercial, professional and economic crime, as well as corruption, glean paltry results, often resulting in a few paragraphs of acknowledgement, if anything appears at all (Stephenson 1992).

4. There can be physical costs in the illegal pursuit of economic goals, as in corporate manslaughter or occupational health and safety standards, just as elites can be involved in violent conventional crimes. In both of these cases however the violence often overshadows the 'white collar aspect', the position of the offender or the economic sphere, as violence is one of the major characteristics of newsworthiness.

5. It is worth noting that, like street crime before it, white collar crime is viewed as a male preserve. Realistically, however, one must examine the variables of gender in the light of opportunity.

6. See Sutherland, E. 1983 and Nelkin, D. 1994.

7. See Levi, 1987: preface.

8. It is apparent that control of street crime often takes precedent over other aspects of research for myriad reasons, however street crime has had the benefit of many decades as a flooded discipline.

9. Such as seriousness, ironic and unusual circumstances, bizarre or sexual elements, dramatic events and high status of the actors involved.

10. This number was arrived at by reviewing television viewing schedules for the month of May 1994. The number is not an average of the month's viewing but rather a calculation of the lowest number of articles in any week. It does not include the satellite channels which would presumably raise the number.

11. This number was arrived at by recording the number of articles pertaining to white collar crime in the months of June and December 1992. It is an average of the daily offerings of white collar crime stories in aggregate, over all of the national daily and Sunday newspapers, excluding the *Sunday Sport*.

12. This would include any article about an actual white collar crime or criminal, new legislation pertaining to the control of white collar crime or information focusing on a regulatory or prosecutorial agency pertaining to white collar crime.

13. Each of the tables was constructed from news clippings from the SFO media library. The agency hired by the SFO was told to extract all articles pertaining to white collar crime (see note 12) and articles containing infor-

mation specifically about any of the SFO cases, individuals involved in SFO cases or articles with 'fraud' or 'serious fraud' in them.

14. This category excludes the evening newspapers and is selective in that it does not include some of the 'extreme end' national tabloids.

15. This number illustrates the difficulty of measuring stories by the space they cover, the amount of words included or just by the article, that is whenever a new headline or title appears, which may or may not be by a different author. Between 13–15 June 1992 the coverage of white collar cases, primarily Maxwell stories were given several pages of coverage in a large section on white collar crime. The difficulty in solely counting the number of articles becomes evident in a situation such as this when each 'article', as designated by a headline or writing in bold may be subsections of a wider article, all written by the same individual. This is why measuring square inches or counting words is often necessary for depth content analysis.

16. The *Sun*, 20 June 1992.

17. The *Guardian*, 20 June 1992.

18. The *Daily Express*, 6 June 1994.

19. 20 June 1992.

20. 20 June 1992.

21. *The Times*, 20 June 1992.

22. The *Independent*, 20 June 1992.

23. The *Financial Times*, 20 June 1992.

24. The *Daily Telegraph*, 20 June 1992.

25. 8 June 1994.

26. The *Independent*'s 'Column Eight' carried a story called 'Making a meal of the Maxwells' and ran the lunch and moped story complete with an intimation within the text of the food ordered, highlighting the fact that clear-cut lines cannot always be drawn between the two categories.

27. This term is first used in D.M. White, 'The gatekeeper: A case study in the selection of news', *Journalism Quarterly*, 27, 4, Fall 1950, pp. 383–90.

28. The personal characteristics of a victim and/or offender though are all important in news of conventional crime.

29. The British Crime Survey (1982, 1984, 1988, 1992) provides additional indices to the crime statistics compiled by the police. The representative sample of more than 10,000 individuals in England and Wales does not cover white collar offences as they 'cannot be readily covered in household surveys' (BCS 1993: vii).

30. They cite information from the Islington Crime Survey to extend issues of victimisation to review white collar offences. 'The victimisation of individuals as consumers, tenants, and workers, then can be considered to be more extensive than is true of street crimes' (Pearce 1990: 49).

31. The *Daily Mirror*, 8 June 1992.

32. The *Daily Mail*, 8 June 1992.

33. The *Daily Telegraph*, 8 June 1992.

34. Throughout this chapter I have utilised words such as offender and criminal, pertaining to white collar crime. It is important to note however that these are not the terms of the media, who prefer to describe them in other ways such as 'ousted executive' or 'fraudster' to name but a few.

35. The *Daily Telegraph*, 7 and 8 June 1992.
36. The *Observer*, 7 June 1992.
37. The *Daily Mirror*, 8 June 1992.
38. 'How Maxwell hoodwinked the DTI', the *Observer*, 7 June 1992.
39. Hugh Stutfield, 'The higher rascality', *National Review*, 31 March 1988 p. 75.
40. See 'The Avengers', pp. 201–5.
41. These are some of the common symptoms of which the media and the public associate with fear of crime. It may well be worth investigating if 'fear' in terms of white collar crime, an offence rarely linked in the collective mind with *physical* danger and behaviour modification, would need to be re-defined.
42. One questions whether or not there are elevated fears of white collar crime amongst business professionals.
43. The exception perhaps being the Press Office of the Serious Fraud Office.
44. Indeed much of the statistics on white collar crime are put together by academics with the help of crime control, financial and/or governmental agencies, or are extrapolated from American estimates, with the exception of the City of London statistics on fraud.
45. The Serious Fraud Office was created by Section 1 of the Criminal Justice Act 1987, Chapter 38, as part of a larger government initiative to combat fraud and regulate financial markets.
46. The Fraud Investigation Group (FIG) of the Crown Prosecution Service was the predecessor of the SFO and continues to play an important role in the processing of fraud. FIG, however, has never acquired the level of media attention which has alternatively cursed and graced the SFO.
47. Fraud Trials Committee Report, 9 December 1985: 1.
48. The lower monetary limit of an SFO case is £5 million.
49. A result sheet basically details each case; defendants, conviction, sentence etc.
50. This could also be pertinent in the case of a high status offender involved in a street crime.
51. Loss of confidence and growth of distrust in the ruling class and their provinces – government and finance – have been cited as major impetuses to sustain the relative historical silence surrounding white collar crime.
52. An allusion to the *New York Times*' motto.
53. Later he had a disqualification order made against him under Section 59 of the Financial Services Act 1986. Levitt will be effectively banned from employment in connection with investment business with the consent of the Securities and Investments Board (SIB). The ban was the first of its kind against an individual in the United Kingdom.

Bibliography

Bauer, W. (1989) 'Crime in the 1990s: A federal perspective', *Federal Probation*, 53.
Bennett, T.H. (1989) *Tackling Fear of Crime: A Review of Policy Options*, cited in Home Office (1989).

Bologna, J. (1993) *Corporate Fraud* (Boston: Butterworth-Heinemann).

Chibnall, S. (1977) *Law and Order News: An Analysis of Crime Reporting in the British Press* (London: Tavistock Publications).

Clarke, R. (1989) 'Insurance fraud', *British Journal of Criminology*, 29, 1, pp. 1–20.

Clinard, M.B. and Quinney, R. (1973) *Criminal Behavior Systems: A Typology* (New York: Rinehart & Winston).

Clinard, M. and Yeager, P. (1978) 'Corporate Crime: Issues in Research', in *Criminology* 16 (August), pp. 255–72.

Clinard, M.B. and Young, J. (eds) (revised 1981) *The Manufacture of News: Deviance, Social Problems and the Mass Media* (London: Constable).

Conklin, J.E. (1977) *Illegal but not Criminal: Business Crime in America* (Englewood Cliffs: Prentice Hall).

Croall, H. (1987) *Crimes Against the Consumer: An Analysis of the Nature, Extent, Regulation and Sanctioning of 'Trading Offences'*, unpublished PhD thesis, University of London.

Croall, H. (1991) 'Sentencing the business offender', *Howard Journal of Criminal Justice*, 30(4), pp. 280–92.

Croll, P. (1974) 'The deviant image', unpublished paper presented at the British Sociological Association Mass Communications Study Group.

Curran, J., Gurevitch, M. and Woollacott, J. (eds) (1977) *Mass Communication and Society* (London: Edward Arnold/Open University Press).

Curran, J. and Seaton, J. (1988) *Power Without Responsibility: The Press and Broadcasting in Britain* (London: Routledge).

Ellis, J. (1982) 'Visible Fictions', in Bocock, R. and Thompson, K. (eds) (1992) *Social and Cultural Forms of Modernity* (Cambridge: Polity Press in association with The Open University).

Ericson, R., Baranek, P.M. and Chan, B.L. (1987) *Visualising Deviance: A Study of News Organisations* (Toronto: University of Toronto Press).

Ericson, R., Baranek, P.M. and Chan, B.L. (1989) *Negotiating Control: A Study of News Sources* (Toronto: University of Toronto Press).

Ericson, R., Baranek, P.M. and Chan, B.L. (1991) *Representing Order: Crime, Law and Justice in the News Media* (Buckingham: Open University Press).

Ermann, M.D. and Lundman, R.J. (eds) (1987) *Corporate and Governmental Deviance* (third edn) (New York: Oxford University Press).

Graber, D. (1980) *Crime News and the Public* (New York: Praeger).

Goring, C. (1913) *The English Convict* (abridged edn, 1919) (London: HMSO).

Grabosky, P. and Wilson, P. (1989) *How Crime is Reported* (Sydney: Pluto Press).

Gunter, B. (1987) *Television and the Fear of Crime* (London: John Libbey and Company Limited).

Hobedell, K. and Stanko, E.A. (1989) *Men Talk: on Becoming Victims of Physical Assault*, cited in Home Office (1989).

Hoch, P. (1974) *The Newspaper Game* (London: Calder & Boyars).

Hall, S., Critcher, C., Jefferson, T., Clarke, J. and Roberts, B. (1978) *Policing the Crisis: Mugging, the State and Law and Order* (London: Macmillan).

Home Office (1989) Home Office Standing Conference on Crime Prevention, *Report of the Working Group on the Fear of Crime* (London: HMSO).

Janowitz, M. (1975) 'Professional models in journalism: The gatekeeper and the advocate', *Journalism Quarterly*, 52.

Last, P. and Jackson, S. (1989) *The Bristol Fear and Risk of Crime Project: A Preliminary Report on Fear of Crime*, Avon and Somerset Constabulary.

Leigh, L.H. (ed.) (1980) *Economic Crime in Europe* (London: Macmillan).

Lemert, J.B. (1989) *Criticizing the Media: Empirical Approaches* (London: Sage).

Levi, M. (1987) *Regulating Fraud: White Collar Crime and the Criminal Process* (London: Tavistock).

Levi, M. (forthcoming) *White Collar Crime in the Media*.

Levi, M. (1991) 'Sentencing white collar crime in the dark?: Reflections on the Guinness four', *Howard Journal of Criminal Justice*, in Croall, H. (1992) *White Collar Crime* (Buckingham: Open University Press).

Lombroso, C. (1876) *L'Uomo Delinquente* (Turin: Fratelli Bocca). See Lombroso-Ferrero, G. (1911) *Criminal Man: According to the Classification of Cesare Lombroso* (New York: Putnam, 1972, New Jersey: Patterson Smith).

Mawby, R.I. and Walklate, S. (1994) *Critical Victimology* (London: Sage).

McBarnett, D. (1988) 'Law policy and legal avoidance: Can law effectively implement egalitarian policies?', *Journal of Law and Society*, 15, 1, pp. 113–21.

Naylor, (1990) 'The use of criminal sanctions by UK and USA authorities for insider trading: How can the two systems learn from each other', *Company Lawyer*, 11, 3, pp. 53–61; 11, 5, pp. 83–91.

Nelkin, D. (1994) 'White Collar Crime', in Maguire, M., Morgan, R. and Reiner, R., *The Oxford Handbook on Criminology* (Oxford: Oxford University Press).

Parsons, W. (1991) *The Power of the Financial Press: Journalism and Economic Opinion in Britain and America* (Aldershot: Edward Elgar).

Robb, G. (1992) *White Collar Crime in Modern England: Financial Fraud and Business Morality 1845–1929* (Cambridge: Cambridge University Press).

Roshier, R. (1973) 'The selection of crime news by the press', in Cohen, S. and Young, J. (eds), *The Manufacture of News: Deviance, Social Problems and the Mass Media* (London: Constable).

Schrager, L.S. and Short, J.F. (1980) 'How serious a crime? Perceptions of organisational and common crimes', in Geis, G. and Stotland, E. (eds), *White Collar Crime: Theory and Research* (New York: Sage).

Schiller, D. (1981) *Objectivity and the News: The Public and the Rise of Commercial Journalism* (Philadelphia: University of Pennsylvania Press).

Siebert, S., Peterson, T. and Schramm, W. (1956) *Four Theories of the Press* (Champaign, IL: University of Illinois Press).

Stephenson, A.E. (1992) 'Corporate crime: An examination of media coverage', unpublished MPhil thesis, Cambridge University.

Sutherland, E. (1949) *White Collar Crime* (New York: Holt, Rinehart & Winston).

Sutherland, E. (1983) *White Collar Crime: The Uncut Version* (New Haven: Yale University Press).

Terry, W.C. (1984) 'Crime and the news', in Surette, R., *Justice and the Media* (Illinois: Charles C. Thomas).

Tuchman, G. (1973) 'Objectivity as strategic ritual: An examination of newsmen's notions of objectivity', *American Journal of Sociology*, 77, pp. 660–79.

Wilkins, L. (1964) *Social Deviance: Social Policy, Action and Research* (London: Tavistock).

Zedner, L. (1994) 'Victims', in Maguire, M., Morgan, R. and Reiner, R., *The Oxford Handbook on Criminology* (Oxford: Oxford University Press).

8 A Fair Cop?
Viewing the Effects of the Canteen Culture in *Prime Suspect* and *Between The Lines*

Mary Eaton

The mass media are widely recognised as an informal but effective form of social control[1] while the police are clearly part of the formal control structure of any society. The abiding popularity of TV programmes featuring police activity attests to the potency of this combination. Such programmes provide ways of transmitting the values that underpin the ordering of society and, in some cases, mounting a critique of those values. This chapter examines the critique of the police mounted by two recent British TV series: *Prime Suspect I, II* and *III* (Granada 1991, 1992, 1993) and *Between The Lines*' first and second series (BBC 1992, 1993). *Prime Suspect* is explicitly concerned with sexism within the police while *Between The Lines* focuses on corruption and collusion. I argue that these issues are all linked by a police subculture or 'canteen culture', from which they arise and by which they are sustained: sexism is a symptom of a malaise which is also manifest in corruption since both arise from the masculinity endorsed by police subculture. The argument is supported by reference to the programmes, to published research and by interviews with men and women serving with London's Metropolitan Police Force (the Met.).

Over ten years ago, as part of a study of the treatment of women within the British criminal justice system, I interviewed 100 serving officers from the Met.[2] Among those officers of different ranks, uniformed and CID, were 13 women. Although the focus of the interviews lay elsewhere the issue of women as police arose frequently with both men and women interviewees. Women were aware of being different but also of having to deal with attributed differences which they did not necessarily accept. Some men expressed concern at the behaviour and attitudes they, as men, felt compelled to manifest. Other men commented on the problems they perceived with women colleagues. Pursuing these themes lay beyond the scope of the research at that time, however, they were given a very public airing by the screening of the original *Prime Suspect* in 1991[3] and by the media coverage which followed. For the purpose of this chapter I talked to Detective Chief Inspector Jackie

Malton who collaborated with Lynda La Plante in the making of *Prime Suspect*. I also talked to eight other women, of differing ages and ranks, currently serving in the Met. While the first set of interviews took place within the police stations in which the officers were working, the second set took place in a variety of informal settings including cafes, wine bars and individuals' homes. However, the experiences of the members of the second group confirmed and extended the themes which arose in the first interviews. Ten years after I had first been alerted to the problem, women both outside and inside the police were still being defined in terms of their relationship to the masculinity endorsed by the police subculture. The position of women officers, as both women and police, posed a problem for the women and for their colleagues. Furthermore these experiences are echoed by the subjects of other research in the UK and the US.[4]

In the UK the Equal Opportunities legislation of 1974 gave women police officers an equal status (on paper) with men in an integrated police force. Before that time women worked in a separate section dealing with incidents considered suitable for them, particularly those involving children and domestic matters. Twenty years after legislation uniting the force women constitute 13 per cent of police officers in the UK, and that 13 per cent is concentrated in the lower ranks. Of the 173 most senior officers in England and Wales only five are women. In the Metropolitan Police Force, which has campaigned for equal opportunities, there are only 65 women holding the rank of inspector or above.[5] A similar situation of integration followed by minority status exists in the US.[6]

Sociological studies in both the UK and the US have chronicled the persistent harassment that women face from fellow officers.[7] Furthermore policies and practices aimed at creating equal opportunities for women are routinely subverted by a culture which reproduces the status quo and the place of women within a traditional femininity. The Home Office may produce circulars on part-time working so that women can combine police work and domestic duties but such potential for change is confounded when these pamphlets are not distributed by all police forces.[8]

In an occupational group which is traditionally the preserve of men, where men still dominate in numbers and authority, the subculture is an effective means of endorsing the status quo. The masculinity endorsed by police subculture conforms to the pattern of behaviour which has been described as 'hegemonic masculinity'.[9] This pattern achieves dominance, both within the police and beyond, not because the majority of men conform to this pattern of behaviour but because it is given high status even by those who neither conform to it nor benefit from it. The dominance of this form of masculinity can be seen in much of the daily output from the mass media. It is particularly noticeable in TV series based on police work.

Policing on the TV screen

Police TV series, in the UK and the US, have undergone well-documented changes in the past 30 years.[10] Sparks[11] discusses the move from a reassuring celebration of community in *Dixon of Dock Green* to a more realistic presentation of police life in *Z Cars*, to a focus on those aspects of police work which routinely encounter violence, such as the Flying Squad, with *The Sweeney*. In the US too he notes a similar move from series which celebrate the due process of law enforcement, like *Dragnet* and *The Untouchables*, to those which celebrate action by heroic police officers such as Kojak, Cannon, Rockford, Starsky and Hutch. Throughout this period the police officer has been presented as the tough crime fighter, upholding the good, protecting the weak and safeguarding society. He, and it usually is he, is the hero of gladiatorial struggles between good and evil, sometimes breaking the rules to achieve his nobler ends. Nor are such images confined to the TV screen. Researchers into police subculture have found that its values are also those associated with conflict, daring and white male supremacy.[12] This has implications for those who do not fit easily into the subcultural model of the police officer. Women in particular are perceived as odd, unusual, 'other'. This fact has been recognised and exploited by the mass media.

Women as police and detectives are neither unknown nor new to the TV screen. However, as Gamman points out, the eponymous policewomen played by Angie Dickinson, Charlie's Angels and Emma Peel of *The Avengers* all demonstrate glamour rather than strength in the accomplishment of their tasks and they work under the direction of men.[13] Thus they leave unchallenged traditional representations of femininity and masculinity. Gender divisions have been even more strongly emphasised where male/female partnerships are the focus of the TV series. In the series *Dempsey and Makepeace* a small, upper-class, British woman was partnered with a large, working-class American man. While the series gave an opportunity for contrasting class and cultural styles the main emphasis was on the exaggerated forms of femininity and masculinity being played out by Makepeace and Dempsey respectively.[14]

There are exceptions to such representations. In Britain we have seen *The Gentle Touch* and *Juliet Bravo* and from the US there is *Cagney and Lacey*. All three series present women as efficient police officers coping competently in a male world. But the problems posed by the male world are presented as the problems caused by individuals. There is little to suggest that sexism is structural and, furthermore, that it has deleterious consequences for the expressed objectives of the police force. The masculine ethos of police subculture, recognised by researchers, is routinely reinforced by the mass media. What then, are the implications of this for those who do not conform to the accepted image of the police officer? How do women, in particular, operate within this structure? Furthermore, what happens when policing is organised around an informal value system which runs contrary to the formal rule of law not only in its disregard for equal opportunities legislation but also in 'looking after its own?'

Constructing hegemonic masculinity

In reality the model of masculinity espoused by police subculture and endorsed by the mass media poses a problem not only for women and a few marginalised men but also for the majority of policemen. This problem centres on the fact that cultural perceptions of doing police work are at variance with the everyday experiences of police officers.

Many officers consider real police work to be about fighting serious crime[15] and this is the image promoted by most media dramatisations of police work. However, there are few opportunities for most police officers to take part in dramatic crime fighting. The reality of much of a police officer's shift is mundane patrolling, uneventful encounters with the public, paperwork and possibly some petty offenders. Officers are daily presented with the problem of structuring their experience to confirm the picture of themselves as real police. As Holdaway has described, canteen conversation is frequently structured around tales of risk and adventure and this bolsters the image of real crime fighting performed with skill and daring.[16]

Why, then, do police officers behave as they do? What is the point or purpose of the tall tales, the bluff bravado, the construction of an image of their world which contrasts sharply with mundane reality, a reality which involves long, uneventful hours driving through suburbs or walking a residential beat? The answer can be found in the police officer's relationship to the dominant masculinity within contemporary western society. The activities of police officers may best be understood as the routine re-creation of a gender role from which they gain status by association: 'Hegemonic masculinity is always constructed in relation to various subordinated masculinities as well as in relation to women. The interplay between different forms of masculinity is an important part of how a patriarchal social order works.'[17]

Other sexualities are recognised and lived out but their status and acceptability is gauged by their association with the dominant sexuality. While recognising the plurality of masculinities and femininities Connell finds no hegemonic femininity comparable in status to hegemonic masculinity.[18] Femininity is not about dominance. However, there is a recognised form of preferred femininity. This is the form which most clearly accepts, and adapts to, hegemonic masculinity. For younger women it involves sexual availability, for older women it involves motherhood.

If gender divisions are recognised as underpinning the status quo as surely as class divisions and racism then the influence of the police subculture becomes particularly significant. The police play an obvious role in the maintenance of order within society and, thereby, in the reproduction of the prevailing social structure. This role is usually understood in relation to law enforcement and police discretion[19] but it may also be seen in relation to the values endorsed within the police subculture.

Within the police force this dominant, or hegemonic, masculinity can be seen to present problems not only for the existence of women officers but also for the efficiency of many men. For women there is the problem of not being seen as real police officers,[20] for men there is a pressure to conform to a model of masculinity which may reduce their effectiveness as police officers: 'police work involves dealing with people (including women) in a sensitive and sympathetic manner ... the denigration of women implicit in canteen talk is also a devaluing of qualities associated with women that are actually required in much police work'.[21]

Police officers can be seen as men who not only endorse but also attempt to act out the hegemonic masculinity. This masculinity is held in favourable contrast to other manifestations of sexuality: to less macho masculinities, particularly homosexualities, and to all femininities. This has an effect on police responses to each other and to the general public: 'While gay men, by their "refusal" to conform to the "normal" image of masculinity effectively have their sexuality policed, all women ... have their sexuality policed through gender-based notions of femininity.'[22]

Nor is such 'policing' confined to the general public. Police culture marginalises any officer who cannot be recognised as a bearer of hegemonic masculinity. This involves not only women but also homosexual men. Burke presents biographical accounts of the ways in which homosexual officers of both sexes are ostracised and victimised.[23] Official attempts to challenge the subculture and change practice are likely to meet with apparent conformity but no real change. The discipline structure of the police force may deny the possibility of overt resistance but the culture promotes covert resistance. Officers facing promotion boards may give lip-service to equal opportunities while back at the station they endorse the canteen culture:

> When I went for my Inspector's board, I was asked how I would react to, and treat a homosexual officer in my group. Of course I told them what they wanted to hear, and not that I would really make his life hell − until I had persuaded him that it would be best for everyone if he resigned.[24]

Constructing acceptable femininity

Hegemonic masculinity marginalises other masculinities: it also defines as 'other' all femininities, all ways of being a woman. Some femininities are acceptable to hegemonic masculinity because of the ways in which they respond to or are accommodated within the dominant sexuality. The virtuous woman, the good wife, the good mother are all compatible with hegemonic masculinity while accepting a subordinate status and concomitant loyalty to men rather than to other women.

Thus it is that a male superintendent can tell me that he is sympathetic to women who stand by their criminal men folk:

> when they [women] become entangled with the criminal element they are very supportive of their spouse or partner. I don't agree with what they do but I understand the problem. There is a lot of support by women which does create problems for us, although I have a sneaking sympathy for them.

The loyal woman is endorsing hegemonic masculinity. She is also contributing to the definition of the disloyal woman as deviant, so providing a justification for the notorious police reluctance to become involved in domestic disputes.[25] Speaking of domestic violence one police constable told me:

> Women have got this tendency, don't know why, but if they've got a husband who say gets drunk and beats her up or whatever, they will go and get a Court Order. Frequently these Court Orders now cover arrest, which is OK, there's no problem there, but this is

where the crunch comes. The women have the man back, are quite happy with him living there, while he's bringing in the money, but as soon as he goes out and gets drunk, she waves this little bit of paper in front of his face and calls us. We've got no option; he's to be arrested. But women use it just as a means to suit themselves.

There is little sympathy here for the woman facing drunkenness and the threat of violence Nor was it only policemen who displayed this attitude. One policewoman told me:

If you go into a domestic dispute, nearly nine times out of ten it's the woman's fault – one I can think of – she's got an injunction against her husband. He can live in the living room until seven in the morning and then he's got to leave the house and he can come back at seven in the evening, but he's not allowed to leave the living room without her permission. So we get called there when he goes to the bathroom, or goes in the kitchen, petty things, but if you're going to a domestic dispute it's guaranteed it's the women at fault.

Accepted femininity does not complain, accepts her lot, and values hegemonic masculinity above all other sexualities. Women are acceptable to the extent that they accept the authority of men. I was frequently told, by male officers, about instances in which women showed a preference for men over other women, and the other woman was often a fellow officer. Speaking of a woman 'streaker' at a local sports ground, a male Detective Constable remarked: 'The nicest part of the whole thing was that she said to one of the journalists who interviewed her that the police had been marvellous to her except for one policewoman, and she thought she was a bit jealous.'

Another told me of the rapport between women prostitutes and policemen: 'Of course prostitutes are famous for smacking WPCs; prostitutes don't mind being arrested by men, they do not like being arrested by women.' Such valorisation of men is obviously important to their dominance but it may owe more to subcultural belief than to reality. A policewoman who had worked as a member of a special squad set up to deal with prostitutes in Mayfair had a different perspective:

We worked in pairs, two women together. At first it wasn't known how we'd get on because it's always been said that women policing women have problems, especially with prostitutes. When we were at training school we were told that you won't have many dealings with prostitutes because they get on better with the men. We found the opposite case. We got on very well with the girls, I think because we saw the female aspect of it. We'd sit and we could feel for them.

A lot of them were unemployed, had little children at home, and no husband, no man even. So they thought that was the best way to get some money together. And we could identify with them being in a real predicament.

Here a woman officer contrasts her own experience with the cultural myths concerning female rivalry. Sadly, as she acknowledges, such myths structure the reality of the working situation and so limit the opportunities for effective challenge. The sympathetic tone of this woman officer is very different from that used by most of her male colleagues when speaking of prostitutes. Within the police subculture the relationship between officers and prostitutes is seen as a game; indeed the colloquial phrase 'on the game' encapsulates this. Arrest and trial are represented as inevitable hazards with no ill will borne by participants to each other as individuals. No man presented such encounters as problematic. On the contrary prostitutes were spoken of as one group of women who seemed not to present a problem to the police since they conform to expectations. In this they differed from many other women encountered.

Policewoman: a problematic category

Any policewoman, by her presence, by her sex, is a challenge to the masculine profile of the police officer. If the police officer typifies hegemonic masculinity then any officer who does not do so is a challenge to that model. This is a culture in which women are defined primarily as women: to be classified according to their relationship to men, rather than as colleagues in a working partnership. One young woman with three years' service as a police officer told me of her experience while at Hendon Training School.

There was this trick the men decided to play on me to find out if I was a bike or a dyke. One of them got into my room and was in my bed without any clothes on. The idea was to test my reaction. Would I run away screaming or would I leap into bed with him? The trouble was I didn't notice he was there. I was pottering about getting ready for bed and by the time I pulled back the duvet and found him he'd begun to feel rather silly. He was OK; he agreed to say I was an all right person because I didn't make a fuss about him being there.

This incident is quoted at length because it illustrates so many aspects of the police subculture, including not only the prevalence of hegemonic masculinity among men but also the incorporation of women within this model. The young women telling me the story revealed no sense of outrage at this incident. Yet consider what she is accepting by her incorporation into the culture. She accords this man the right to intrude into her private space; to investigate her sexuality; to assume that only a lesbian would resist his advances to see her not as a police officer but as a deviant women, either oversexed or under-/inappropriately sexed. The woman even accords him the power to define the situation ('he agreed to say I was an all right person') thus according him a structural superiority which overrides the situational deficiencies of his circumstances. From such contexts the outsider status of the woman officer is continually endorsed.

The dominant masculinity endorsed by the cultural code underlies routine interaction between men and between men and women, both off and on the screen. It defines not only acceptable ways of being a man but also acceptable ways of being a woman. The 'real-life situation' described above is one manifestation. Another is the background to a media representation. In the original episode of *Cagney and Lacey* the part of Christine Cagney was played by Meg Forster, who was subsequently considered 'too butch' by CBS. For the long-running series the part was given to a more glamorous actress, Sharon Gless.[26] There is no public space for a critique of acceptable femininity even in a series which is prepared to mount a critique of dominant structures and attitudes in different areas, for example ethnicity, environment and other aspects of sexual oppression. Perhaps this is the inevitable consequence of a series which leaves unexamined the structural position of the police in the society in which they operate, and of an institution (the mass media) which itself plays an important role in the reinforcement of dominant ideologies.

Prime Suspect's Jane Tennison: a force to be reckoned with

Prime Suspect differs from its forerunners. From the beginning it could be seen as a critique of the position of women, as women, within the police. Devised and written by Lynda La Plante, *Prime Suspect* was recognised as groundbreaking in its depiction of a policewoman operating as a detective in conditions of outright and all-pervading hostility to a woman in this role. The protagonist, Detective Chief Inspector (DCI) Jane Tennison, is fighting not only the criminals but

also her colleagues in the force. The impact of this series is strengthened by the rigour with which Lynda La Plante researched the main
character. Indeed that the fictional DCI Jane Tennison is based on the
professional life of the real-life DCI Jackie Malton is a matter of public
record and media attention (see, for example, the *Daily Telegraph*, 10
April 1991; the *Independent*, 15 June 1993; the *Daily Mirror*, 2 December
1993; *The Times*, 7 February 1994). Speaking of the verisimilitude of
the series Jackie Malton said: 'About her professional life there's nothing
in the series that hasn't happened to me.'

Prime Suspect does not merely include the police subculture as one
aspect of the background to the story; the oppressive force of hegemonic
masculinity is a real enemy which our heroine faces. As the series
progresses we see that she manages to win battles, but the war continues.

Prime Suspect I opens with our heroine, a senior woman detective,
talking to another woman officer in the women's lavatories. A young
male rushes in with exciting news, calling 'Hey girls', but stops on recognising the senior officer and says 'Oh, sorry ma'am.' The junior male
assumes that not even the women's lavatories are out of bounds to him,
that any woman may be accosted or interrupted by him, that women
present will be powerless 'girls'. The presumed low status of women who
are not even afforded their own space is thus clearly presented to the
viewers.

The next shot reinforces the message. Our heroine is now squashed
at the back of a lift crowded with senior men who are loudly discussing
the current excitement of a case reported the previous night and now
almost solved. DCI Jane Tennison is again ignored and marginalised:
her existence is not acknowledged.

The third shot shows Jane Tennison asking about the time the case
was reported to the station. Although she was on duty no attempt was
made to contact her; instead an off-duty male colleague was brought
in. As a professional she is being denied the opportunity to practise. When
the officer in charge of the case has a heart attack and dies Jane Tennison
asks to be allowed to take over the case, and points out that in 18 months
on the murder squad she has never been put in charge of an investigation, despite her experience and rank.

Her request is granted. Jane Tennison is put in charge despite the
hostility of the men she commands. Many of the subsequent scenes
demonstrate Tennison's competence as a police officer and a detective.
She does not blanche at mutilated bodies while her male assistant
appears queasy. She is not fazed by the repellent facts of the case. She
finds flaws in the original investigation.

As Tennison becomes more professionally involved in the case the audience is continually reminded of the background to her work. Scenes at a boxing benefit for the dead colleague's family reinforce the masculinity of the subculture: the sexist jokes, the alcohol consumption, the violence. This is a game that only men can play.

Meanwhile Tennison contends not only with the dismissive attitude of her colleagues but also with the equally frustrating expectations of her male cohabitee. He wants her to play a traditional wifely role: to care for his visiting child, to cater for his colleagues and to focus her whole attention on him. He complains that 'if the phone rings I don't exist'. When the complications of the murder investigation make her late for a dinner he says 'I just wanted you to do something for me for a change.' He leaves her. Sexism and sexist expectations are not confined to the police.

In her work Jane Tennison experiences success. Not only is she as good as the men, but in some circumstances her skills as a woman give her an advantage. Prostitutes are willing to talk to her, recognising her as non-judgemental. A suspect's wife will give details of her sexual humiliation only to another woman. As *Prime Suspect I* draws to a close Jane Tennison is reduced to tears, not by the human misery she has to deal with, not by the aggression of hostile colleagues, not even by the rejection of her lover. It is the recognition that she is accorded, the hardwon respect of her team, her professional acceptance that moves her as nothing else does.

The problematic woman: critique or collusion?

The heroine of *Prime Suspect* shows that women can be good police officers, can even overcome the obstacles placed in their way by the prevailing culture. In so doing the series challenges the status quo. *Prime Suspect II* and *Prime Suspect III* take us further along the career, professional and personal, of DCI Jane Tennison. However, the challenge to the status quo posed by Tennison's professional competence is considerably weakened by the presentation of her personal life. Here Jane Tennison is not a success but demonstrates domestic inadequacy, relational failure and non-motherhood.

The hegemonic masculinity of the police subculture declares that only real men can be real police. Thus no woman can be a good police officer, and given the status of women within this framework it is easy to recognise that competence by a woman would lower the prestige of real police work. Does *Prime Suspect* challenge that model? Not really, because while Jane Tennison is clearly a good/real police officer we are invited to entertain doubts about her validity as woman. These doubts are frequently expressed by men. The hostile Sgt Otley suggests that she might be a lesbian; her lover comments on her ruthless determination to pursue her suspect; a victim's boyfriend, appalled at her seeming invulnerability asks: 'What sort of person are you?' And that is the question which remains at the end of the three series. Even the actress who plays the character and has won awards for doing so said: 'I never really liked Jane Tennison's brutality or her selfishness, and I don't like her job and could never be involved in a profession like it.'[27]

Close inspection shows that the triumphs achieved by Jane Tennison are bought at a high price: a successful detective but not a successful woman. Of course it may be argued that this is merely an accurate depiction. Professional women are frequently expected to act as men without the supportive domestic infrastructure, and to act as women within their private lives, providing that structure for others regardless of professional commitments. Women do not easily fit into structures designed to celebrate masculinity in the form endorsed by the police subculture. However, it would be heartening to see a critical exploration of this subculture rather than attempts, albeit successful, of a woman to be accepted into it.

There is potential in the use of marginalised characters to explore the culture through the eyes of the stranger. Through different assumptions there is the possibility of challenge. The horror encountered in police work, the acceptance of brutality as part of a day's work, become shocking when we see a woman experiencing this, and being inured to it. But should we not be asking questions about the impact of such events on policemen? Do we not collude with hegemonic masculinity when we expect that men will remain unmoved by scenes of violence and degradation? Speaking of the prevalence of heavy drinking within the police subculture, one officer told me: 'We drink on the pain; we drink to numb the pain.'

Hegemonic masculinity does not admit to human suffering. The male hero is above such reaction. He does as other men do in the situation, he buys into the dominant myth which helps him to endure but not to challenge or change the situation.

Exclusion, inclusion, collusion: the problem of corruption

With the character of Jane Tennison it is possible to demonstrate the difficulties faced by women in a social and professional context where formal rules and regulations are contradicted by custom and practice. However, the dilemma posed by hegemonic masculinity is not just about equal rights and equal opportunities for other sexualities. The celebration of hegemonic masculinity involves a bonding, a solidarity, an unquestioning loyalty to those defined by the culture as insiders, as 'one of us'. Loyalty to individuals, rather than to values or principles, all too easily becomes collusion. Hegemonic masculinity becomes a justification for corruption and this has implications for the rule of law in its widest sense.

Prime Suspect dramatises a practice which has been sociologically documented. Women police officers are excluded from male colleagues' socialisation and from interesting work assignments.[28] However, such exclusion may be seen as part of a process contributing to corruption within the police force. Recognising the hegemonic masculinity of the police subculture Smith and Gray comment on 'the emphasis placed on masculine solidarity and on backing up other men in the group especially when they are in the wrong'.[29]

Such 'masculine solidarity' has particular significance in the light of media accounts revealing police corruption to be systematic and widespread in many forces. Collusion appears to be an obligation within the subculture and an attribute of hegemonic masculinity.

Officers who refuse to co-operate on such matters find themselves ostracised and victimised. The experience of Inspector Peter Jackson of the Greater Manchester police is one such example. Having led a successful inquiry into the corruption of a constable the Inspector was praised and promised promotion. However, the inquiry revealed that senior officers were also involved in corrupt practices and when Jackson wanted these to be investigated he met immediate opposition:

> Within days I was being condemned as treacherous, incompetent, dishonest, and mentally unstable ... A vicious campaign was launched to undermine my credibility and integrity ... It is this kind of unhealthy atmosphere which makes possible cases such as the Guildford Four.[30]

Hegemonic masculinity demands allegiance to the subculture and the values this promotes, even when these run contrary to the explicit aims of the organisation. Excluded from the subculture, women are less likely to be enmeshed in the corruption which it promotes. This has been recognised elsewhere:

> The comforting notion that police turpitude was limited to 'rotten apples' has given way to alarm that the tree itself is horribly diseased.

However, among the myriad recent allegations of police malpractice, nowhere have I come across a woman officer who has been accused of wrongdoing or suspended from duty.[31]

A former criminal who had furthered her career by providing regular bribes to the police writes of her final arrest:

My flat was full of Flying Squad including one WPC Saint. I mention Ms Saint because if she had not been present I could have bought the lads off and that would have been that. I am pretty sure of this because the two I approached on this matter assured me ... that they were 'sick as pigs' not to get an earner.[32]

The relationship between masculinity and corruption within the police is a central focus of *Between The Lines*. However, before looking at the way this theme is explored by a TV series, it is illuminating to consider the situation encountered by a sociologist in the US for whom this phenomenon became a subject of investigation.

The exclusion of women because they cannot be trusted to collude becomes a focus of discussion in Jennifer Hunt's paper on the role of the female researcher in police subculture.[33] Hunt was involved in participant observation with New York police officers. She was aware that as a woman her presence was resented both as a challenge to the masculinity of their image and as a threat to their illicit activities. Hunt presents the policeman's world view as one which distinguishes between the private and the public, placing women in the private, clean and virtuous realm of the home and men in the public, messy and necessarily corrupt realm of the outside world. From this perspective men who do not wish to be part of such corruption must undertake the more feminine aspects of police work away from the public realm of the street:

In order to avoid involvement in illicit activity, honest men may transfer to inside units such as juvenile aid, research and planning, or the police academy. However, they tend to lose their manhood in the process. In contrast, the cop who joins elite crime-fighting units such as highway, homicide or narcotics, may increase his participation in illicit activity and, at the same time, affirm his masculinity.[34]

As a woman and a sociologist Hunt is aware of the factors which make it difficult for her to be accepted by the policemen she wishes to associate with for the purposes of study:

As a civilian and a moral woman I represented the formal order of law and the inside world of the academy ... Given my gender and formal orientation, many policemen assumed that I would naively report their activities to the department out of a sense of moral responsibility.[35]

In her paper she describes and discusses how she evolved a new gender role as 'street-woman-researcher'. She also gives a further demonstration of the way in which police subculture endorses corruption as a part of the hegemonic masculinity. The presence and influence of women, and of men who do not conform, is a threat not only to the symbolic world of gender models but also to the material benefits of corrupt practice. Hegemonic masculinity endorses different roles for men and women. In accepting that 'boys will be boys' the culture recognises that rule breaking is condoned within masculinity. When the rule breaking is serious and the masculinity is hegemonic there is a problem.

Between The Lines: investigating officers

Corruption and attempts to challenge corruption are the themes of *Between The Lines*. Devised by J.C. Wilsher this series explores the professional and personal lives of a team from the Criminal Investigation Bureau (CIB) of the London Metropolitan Police Force. The team, two men and a woman, investigate police officers who have become the subject of an official complaint. Complicity in corruption or cover-up is the focus, rather than sexism, but the Met. appears much the same as it does in *Prime Suspect*. There are few senior women above the rank of inspector. Within the CIB the most senior woman shown is Sergeant Maureen Connell who with Inspector Harry Naylor and Superintendent Tony Clarke makes up the team which is the focus of the series. The male camaraderie of Masonic dinners and heavy drinking sessions in pubs and clubs once again forms a background to the episodes which further a storyline. However, while in *Prime Suspect* these male enclaves serve to underline the exclusion of women officers, both socially and professionally, in *Between The Lines* the male bonding underlies the collusion in corrupt practices. The theme of 'you don't grass on your mates' runs through the series and provides the work of the CIB team. In one episode an otherwise honest sergeant has overlooked a detective inspector's malpractice. The sergeant is eventually persuaded to provide the piece of key evidence which will expose the detective's conduct. It is the sergeant who is ostracised and victimised by his colleagues and the Masonic oath of loyalty is used to suggest that further harm may come to him. He commits suicide.

The work of the CIB addresses complaints that officers have not followed proper procedures in the gathering of evidence, in the treatment of suspects and in their dealings with known criminals. The CIB works against two prevailing values within the Met. and other police forces. The first is the widespread believe that it is acceptable to break the rules to bring villains to justice, the second that it is not acceptable to betray a colleague. In attempting to uphold the law in relation to those charged with upholding the law the officers of the CIB challenge a code held more strongly than any legal statute or professional regulation.

Episodes of *Between The Lines* are scripted by individual members of a team of writers including J.C. Wilsher. Each series consists of a number of episodes, each complete in itself in relation to one story while developing another storyline which runs throughout the series. The characters of the main protagonists are also developed as the series progresses. From the beginning of the first series the private life of Super-intendent Tony Clarke is a focus for the storyline and in both the first and second series his private life becomes enmeshed with the investi-gation that forms the ongoing storyline of the series. In Clarke we see a celebration of many of those aspects of hegemonic masculinity which are endorsed by police subculture. He attracts, and is attracted to, women. He drinks, swears, loses his temper and has no time for the refined courtesies of polite exchange. In this he is contrasted with a calmly efficient but much less interesting colleague, Superintendent Graves. Personally flawed, with a chaotic private life, Clarke is presented as a likeable rogue but one who, initially at least, is beyond corruption in professional matters. Comparing Clarke to the more cold-blooded Graves, his commanding officer remarks to Graves: 'The extent to which Clarke frequently pisses me off pales into insignificance beside my intense and permanent dislike of you.'

In the first series we see the breakup of Clarke's marriage precipitated by his affairs with a junior police officer and an eminent journalist. In the second series we see the developing relationship with a senior civil servant. Clarke's heterosexuality is constantly invoked in relation to his own conduct and that of other officers.

Little is seen of Harry Naylor's private life in the first series, but it forms part of the story of the second series. In the first series we are given two indications that Naylor is a happily married man and no indications to the contrary. In episode six of the first series the team are investigating a case in Liverpool. Explaining Naylor's brusqueness, Connell comments that he hates being away from home. In the final episode of the first series we learn that Naylor is to take part in a ballroom dancing competition with his wife. In the second series Harry Naylor is revealed more fully as an undemonstrative but affectionate husband. His wife has developed Multiple Sclerosis and he takes on extra work, without his superiors' permission, to pay for private care for her. In both series the character of Harry Naylor is that of a slightly cynical, world-weary cop with a strong sense of justice. His reticence about his wife and his ballroom dancing can be seen as a way of preserving his affinity with the police subculture. Points of difference are not discussed.

All members of the CIB present a challenge to the police subculture and the hegemonic masculinity which it endorses. That 'you don't grass on your mates' is an oft-repeated tenet. Officers serving with the CIB are subverting this tenet, as the text of the series frequently reminds us. Perhaps this is why Clarke and Naylor are in other ways such an embodiment of the values of that culture. For the series to work it is important that the viewers see them as real police officers doing real police work. What then of Maureen Connell? How are the issues concerning women police officers to be resolved when the character is further distanced from the culture by her role in the CIB?

The emphasis in the first series is on Sergeant Connell as an efficient police officer. We see her working as a member of the team and, 'under cover', on her own. Significantly she is the only one of the team who, by the end of the second series, has not compromised the ethical standards of her job. Indeed she stands as a warning against excessive zeal. In episode two Clarke, infuriated by the inhumanity of a member of the public, declares: 'I'm gonna have him, I'm gonna hang him out to dry.' Connell reminds him: 'It's not down to us. It's not our brief.'

While in the first series we see Maureen Connell at work we see little of her off duty. The private life of this character is developed by allusion and suggestion. In episode four a hostile officer under investigation decides that as there is no Mr Connell 'she's gotta be a dyke'. At a party Tony Clarke's wife reveals her suspicions that he is having an affair with Connell. To this charge Connell replies: 'You really have got hold of the wrong end of the stick — in fact you couldn't be more wrong.' Clarke takes his wife away before any more is said.

The real cause of Sue Clarke's suspicions is PC Jenny Dean, with whom Tony Clarke has a turbulent relationship. Following a row with Clarke in episode five, Jenny Dean goes out for the evening with her former colleague now working under cover, Maureen Connell. At the end of the evening we see both women in Dean's flat drinking coffee. Dean is fearful of investigation by the CIB because of her part in an important case. She is clearly looking for allies and she makes a sexual overture to Connell, who tells her: 'I don't mind being called a dyke — what worries me is that you seem to think I'm a stupid dyke.'

By episode eight Tony Clarke's marriage is over and he is living out of suitcases and sleeping in his car. He gratefully accepts the offer of the spare bed at Maureen Connell's flat. Once there he propositions Connell who gently refuses saying: 'you're just not my type'.

On such remarks, and in the absence of any contradictory characterisation, is a picture of Maureen Connell as a lesbian suggested to the viewer. However, the whole edifice of this representation is demolished by the opening episode of the second series. Maureen Connell is now living with a man and this relationship continues into the new series although it is threatened by the demands of her work. Yet it is in this series, which begins with an apparent denial of Connell's lesbianism, that the character is fully developed as a lesbian. As the series ends Connell makes a public statement of her sexuality by taking her woman lover to a police social function. As the second series ends Connell is promoted and leaves the CIB. In the third series, screened during the Autumn of 1994, she has left the Met. There is, therefore, no addressing of the issues raised by the presence of an acknowledged lesbian within the police force. Nevertheless the creators of *Between The Lines* have gone further than those of other series in addressing issues of sexual marginalisation. Writing of *Cagney and Lacey*, Gamman comments: 'While male homosexuals have appeared ... and male homosexuality has been discussed, lesbianism seems to be the "repressed" of the series.'[36]

Prime Suspect, which has done so much to reveal the forces operating against women officers, has also addressed other issues of oppression and exclusion. *Prime Suspect II* explored racism while *Prime Suspect III* dealt with a range of issues around male homosexuality ranging from rent boys to drag artists, and even included a gay male police officer. Yet lesbianism is unaddressed in *Prime Suspect* and exists only as a category of abuse.

Gender and justice

With *Between The Lines* and *Prime Suspect* we see media explorations of the cultural underpinnings of the police force. Charged with preserving the good order of society the police force appears more concerned with preserving its own traditions of order and dominance. Central to that tradition is a hegemonic masculinity which marginalises and excludes other ways of being a police officer and doing police work. The consequences are apparent in the police corruption scandals of the 1970s and the miscarriages of justice which have increasingly come to light in the 1980s and 1990s. Among these is the case of Assistant Chief Constable Alison Halford, formerly Britain's most senior policewoman.

Having been passed over for promotion in favour of less experienced and less qualified men, in 1990 she brought a complaint of sex discrimination against her Chief Constable, the Home Secretary and HMI. After much public recrimination and counter-accusation the case was settled out of court. Discussing the isolation of a woman in this position, a recent account highlights the problems caused not only for the woman but also for the future of the organisation:

> None of the men with whom she worked ... was ever confronted by a woman in their professional midst who was his equal. Nor were these men ever in the position in which she found herself, of being surrounded only by otherness, being denied supervision or support by anyone who knew how that felt, or who knew what difference might bring to the organisation's professional repertoire.[37]

As a woman, Alison Halford was different, furthermore she tried to make a difference. She tried to bring about change and found herself ostracised and ultimately excluded. The police force suffered the loss of an efficient officer and the timely introduction of practices to facilitate effective policing in an area of strife and division. The accusations against her emphasised her difference from her male colleagues. However, the police force pays a price for homogeneity and conformity to the values of hegemonic masculinity. This is explored in *Prime Suspect* and *Between The Lines*. Unlike some of their more anodyne predecessors, both series question not only the behaviour of individuals within the police force but also the values that permeate the organisation.

When they function as a critique, media representations, documentary or drama are able to raise questions about the relationships between a society and the institutions which serve that society, and about the way this affects and is affected by the men and women within those institutions. With *Prime Suspect*, and even more so with *Between The Lines*, questions of gender become central to the operational practices and concerns of the police; issues of equal opportunities can then be seen as vital to the good order of a police force and of the society it claims to serve.

The hegemonic masculinity fostered by the canteen culture of the police can be recognised as ultimately destructive not only of the moral well-being of men and women within the police but also of the processes of justice and accountability that should characterise the work of a police force within a democracy. But in mounting a critique of this culture both programmes also remind the viewers of the opposition to that critique, an opposition with which many viewers may collude. With *Prime Suspect* we are reminded that what we find shocking if presented to a woman is acceptable when encountered by a man. The viewers' incorporation into the hegemonic masculinity usually precludes any outrage at the exposure to brutality and brutalising processes which characterise certain aspects of police work. In *Between The Lines* we are reminded that there is a constant temptation, endorsed by the culture, to allow the ends to justify the means. In the final episode of the first series, Tony Clarke's superior comments:

> The Met. has never been cleaner, I can tell you that for a fact. It's also a fact that our clear-up rate for crime is at an all-time low. What conclusion you draw ... is entirely up to you.

Prime Suspect and *Between The Lines* have presented the viewer with the possibility of concluding that hegemonic masculinity may be a damaging and destructive force but it is one which underpins much of what we take for granted in our understanding of law enforcement and good order. This explains not only the importance of challenge but also the strength of resistance.

Acknowledgements

I am very grateful to Professor Frances Heidensohn and Detective Chief Inspector Jackie Malton for their constructive criticism and advice, to David Kidd-Hewitt for his elucidating editorial comments and to Catherine Goddard for patiently processing these words.

Notes and references

1. Kidd-Hewitt, D., 'Crime and the Media: A Criminological Perspective', Ch.1 in this volume.
2. Eaton, M., 'Familial ideology and summary justice', unpublished PhD thesis, (The London School of Economics and Political Science, University of London, 1984).
3. Granada Television, 1991.
4. Heidensohn, F., *Women in Control? The Role of Women in Law Enforcement* (Oxford: Oxford University Press, 1992).
5. *The Times*, 7 February 1994.
6. Heidensohn, F., *Women in Control?*
7. Jones, S., *Policewomen and Equality: Formal Policy v. Informal Practice* (London: Macmillan, 1986). See also Heidensohn, F., *Women in Control?*
8. *The Times*, 7 February 1994.
9. Connell, R.W., *Gender and Power* (Oxford: Polity Press, 1987).
10. Clarke, A., 'Holding the blue lamp: Television and the police in Britain', *Crime and Social Justice*, 19: 1983, pp. 44–51. See also Clarke, A., 'This is not

the boy scouts: Television police series and definitions of law and order', in Bennett, T., Mercer, C. and Woolacott, J. (eds), *Popular Culture and Social Relations* (Buckingham: Open University Press, 1986).

11. Sparks, R., *Television and the Drama of Crime: Moral Tales and the Place of Crime in Public life* (Buckingham: Open University Press, 1992).

12. Young, M., *An Inside Job* (Oxford: Clarendon Press, 1991). See also Reiner, R., *The Politics of the Police* (Brighton: Wheatsheaf, 1985), Holdaway, S., *Inside the British Police: A Force at Work* (Oxford: Basil Blackwell, 1983) and Bittner, E., *Aspects of Police Work* (Boston: Northeastern University Press, 1990).

13. Gamman, L., 'Watching the detectives', in Gamman, L. and Marshment, M. (eds), *The Female Gaze* (London: Women's Press, 1994).

14. Gamman L., 'Watching the detectives'.

15. Punch, M., 'The secret social service', in Holdaway, S. (ed.) (1979). See also Reiner, R., *Politics of the Police*.

16. Holdaway, S., *Inside the British Police*.

17. Connell, R.W., *Gender and Power*.

18. Connell, R.W., *Gender and Power*.

19. McBarnet, D., 'The police and the state: Arrest, legality and the law', in Littlejohn, G., Smart, B., Wakefield, J. and Yuval-Davis, N. (eds), *Power and the State* (London: Croom Helm, 1978).

20. Jones, S., *Police women* and Heidensohn, F., *Women in Control?*

21. Smith, D.J. and Gray, J., *Police and People in London: The PSI Report* (London: Gower, 1985).

22. Brogden, M., Jefferson, T. and Walklate, S., *Introducing Policework* (London: Unwin Hyman, 1988).

23. Burke, M., *Coming Out of the Blue* (London: Cassell, 1993).

24. Burke, M., *Coming Out of the Blue*.

25. McCann, K., 'Battered women and the law: The limitations of the legislation', in Brophy, J. and Smart, C. (eds), *Women-in-Law* (London: Routledge & Keegan Paul, 1985).

26. Gamman, L., 'Watching the detectives'.

27. The *Irish Times*, 18 December 1993.

28. Smith, D.G. and Gray, J., *Police and People*.

29. Smith, D.G. and Gray, J., *Police and People*.

30. The *Guardian*, 3 January 1990, p. 1.

31. Chesshyre, R., 'Softly, softly', *New Statesman*, 24 November 1989.

32. Tchaikovsky, C., 'Looking for trouble', in Carlen, P., Hicks, J., O'Donoghue, J., Christina, D. and Tchaikovsky, C., *Criminal Women* (Oxford: Polity Press, 1985).

33. Hunt, J., 'The development and rapport through the negotiation of gender in field work among police', *Human Organisation*, 43, 4, 1989.

34. Hunt, J., 'Development and rapport'.

35. Hunt, J., 'Development and rapport'.

36. Gamman, L., 'Watching the detectives'.

37. Campbell, B., *Goliath: Britain's Dangerous Places* (London: Methuen, 1993).

9 Prime Time Punishment: The British Prison and Television

Paul Mason

On Monday 23 January 1995 Channel Four News were leaked a prison service memo outlining government plans for prison expenditure over the coming years. What was so striking about the content was not the cut in prison spending, nor the predicted increase in the prison population, but the areas targeted by the government for allocation of available funds: security and public relations. In recent months prison has dominated the headlines in Britain with the escapes from Parkhurst and Whitemoor, the suicides at Wöld and Feltham remand centre as well as the alleged suicide of Fred West at Winson Green. The point here is that the leaked memo was clear evidence of government policy reacting to the media: that prison security and its perception by the public are the two most important current issues, issues decided by the media.

Not since the 1960s have the prison systems of England and Wales come under such close scrutiny. The Criminal Justice and Public Order Act 1994 and the Woolf Report[1] contain major policy changes and recommendations. All of this means that prisons and the prison system have been the subject of much media attention, specifically from television.

The principal aim of this chapter is to discuss notions of visibility of punishment and the relationship of the viewer to images of incarceration on the television screen. With the abolition of capital punishment, the spectacle of public hangings, gallows and the stocks came the loss of visible punishment: punitive measures disappeared behind the walls of prison. What I intend to argue is that although the ability to witness punishment disappeared the desire to see continued, and thus television replaced the gallows and the stocks, in the form of the prison programme.

In discussing visibility in this form, two more specific questions need to be addressed. First, why are televisual images of prison an important area for research and why, thus far, has there been such a paucity of research in the area? Secondly, what kind of agenda and production techniques do the programmes adopt in communicating themes of incarceration and punishment to the television audience?

Prisons and television: a dearth of research

Existing literature

Given the importance of television's relationship with prisons it is puzzling that both penologists and criminologists as well as writers of television criticism have overlooked such a significant area. Even including film, there has been surprisingly little written on prisons in the media. Why should this be? One explanation may be that programmes concerning prison do not fall neatly into one specific genre; it is not like discussing, say, game shows: prisons appear across genres and as such seem to have been overlooked. Nellis and Hale[2] comment on this problem regarding prisons in film: 'scenes of imprisonment occur in all different types of ... film ... like *A Man For All Seasons*, swashbuckling melodramas like *The Count Of Monte Cristo* and even in westerns, *There Was A Crooked Man* for example' (p. 6). And so it is with television: prisons occur in comedies (for example *Minder*); soap operas such as *Eastenders*; dramas (for example *A Sense of Freedom*); films (for example *McVicar*); and, most commonly, prisons have been the subject of documentaries and current affairs programmes (*Panorama* and *World In Action* to name but two).

A second reason for the lack of research is the subject matter itself: prisons on television cut across several disciplines. Criminologists are interested in the prison itself and questions of punishment but do not discuss the role of the media in any depth, while cultural studies work concerned with crime and television tends to centre on the fictional depictions of the police,[3] crime reporting in television news[4] and the United States research tradition of 'prime time crime'.[5] Only in film is the representation of prison discussed, and even here research is sparce.[6]

Current research

Space precludes a detailed discussion of the current research project on which this chapter is based, but some cursory points need to be made. The project concerns the depiction of English and Scottish prisons on terrestrial British television from 1980 to 1991. The time period begins with the eight-part *Strangeways* series, the fruit of William Whitelaw's 'open policy' with regard to the publicity of prisons. It ends with a rerun of the series in 1990, following the prison riots at Strangeways and elsewhere in April 1990.

There was clearly a need to restrict the kinds of institutions dealt with by the programmes and the category chosen for the present study was those programmes dealing with male, adult prisons, which includes local, dispersal, training, open and closed institutions. Regarding genre, films, plays and drama, comedy and documentaries broadcast within the time period were all included. News items could not be included due to the vast quantity of material and the fragmented nature of news reports and their coverage of prisons. A further restriction was that 'prison programmes' were defined as having a significant number of scenes set in or concerned with prison, hence the plethora of shows which contain odd scenes of prison, but whose content is concerned with other matters, were excluded.

After several approaches and pilot analyses of a number of programmes a textual method was adopted and programmes were analysed on a number of layers, beginning with a description of the narrative structure, through issues of agenda and production techniques and ending with theories of visibility and punishment. The three programmes discussed later are examples of this approach.

In tracing the programmes from 1980 to 1991 using the broadcast guide of *The Times*, some interesting patterns and statistics emerged. In total the trawl generated 196 programmes, of which 41 were repeats, the most common being episodes of *Porridge*, which accounted for 19 repeats as well as two repeats of the film *Porridge The Movie*. With regard to channel distribution, Channel Four's prison programme output amounted to 21, a mere 10.7 per cent of the total compared with BBC2's output of 55 programmes, 28 per cent. BBC2 had twice as many documentaries as BBC1 and, although BBC1's total output was higher, over half of the 62 programmes broadcast on BBC1 were episodes of *Porridge* (38). In terms of genre, it comes as no surprise that there were far more *documentaries* concerning prisons than anything else, and they accounted for 56.1 per cent of the total number of prison programmes shown over the ten-year sample. It is undoubtedly the nature of the subject matter that dictates the most suitable genre, and the combination of topicality and limited knowledge of the audience make prisons a suitable subject for the documentary, underlined by the genre's consistency over the sample, averaging over nine documentaries a year. Prison and comedy on television was, unsurprisingly, dominated by *Porridge*, giving a rather distorted view of the genre when compared to the number of dramas, which were not only repeated less but also tend to be either one-offs or short series. The film category was the lowest category, as expected, and only *McVicar* fitted the research criteria.

Iconography and production techniques: three examples

The programmes

In order to discuss television's treatment of the prison I have chosen three programmes from one strand of the current research sample. These illustrate the principal themes explored by television in its representations of prison and from this more specific points can be made about production techniques, agenda and questions of prison iconography.

The three programmes are all documentaries concerned with Prison Rule 43, a prison regulation dealing with the segregation of inmates. Rule 43 (a) can be requested by an inmate for his own protection. He will then be segregated from other prisoners: this is most commonly used by sex offenders. Rule 43 (b) is used to segregate an inmate from others because he is seen as a danger or threat to them. I have chosen these programmes for two principal reasons. First, because they deal explicitly with confinement and themes of punishment, issues I wish to discuss in relation to visibility later; and secondly, they are representative of the changes over the ten-year sample period, 1980–91, in prison television. The three programmes are *Strangeways*: 'They Call Us Beasts', first broadcast on BBC2 in 1980, *Brass Tacks Reports*: 'Solitary', also on BBC2, in 1982; and *This Week*: 'Sex Offenders – Prisoners or Patients?' shown on the ITV network in 1989.

As part of the 'open policy' regarding prisons announced by the then Home Secretary William Whitelaw in 1980, Rex Bloomstein was permitted to make an eight-part documentary series about the local Manchester prison known as 'Strangeways'. At the time it was described by the *Guardian* as 'a frank and uninhibited series about life in prison'.[7] Transmitted over eight consecutive weeks in November and December 1980, its aim was to communicate to the viewer what life inside was like, with each self-contained episode covering a different aspect of prison life. 'They Call Us Beasts' was the sixth episode and was concerned with inmates on C1 landing: that part of the prison where inmates on Rule 43 (a) are sent. 'Solitary' was part of the *Brass Tacks Reports* series. This programme was a critical inquiry into the operation and use of Rule 43 (b). It featured two inmates' accounts of their experience in prison as well as criticisms of the use of Rule 43. *This Week* was a weekly current affairs programme which aimed to report on pressing contemporary issues which it considered to be of importance to the public. It was fronted by John Taylor, presented as the reporter on the scene, and in this respect the programme was more like an extended news report than a self-contained programme. 'Sex Offenders – Patients Or Prisoners?', broadcast in December 1989, was a 30-minute programme dealing with the treatment of sex offenders in prison.

Strangeways: *'They Call Us Beasts'*

In the early scenes of 'They Call Us Beasts' the emphasis is on the hatred other inmates have for those on C1 landing. There are clear shouts of 'beast' as inmates collect their food and two open elicit interviews confirm this view when one inmate says: 'The cons will go up to that man and give him a beating, may cut him up by beating him up.' As if to stress the reality of this claim, two or three scenes later an inmate asks to go on Rule 43 (a) (and therefore C1 landing) because he has been attacked – 'They tried to murder me this morning sir, carve me up' he tells the governor.

Having illustrated what Rule 43 (a) involves, *Strangeways* develops its central theme, achieved through two conversations: one between two prison officers and the other between three inmates. Both conversations relate to the same topic – whether all inmates on C1 landing should be tarred with the same brush and called beasts. The two conversations do not run concurrently, but are mixed up, and the camera cuts between the two as they develop. Both debates have two proponents: one inmate defends his actions of hitting an inmate on C1 even though he had no idea of the other's offence, while one of the prison officers expresses the view that 90 per cent of the officers 'dislike the blokes down here as much as the cons'. The opposing view comes from another inmate who says that not everyone on the landing is 'a sex case', and the other officer who says it is wrong to shout 'beast' at all the inmates on the wing. In previous episodes called 'Cons' and 'Screws' inmates and officers were depicted on different sides. Here, they are cleverly used in juxtaposition to create a sense of homogeneity and therefore accentuate the point about the misunderstanding of Rule 43 (a).

So as not to omit the issue of sex offenders there are two subsequent interviews with inmates who have committed offences against children. Both interviews are quite long, with very little interruption from the interviewer. In the first a man who appears to be about 60 admits to committing indecent assault on a nine-year-old child. The initial repulsion of the viewer at hearing this is partly eroded as the interview progresses. As the shot gets tighter and zooms in close on the face of the inmate, he describes how he doesn't know he has committed these offences and has no sexual interest in his victims whatsoever. Although there is no attempt by the programme to condone his actions it does try to elicit some sympathy. A similar technique is used in the second interview: again there is initial shock when the man says he was found guilty of GBH on a 23-month-old baby. However, the long narration of events by the inmate reveals various tensions in his life which, in part, are recognisable to the viewer as extenuating circumstances.

Both interviews have long pauses and only rarely does the interviewer ask another question, as if to allow both men to explain their actions as best they can. In summarising the interviews, and before a scene concerning parole, the voiceover makes the following observation:

> It is much easier to condemn the sex offender in our society than to understand or cure him. There are no simple solutions to long-standing problems of neglect, inadequacy, obsession. Least of all in the human warehouse that is Strangeways where gross overcrowding places impossible demands on welfare and psychiatric services.

This serves both to underline further the difficulties in understanding sex offenders and also as a link to the next scene of a local review committee discussing possible parole for a man who has 'committed a serious sexual assault on a boy'. The treatment of sex offenders by *Strangeways* avoids the temptation to play on audience inquisitiveness about such people, but instead attempts to portray them as people with difficulties and problems. Hence the lengthy interviews with the two inmates and the two interwoven debates.

The remainder of the episode is devoted to a problem introduced by the commentary:

> In prison you have to live with strangers. You have to share a living, breathing, eating space of 12 feet by 8 and try to adapt to other convicted men ... but tensions inevitably arise when three men are locked in a cell for most of the day and night especially where sexual relations are concerned.

What follows is a long discussion between the three inmates of a cell, two of whom are having a homosexual relationship. Using the fly-on-the-wall camera style, the audience is able to follow the tensions between the men. The programme follows this problem to its conclusion when the senior prison officer moves two of the inmates out of the cell and puts 'Steve' in solitary. It transpires that his homosexuality has caused problems in the prison before and he is sent 'down the block', not for punishment but for his own good.

The feeling throughout these scenes is that the audience is witnessing 'real-life' tension as it happens. 'They Call Us Beasts' is about life in C1 rather than simply about sex offenders and this incident serves as further evidence. The voiceover provides the postscript to the incident, and the final comment of the programme, when he tells the audience that 'Steve' spent the next three months – the rest of his sentence – in the punishment block.

Despite the provocative title *Strangeways* does not go the way of other programmes about sex offenders and foreground their danger, its principal concern is with life as it appears on C1 landing. The audience is introduced to various inmates on the wing, some of whom have committed sexual offences, but there is more emphasis on the inmates themselves and how they relate to each other rather than on the danger they pose to the public.

There is certainly some sympathy elicited for the two interviewed inmates, which was communicated both by allowing the inmates to talk at length about their crimes without morally loaded questions being thrown at them by the interviewer; and by the stance taken by the voiceover, illustrated in the comments quoted above – although both these instances worked on a more propositional level than anything overt. The programme also attempted to depict both the mundane nature of prison life and the routine of its inmates by long sequences of shots of slop buckets being emptied, inmates collecting their food and walking along landings. These scenes were not accompanied by anything other than the prison sounds that were present at the time – whistling, shouting, doors slamming and so on.

In communicating these themes *Strangeways* used the inhabitants of the prison rather than any academics, footage of other prisons or commentary. Consequently interviews and the verite camera work were used extensively. When Rule 43 (a) needed explaining in more detail, a scene where an officer was explaining it to an inmate was used rather than the voiceover. The issue of granting parole to sex offenders was dealt with by way of fly-on-the-wall footage of a parole meeting. This technique was in keeping with one of the main aims of the series – to show the audience what life in *Strangeways* was like. The camera was often seen in amongst the inmates – being shouted at by other inmates and collecting food with them. Commentary was sparce, though used to good effect when it made critical points about those on C1 landing. Its main role was that of imparting additional information, either telling the viewer what happened in the future or giving names and circumstances of certain inmates when necessary.

As with the rest of the series, the lack of commentary allowed the pictures to take on a greater significance. With many silent moments both in interviews and with other shot sequences the pictures communicated all the audience needed. There was an absence of the stock shots of landings, bars and cells – these were only used when they came into shot because the camera was following an inmate rather than as a technique for linking scenes together or as a background for commentary.

'They Call Us Beasts' was designed as part of the *Strangeways* series but could also be viewed as a self-contained episode. The extensive verite camera work and open elicit interviews enabled viewers to submerge themselves in C1 landing. The audience was invited to listen to the arguments and to be involved in the tensions when three men have to share a cell. They were able to make their own decisions about parole for a sex offender by listening to all the relevant facts. Finally they could decide whether all Rule 43 (a) inmates really are the beasts the rest of the prison says they are.

Brass Tacks Reports: 'Solitary'

In contrast to *Strangeways*, 'Solitary' concentrates more specifically on two inmates – Robert Maudsley, who has spent four years in solitary confinement, and who is introduced at the beginning of the programme as 'probably Britain's most dangerous prisoner'; and Douglas Wakefield, who has also spent years in solitary confinement. Although not clearly divisible into two sections, 'Solitary' develops from emphasising the danger and violence of both Wakefield and Maudsley, to using them critically to analyse the use of solitary confinement in British prisons.

To this end, the opening scenes serve as an introduction to Maudsley. The voiceover is quick to inform the audience of his crimes, stressing their violent nature: 'Robert Maudsley is the killer of four people, three of them fellow inmates who were brutally stabbed and garotted.' The security surrounding Maudsley's movements within Wakefield Segregation Unit is also emphasised: the viewer is told that 'wherever he goes, whatever he does' there are always five prison officers with him. This is accompanied by footage of Maudsley having a shower with several prison officers outside the cubicle watching him. The camera also dwells on Maudsley's cell, described as 'unique in Britain with two doors, one of them a heavily barred and meshed inner gate'. Such an introduction creates a degree of tension which dehumanises Maudsley and establishes an image of captivity. It is only after this introduction that some of the tension is released with an interview with the softly spoken and quiet Maudsley, discussing his feelings of depression and the isolation of his cell.

A similar approach is taken with the other prisoner discussed by the programme. Following the interview with Maudsley, the audience is told that there is another man who has also spent over four years in solitary. He, like Maudsley, is introduced via the offences he committed:

'Douglas Wakefield, now in Alberny prison, is serving a double life sentence for murder, manslaughter and the attempted murder of a prison officer.'

The visuals which accompany the commentary consist of a slow zoom on a passport photo of Wakefield, which accentuates both the danger and mystery of this man. Indeed, although no reason is given, Wakefield is never seen in the programme – there are reconstructions of him in solitary with an actor but no actual footage. This is given a dramatic edge by the commentary: '*Brass Tacks Reports* has reconstructed parts of Douglas Wakefield's life in solitary confinement. The thoughts, the allegations, the descriptions are his – it presents one man's view of life in solitude.'

There are then several scenes in which extracts from Wakefield's book are read, while an actor plays them out on screen. In contrast to Maudsley, Wakefield's dangerous image is not dispelled by personal interviews or shots of him in the prison. The reconstructions merely add to the anonymity that surrounds him, especially since the programme makes no attempt to explain why it uses a reconstruction rather than Wakefield himself.

Following an exploration of Rule 43 (b) and its implications, the programme widens its scope to include discussions on a number of inmates currently held in solitary confinement. In similar fashion to the introductions of Maudsley and Wakefield the commentary recounts the offences committed and sentences served by each of these men. In distinguishing Maudsley from these men the programme follows 'Robert Maudsley's daily life'.

The camera follows Maudsley going to and from his cell, eating his food, listening to the radio, while the voiceover provides the detail with comments like 'what he sits on is made from cardboard' and 'every course is eaten with the same plastic spoon'. After another interview clip in which Maudsley describes what he does day to day, the programme moves on to explain the history of solitary confinement, and in particular the '[its] mental and physical rigours'. There are newspaper clippings which depict the controversy of the 'control units' of the 1970s, followed by an open elicit interview with a former inmate, Michael Williams, who describes what the control units were like. Other talking heads also criticise the use of Rule 43 (b), specifically the mothers of Alan Brown and Peter Searle, the latter describing how her son spent 47 days in a 'strongbox', supposed to be used for only very short periods. This was also the complaint of Douglas Wakefield who, the programme explains, says he was detained in the strongbox in Leeds for 156 days. This period is again reconstructed with extracts from

Wakefield's book being read. The programme is now far more critical of solitary confinement than it was at the beginning, and uses more examples than simply Maudsley and Wakefield although they, and particularly Maudsley, are used as a vehicle for a critical investigation of Rule 43 (b).

In continuing the explanation of Maudsley's daily routine, there are several scenes devoted to the small privileges 'which take on great importance' to Maudsley, such as the refusal of a budgie and a football in the exercise yard. The programme has now stepped up its criticism of Maudsley's treatment, accentuated by the interview with him through the heavily meshed fence in his exercise yard. References to the European Court of Human Rights are also made by the voiceover regarding the effects of solitary confinement on inmates' health. These are further underscored by a forensic psychiatrist who lists the side-effects of long periods in solitary.

Following Governor Dunbar's explanation of future plans for Maudsley's cell the programme ends in silence, with footage of Maudsley going about his daily routine. In a strong and thought-provoking last scene after the credits, the commentator shouts up to Maudsley's cell, asking whether he can see the light. The camera zooms in on the wire which covers the outside of his cell and Maudsley shouts back: 'If I crouch down on the floor I can see about half an inch of sky.' The picture fades to black and the programme ends.

Although opening with themes of danger and violence, *Brass Tacks Reports* was primarily concerned with the injustice of the extensive use of Rule 43 (b) in British prisons. This motif was explored through Maudsley personally, in interview; and Wakefield, vicariously, in reconstruction. Both are powerful indictments on solitary confinement, particularly Maudsley whom the programme successfully represented in a sympathetic light in interview. The programme did not, however, lose sight of his past and the opening few minutes served as a reminder of his crimes. This nevertheless lent weight to the propositional discourse which argued for some form of basic human existence in prison which Maudsley and Wakefield do not receive.

As with other programmes concerned with Rule 43 prisoners, the early focus on danger and brutality served to attract the audience from the outset by appealing to their voyeuristic nature: here is a programme about a man who has taken other men's lives – look how he is punished. To this end Maudsley's lifestyle is examined closely – how he spends his day, what he eats, how many guards he has and so on. The programme's rationale for this approach was to show how different solitary confinement was from 'normal' prison life. However the concentration on Maudsley, Wakefield and others on Rule 43 (b) again satisfied audience desire to watch others being punished. This was evident not only in the visual, but also in the commentary: '*Brass Tacks*' cameras were allowed to observe Robert Maudsley's daily life ... he sees no other prisoner ... in four years he's seen no film or television ... his only human contact ... is with prison officers.'

In communicating punishment to the audience there were also specific questions asked by the commentator, such as 'What sort of feelings do you experience during the day?' and 'How did you attempt suicide?'

As mentioned earlier, the programme shifted from a treatment of two dangerous inmates to a stance which questions the use of solitary confinement without adequate safeguards. It was designed with factual instances in the foreground, backed with interviews with Maudsley. One of the centrepieces of the programme was the set of mugshots of inmates who are or have been in solitary confinement for long periods; the audience is given information about their crimes and how long they were in solitary, before cutting to interviews with the mothers of two of the inmates and an inmate who was himself in solitary. Such techniques had a dramatic impact in keeping with the tone of the voiceover which was both stern and theatrical: 'Although little known on the outside, Wakefield and Maudsley are labelled inside the prison system as its two most dangerous inmates.'

In visual content the emphasis was on confinement and loss of liberty. There were many shots of Maudsley's cell, close up, to stress the lack of space; and a concentration on bars. These coupled with several shots of the razor wire on the perimeter fence and the continual door slamming all helped to communicate what Maudsley himself described as 'a coffin in which I live 23 hours a day'.

Although *Brass Tacks Reports* could be seen as bringing to light 'the scandal' of the use of solitary confinement in Britain's prisons, arguably it is motivated by a voyeuristic notion of watching others suffer punishment. This is illustrated by the attention to Robert Maudsley's daily routine, the dramatic voiceover stressing the danger to the mental and physical health of inmates kept under those conditions and the visual foregrounding of the conditions in which Maudsley lives. These notions will be explored later.

This Week: '*Sex Offenders – Prisoners or Patients?*'

Much more of a tabloid documentary than the other two, *This Week*'s populist media style is evident from the start with presenter John Taylor's introductory comments:

There are now more sex offenders in prison than ever before and almost nothing is being done to cure them of the urges that led them to commit their crimes – are the child molesters and the rapists being set free to strike again?

This leads immediately into the titles – a compilation of prison images, to be seen later in the programme. The opening scene is a woman sitting in darkness describing her sexual assault, the caption below her reads 'rape victim'. This cuts to a shot of the back of a man's head; the man talks to Taylor (in shot) about assaulting women. The caption on the screen says 'sex attacker'. The first few minutes of the programme are designed to capture the viewer's attention, achieved primarily by using fear: although the programme appears to be concerned with the plight of sex offenders in prison – that the authorities are 'doing little to treat them' – it is in fact creating an image of sex criminals being released back on the streets, ready to reoffend.

Following the introduction and an explanation of Rule 43, the audience is presented with a series of talking heads – a psychiatrist, a probation officer and a prison reformer – who argue that prison merely reinforces sexual fantasies for many sex offenders, summarised by an inmate: 'It's just like a bed of rats in there ... the filth just grows.'

The programme then moves on to discuss possible solutions to this problem and introduces the Vulnerable Prisoner Unit at Channings' Wood prison in Devon. Taylor describes the facilities as 'more humane' and the camera cuts between shots of a workshop with inmates undertaking various activities. Inmates are only visible at a distance and, for the most part, are shown either from the back or side or at a distance. In scenes of a therapy session for inmates which follow, the camera concentrates on inmates' legs and shoes, or extreme close ups of hands, necks and arms. The absence of clear shots of inmates could be due to their own reluctance to have their identity revealed, but it is arguable that such a production technique reinforces the mystery and fear which surrounds the sex offender. This is emphasised by a subsequent interview with an inmate who talks about his experiences in prison. Taylor introduces him as 'serving a long sentence for a series of notorious rapes'. The caption which appears while he is talking reads 'multiple rapist'. In a key interview with this man, the issue at the heart of the programme is revealed:

Taylor: Do you think when you're released in the end you'll still be a danger to the public?

Inmate: That's a hard question that one, I hope not ... but if I had to go back in the system as it was two years ago I'd have no chance.

Taylor: You'd go and rape again?

Inmate: Yeah, I think I would.

Having foregrounded the problem of lack of treatment for sex offenders, *This Week* moves to 'the Annexe', a therapeutic centre based at Wormwood Scrubs. Taylor is seen standing outside the walls of the prison and explains to the audience the function of the Annexe. The camera pans around the paintings-hung walls of a room and shows inmates sitting in a circle discussing their problems. This is the first time any inmate has been shown facing the camera, which contrasts to the danger and fear that the programme has thus far associated with the sex offender. The Annexe is portrayed in a favourable light, both the governor of Wormwood Scrubs and the inmates say it works. 'A former graduate of the Annexe' is interviewed; now back in society he discusses how the therapy helped him.

   Having now given sex offenders an identity, the programme reverts to reinforcing the commonly held fears and attitudes about these men. *This Week* reconstructs the death of 15-year-old Anna Humphries, who was sexually assaulted and killed on her way home from school by 'a man with a history of sex attacks who'd been out of prison just six months'. Taylor explains: 'What happened to her offers a chilling illustration of the price we may be paying for doing too little about sex offenders.'

   In a provocative conclusion Taylor stands with a copy of the Carlisle Report[8] – which recommends treatment for sex offenders before they are granted parole – and says:

> Had the recommendations contained in this report been enforced last year, Anna Humphries might still be alive today ... the Home Office is still considering the Carlisle Report and sex offenders are still being released on to the street without any control.

This comment, coupled with the talking heads of Stephen Shaw of the Prison Reform Trust and psychologist Brain Thomas-Peter, further emphasise the risk such sex offenders pose to the public. As if to underscore the point even further, the final word goes to the former inmate of the Annexe who says:

If you don't care about the offender that's fine, don't give them therapy because you think 'poor chaps they deserve some help to make their lives better'. You must do it for your own sakes, for the sake of children in the streets.

This Week operates on two levels. It foregrounds the difficulties sex offenders face in being sent to prison for long periods without treatment, presented as a journalistic quest to uncover the truth: 'From inside Britain's prisons, *This Week* reports on the growing number of sex offenders and the dangers of putting men behind bars and doing little to treat them.' However, in order to make the programme appeal to the audience, it angles the issue towards danger. From Taylor's opening to the reconstruction of Anna Humphries' death, the programme constantly reminds the viewer that sex offenders are still being let out on to the streets with little or no supervision.

Several techniques are used to establish fear in the minds of the viewer. The most (in)visible is the treatment of the actual offenders. Those inmates who are interviewed are cloaked in darkness or by an obscure camera angle, focused on feet or the back of the head. Clearly it could be argued that maintenance of anonymity is of primary importance in any interview with sex offenders if they are to return, one day, to some degree of normality in society. The particular methods used to obscure the identity of the inmate were not those commonly used – digital squares on the face, voice alterations and so on were conspicuous by their absence. It would seem therefore that the programme set out to reinforce existing viewer opinions about sex criminals in order to rouse anxiety and apprehension in the audience.

This can be further illustrated by the captions that appeared on the screen during the interviews with sex offenders – 'sex attacker', 'multiple rapist'. These replace the usual captions seen during inmate interviews, where details usually include perhaps a first name, the offence, how long they are serving, the prison they are in – all of these details are omitted.

Maintaining the intensity is the language used by Taylor both in his commentary over stock shots of landings and stairwells and in his reporting to the camera. He uses colloquial phrases such as 'walk free' and 'behind bars' which give *This Week* a tabloid newspaper feel, with the same urgency and drama. Taylor constantly refers to inmates as 'the sex offender', there is no attempt to humanise them (save for one scene towards the end). As well as forming the background to his commentary, the external footage of the prison accentuates danger by centring on razor wire and cameras – the potential threat to the public constantly reiterated.

The programme supports its claims by reference to the 'outside world' and therefore the world occupied by the viewer. This is achieved by using 'experts' such as consultant psychiatrist Dr Gerald Silverman, probation officer Christine Vincent and Prison Reform Trust spokesman Stephen Shaw, all of whom repeat the dangers of keeping sex offenders together where they can reinforce their fantasies and be even more of a threat when they are released. The other 'outside world' reference is the reconstruction of the death of Anna Humphries. The reconstruction is shot with the camera as Anna and Taylor leaves out none of the details of where she was attacked, what time of day it was, the circumstances of her walking home alone: all of which accentuate the very real danger to the audience – that it could happen to any girl. Undoubtedly there is a conscious effort to stress the manifest risk of allowing sex offenders to be released without treatment: a 'real-life' example of what happens when sex offenders are not treated for their condition. The subsequent interview with Anna Humphries' mother confirms the stance of the programme.

This Week is problematic in its approach to the issue of sex offenders. Unlike the other programmes in this strand its agenda does not seem to be to bring to the attention of its viewers the scandal in Britain's prisons. Ostensibly it tells of the lack of funds and treatment for men with illnesses which mean they attack women and children. What the programme in fact does is to reinforce the fear of crime – in particular rape and sexual assault – by using the techniques described above. Whether such methods are due to the subject matter, the programme itself or some other variable remains to be seen.

Television and the visibility of punishment

Having discussed in some detail three particular prison programmes, the wider themes of prison on television can now be discussed. The principal area I wish to concentrate on is the concept of visibility with regard to punishment.

Punishment and spectacle

By the middle of the nineteenth century punishment as a spectacle had all but disappeared. But up to this point 'the theatrical representation of pain'[9] had been a crucial element in state justice. From Roman times publicity and spectacle were an important element in punishment, with gladiatorial battles and Christians thrown to the lions in the vast public arenas. The Anglo-Saxons introduced the pillories and stocks in which criminals would be pelted with rotten vegetables and publicly humiliated. These sanctions continued into the thirteenth century, following the abolition of trial by ordeal. Capital punishment in England can be traced to the earliest times, where hanging was the usual method of execution. The function of public punishment went beyond the simplicity of making an example of the condemned. Foucault identifies several other purposes for public forms of punishment.[10] Perhaps the most important was the role of the body: at the crucial moment of execution, the state exacted its power over its subjects – 'the physical strength of the sovereign beating down upon the body of his adversary and mastering it'.[11] However, such terrifying rituals required the public to watch, for without them much of the effect was lost:

> Not only must people know, they must see with their own eyes. Because they must be made to be afraid; but also because they must be the witnesses, the guarantors, of the punishment, and because they must to a certain extent take part in it.[12]

It was however the crowd which, among other things, led to a move away from visible punishment. Public execution days were the symbol of monarchic power, but such order over the masses often disintegrated into mass disorder, and public executions were abolished in 1865.

With the development of prison as a penal sanction came the negation of visible punitive measures. Punishment was concealed behind giant grey walls, all that remained of the public ritual was the trial. A certain dichotomy exists in this development, however, for although the public did not know what went on inside the prison they were certainly made aware of its existence:

> the persistence of castle and fetter as the principal emblems of imprisonment bore no relation to the realities of contemporary discipline, nor were they meant to. They were employed as a consciously deceptive deterrent keeping old fears alive by reflecting a popular, melodramatic picture of the prison back towards the public.[13]

This continues today: externally prisons are very visible in towns and cities, their stark silhouettes dominating the suburban skyline. Even though much of the gothic imagery of impenetrable castles has gone, replaced by a more practical design, their hallmark remains: 'But these muted functional buildings nevertheless project an eloquent and well-understood symbolism, which speaks of unshakeable authority, of stored-up power and of a silent, brooding capacity to control intransigence.'[14]

The desire to watch

What effect then has this shrouding of punishment had on the public? Nellis and Hale argue that, despite the loss of a focus for the public desire to watch punishment, that desire remains: 'the desire to observe punishment does not disappear – it cannot. As it breaks against the walls of prison like a wave, it flows back and is absorbed in numerous images of the punitive.'[15]

The argument here is that society has always harboured and will always harbour a desire to see punishment carried out. Whether this stems from a primeval yearning for revenge against the perpetrator of the crime, or a deep-seated voyeuristic craving, Nellis and Hale argue that it does exist. With the absence of public punitive displays and with prison 'wrapped in an impenetrable veil of secrecy',[16] this desire to see translates into 'fantasies of punishment'.[17] For the purposes of their research, Nellis and Hale identify the prison film as one such fantasy, an idea supported in Querry's work:

> should we decide to think about our prisons we find that we are quite ignorant about them, and that we are forced to call upon the powers of our imaginations – or the imaginations of someone else – to help us with the details of an institution about which we really know very little.[18]

Such an argument can equally be applied to television programmes about prison. The desire to see the wrongdoer punished, to witness society's retribution, is illustrated in both the subject matter of the prison programme and the manner in which it is portrayed.

Taking subject matter first, prison programmes between 1980 and 1991 could be divided into four broad categories: programmes dealing with physical conditions, Rule 43 offenders, atypical or special prison regimes and prison fiction. Notwithstanding the diversity of prison issues covered by the programmes themselves, I would argue that a large proportion emphasise the regime of the prison itself and stress the kinds of punishment that inmates are subjected to. For example, programmes such as *Strangeways*: 'A Human Warehouse' and *Charlie Wing*, both of which can be categorised as concerning physical conditions, stress the routine of punishment. *Charlie Wing* is structured by time slots in the prisoner routine – '07:50 prisoners unlocked and collect breakfast' and '17:00 prisoners given tea' – and stresses the incarceration of such dangerous men and the effect of such punishment, summed up by one inmate of Charlie Wing: 'There's an easy way of doing a sentence and that's conforming. Without giving up your pride,

without giving up your feelings about certain things you can still go along
with the system because it makes sense for you.'

The technique of showing the audience punishment in action, of
making the invisible visible is a constant theme in these programmes.
In 'A Human Warehouse' the use of a Strangeways inmate, 'Terry',
allows the audience to share in the prison experience: we wake up with
Terry in his cell, visit the prison doctor, have meals with him and get
locked up with him. 'A Human Warehouse' is typical of many of the
prison documentaries – it opens up the prison for our inspection, to fulfil
our desire to watch men behind bars. The three programmes discussed
in detail above further substantiate this theme – Robert Maudsley's daily
routine of solitary confinement in *Brass Tacks Reports* and the segregation of sex offenders on C1 landing in *Strangeways*: 'They Call Us
Beasts' in particular.

What techniques does television use to visualise punishment? Clearly
the iconography of prison is important here. There is an emphasis on
bars and fencing, with programmes punctuated throughout by close ups
of perimeter fencing, razor wire and bars on windows. The most
common visualisations of prison however are stock shots of landings,
stairwells, and prisoners milling about, stressing the mundane routine,
the loss of liberty and of freedom of choice of the inmate. Frequently
such techniques are used in conjunction with a voiceover which acts
as omniscient provider of information about the prison, an inmate or
a situation, and as a critic both overtly and through suggestion. Again,
much of the commentary is concerned with the regime of discipline and
correction to which the inmate is subjected:

> D wing is slopping out. This is the everyday scene in the rest of Hull
> prison, no lavatories in cells here and no association for some on this
> overcrowded wing. It houses 200 convicted and unsentenced
> prisoners. They're in their cells for up to 23 hours a day.[19]

Camera work, particularly verite, fly-on-the-wall shots, develop the relationship between viewer and programme further. Frequently prison
programmes adopt the bumpy-style camera to follow inmates around
prison, to listen in on conversations between governor and inmate or
between prison officers. The voyeuristic nature of these programmes
is inescapable: the audience is invited to visit the dangerous and unpredictable world of the prison, to see life as the inmates see it, to have a
relationship, however nebulous, with the cons of Strangeways,[20]
Wormwood Scrubs[21] or Long Lartin.[22] The verite camera work takes
the audience into the cells of the criminal to peer and poke around, to
shift between the ordered world of the viewer and the dark and

dangerous world of the criminal. In order to establish the difference
between the two worlds, programmes often highlight the dangerousness of the inmates:

> David McAlister, serving 19 years for robbery and assault ... Patrick
> McKay is serving five life sentences for manslaughter and robbery ...
> This is Fred Lowe. He is serving two life sentences and 20 years for
> grievous bodily harm, aggravated burglary and attempted robbery. He
> received a third life sentence for the manslaughter of an inmate at
> Gartree prison.[23]

The fascination of the murderer and the consequent punishment meted
out to him is stressed throughout programmes like *40 Minutes*: 'Danger
Men' but, more importantly, for those 40 minutes the audience can live
with the murderer, the serial killer, the sex offender in the knowledge
that when the credits roll they can escape back to their living rooms.
In some ways this relationship between the watcher and the watched
has parallels with the watchers at public executions of old: 'The
vengeance of the people was called upon to become an obtrusive part
of the vengeance of the sovereign'.[24] Foucault continues: 'But above
all ... the people never felt closer to those who paid the penalty than
in those rituals intended to show the horror of the crime and the
invincibility of power.'[25]

Prison programmes provide an opportunity for the audience to share
the world of the criminal and be 'compelled to tread a slippery and ver-
tiginous path'[26] between sympathy and vilification. The unruly mass at
the gallows are now the voyeurs on the sofa.

Conclusion

Prisons will always be part of television, whether as news items, documentaries or drama: the public's fascination with invisible punishment
behind huge walls demands it. How this manifests itself in the future
is less certain, but with interactive television and virtual reality just around
the corner, the relationship between viewer and inmate may get
uncomfortably close.

Programmes

In order of appearance in text:

Strangeways (1): 'A Human Warehouse' 29 October 1980 BBC1 21:25
Strangeways (2): 'The Allegation' 5 November 1980 BBC1 21:25

Strangeways (3): 'Screws' 12 November 1980 BBC1 22:25
Strangeways (4): 'Cons' 19 November 1980 BBC1 21:25
Strangeways (5): 'The Block' 26 November 1980 BBC1 21:25
Strangeways (6): 'They Call Us Beasts' 3 December 1980 BBC1 22:20
Strangeways (7): 'Borstal Boys' 11 December 1980 BBC1 21:25
Strangeways (8): 'Christmas' 17 December 1980 BBC1 21:25
Porridge: 'The Harder They Fall' 23 July 1980 BBC1 19:40
Porridge: 'Just Desserts' 11 January 1982 BBC2 19:55
Porridge: 'Heartbreak Hotel' 18 January 1982 BBC2 19:55
Porridge: 'Disturbing The Peace' 25 January 1982 BBC2 19:55
Porridge: 'Happy Release' 1 February 1982 BBC2 19:55
Porridge: 'No Peace For The Wicked' 28 August 1982 BBC1 19:15
Porridge The Movie 30 December 1982 BBC1 21:15
Porridge: 'Prisoner And Escort' 3 May 1984 BBC1 20:05
Porridge: 'New Faces, Old Hands' 10 May 1984 BBC1 20:05
Porridge: 'The Hustler' 17 May 1984 BBC1 20:05
Porridge: 'An Evening In' 24 May 1984 BBC1 20:05
Porridge: 'A Day Out' 31 May 1984 BBC1 20:05
Porridge: 'Ways And Means' 7 June 1984 BBC1 20:05
Porridge: 'Men Without Women' 14 June 1984 BBC1 20:05
Porridge: 'Poetic Justice' 20 November 1985 BBC1 19:35
Porridge: 'Rough Justice' 27 November 1985 BBC1 19:40
Porridge: 'Pardon Me' 30 November BBC1 17:55
Porridge: 'A Test Of Character' 7 December 1985 BBC1 18:00
Porridge: 'The Final Stretch' 14 December 1985 BBC1 18:00
Porridge: 'Christmas Special' 22 December 1986 BBC1 20:00
McVicar 20 March 1988 ITV 01:10
Brass Tacks Reports: 'Solitary' 27 May 1982 BBC2 21:30
This Week: 'Sex Offenders – Prisoners or Patients?' 7 December 1989
ITV 20:30
Charlie Wing 10 September 1990 ITV 23:15
40 Minutes: 'Danger Men' 19 October 1989 BBC2 21:30

Notes and references

1. *Home Office Prison Disturbances* (Woolf Report), April 1990, Cm, 1456
   (London; HMSO, 1991).
2. Nellis, M. and Hale C., *The Prison Film*, (London: Radical Alternatives to
   Prison, 1982).
3. See for example Clarke, A., 'You're nicked: Television police series and the
   fictional representation of law and order', in Strinati, D. and Wagg, S.
   (eds), *Come On Down? Popular Media Culture in Post-war Britain* (London:

Routledge, 1990); Hurd, G., 'The television presentation of the police', in Bennett, T. (ed.), *Popular Television and Film: A Reader* (London: BFI, 1981); Sparks, R., *Television and the Drama Of Crime: Moral Tales and the Place of Crime in Public Life* (Buckingham: Open University Press, 1992) and Mason, P., *Reading The Bill: An Analysis of the Thames Television Police Drama* (Bristol: Centre For Criminal Justice, 1991).

4. See for example Ericson R., Baranek, P. and Chan, J., *Representing Order: Crime, Law and Justice in the News Media* (Buckingham: Open University Press, 1991) and Schlesinger, P. and Tumber, H., *Reporting Crime: The Media Politics of Criminal Justice* (Oxford: Clarendon Press, 1994).

5. See for a useful summary of some of this work Garafalo, J., 'Crime and the mass media: A selective review of research', *Journal of Research in Crime and Delinquency*, 18, 1981, pp. 319–50.

6. For a brief overview of the prison in film see Nellis, M. and Hale, C., *The Prison Film*. More specific work includes Querry, R., 'The American prison as portrayed in the popular motion pictures of the 1930s' (unpublished PhD thesis, University of New Mexico) on American prison films in the 1930s, and a discussion of the symbolic use of prison in social problem films in the American depression is discussed in Parker, J., 'The organizational environment of the motion picture sector', in Ball-Rokeach, S. and Cantor, M. (eds), *Media, Audience and Social Structure* (Beverly Hills: Sage, 1986) and Roffman, P. and Purdy, J., *The Hollywood Social Problem Film* (Bloomington: Indiana University Press, 1981).

7. *The Guardian*, 16 October 1980.

8. Review Committee on Parole System in England and Wales (Carlisle Report), Cmd 532 (London: HMSO, 1988).

9. Foucault, M., *Discipline and Punish: The Birth of a Prison* (London: Peregrine Books, 1979).

10. Foucault, M., *Discipline and Punish*.

11. Foucault, M., *Discipline and Punish*, p. 49.

12. Foucault, M., *Discipline and Punish*, p. 58.

13. Evans, D. *The Fabrication of Virtue: English Prison Architecture 1750–1840* (Cambridge University Press, 1982), pp. 225–6, quoted in Garland, D., *Punishment and Modern Society* (Oxford: Clarendon Press, 1985), p. 259.

14. Garland, D., *Punishment and Modern Society*, p. 260.

15. Nellis, M. and Hale, C., *The Prison Film*, p. 54.

16. Cohen, S., *Visions of Social Control* (Cambridge: Polity Press, 1985), p. 57.

17. Nellis, M. and Hale, C., *The Prison Film*, p. 62.

18. Querry, R., *The American Prison*, p. 148.

19. From *40 Minutes*: 'Danger Men'.

20. *Strangeways* was first broadcast in November and December 1980.

21. *Prison: Inside Out*, ITV, 30 March 1983.

22. *Dispatches*: 'Voices From Long Lartin', Channel Four, 22 March 1989.

23. From *40 Minutes*: 'Danger Men'.

24. Foucault, M., *Discipline and Punish*, p. 59.

25. Foucault, M., *Discipline and Punish*, p. 63.

26. Nellis, M. and Hale, C., *The Prison Film*, p. 63.

10 Small Crime to Big Time: An Australian Celebrity Self-abduction

Noel Sanders

Networked global media in the late twentieth century base their claim to the legitimacy of their enterprise, as never before, on their ability to synchronise a world-wide audience. This new 'media time', satellitised and patrolled by 'authoritative communities' (the phrase is Barbie Zelizer's,[1] describing journalistic arrangements brought into operation by the JFK assassination) proposes the existence of a universal, spectacular present along with the claim to shape memory of events through an appeal to 'the possession of a common faith' (Zelizer again). Every now and again, however, a breach is made in the system, seducing the means to different advantage. People astute or devious enough to crack and wrest control of the codes play the game – even momentarily – of all seductions: what Baudrillard once called 'the irony of community'.[2]

The celebrity self-abduction is in this sense a specialised subgenre of a technique of media subversion usually called 'terrorist'. Yet while hijackings and hostage takings involve a form of media seduction that these days uniquely provoke Manichaean disapproval (the 'evil spell and stratagem of all unorthodoxies ... a conspiracy of signs', in Baudrillard's words), a well-executed but flawed celebrity self-abduction has a wide popular following and a reception that nears the approval accorded to the failures on talent shows where, temporarily, media negotiate a carnival of amateurism to advance claims for their own professionalism and authority. The contestants all know better: for all the hubris involved, they know (as did Rupert Pupkin) the worth of that famous 15 minutes.

That said, there is nevertheless a gulf between the way amateurs are allowed on to, in particular, TV and the way that small-time celebrities hit the big time through a well-calculated disappearance. As Dale Carter maintains, entry into the star system begins first of all as an induction into 'a system of production that defined [a potential star] as capital to be invested in or raw material to be enriched'.[3] It is significant here that the move from mere celebrity (literally, one who is 'frequented', from the Latin celeber) to stardom is achieved through a sidereal, astronomical transition. While a 'celebrity' suggests a round of routine appearances and adulations that differ not significantly from the pattern of work or domestic activity that is the common lot, stardom is extraterrestrial: a star is near and far away at once, a star disappears only to return but, above all, its brilliance is only a sign of its consumption and death. Yet this is a death which, given the light-years taken for the brightness of its extinction to reach us, is available only by means of simulation. No mistake perhaps that disappearance played as large a part in the star creation of high-flyers such as the aviators Charles Lindbergh and Howard Hughes earlier in the century. As Paul Virilio has it in his *The Aesthetics of Disappearance* : 'To win in the game of life is to create a dichotomy between the marks of one's personal life and those of astro-nomical time, so as to master whatever happens and fulfil immediately what is in the offing.'[4]

When Fairlie Arrow, a torch singer and song stylist at Jupiters Casino on Queensland's Gold Coast, disappeared from her Isle of Capri home on 15 December 1991 it was immediately reported that she was in the clutches of 'an obsessed fan'. On ABC-TV on 17 December Arrow's husband, George Harvey (of the showband the Four Kinsmen) elaborated on the idea of a fatal attraction, asserting that 'if you look at what showbiz is about, it's really about what you aim for ... You aim for people to like your image.' Yet 'image', at the time of her disappearance, was something that Arrow was finding increasingly difficult to sustain. Her work at the casino had of recent times to be supplemented by hoofing at lesser venues. While still a regular performer at Jupiters, Twin Towns Leagues and Seagulls, and having in the past supported dinosaur acts such as Cliff Richard, Gene Pitney and Charlie Pride, it had become evident that increasingly more territory was going to have to be covered to maintain Arrow's faltering career. At the time of the disappearance Arrow was playing the Lone Star Tavern on the Coast, of which her father, Bob, was the manager, and from the evidence of its own advertising the Lone Star may well have loomed as the end of the road for Arrow: 'The Lone Star reflects the old west: Gunfighters' Bar, Dodge City Saloon, Diamond Lil's Showroom, Texas Teahouse, Leroy's Liquor Barn, Santa Fe Express [and] Pullman Club Restaurant.'[5] It was from this estab-lishment that Arrow was said in the first coverage of the 'abduction' to have been followed home by 'a man'.[6]

Until September 1991 Arrow had lived with George Harvey in an isolated farmhouse at Mudgeeraba in the Gold Coast hinterland region. It was there that she maintained, fronting TV cameras after having been found tied up at the side of the road at Mudgeeraba two days after her disappearance, that the mystery man had begun a series of break-ins which had lasted for six months. The intruder had, she said, been an unseen presence at the house, and had (like Arrow herself) showed signs of wanting to 'rearrange her life'.[7] Accounts early in the affair told of him 'living out a fantasy of dressing her up in silk lingerie',[8] and subsequent affirmations attested to him, poltergeist like, rearranging her wardrobe and furniture, preparing meals, washing the dishes, drinking the house liquor and changing stations on the radio when Arrow was out. Indefatiguably, he also wrote messages in lipstick on the mirror ('Don't leave me', and then, ominously, 'U left me'), 'draped lingerie across [Arrow] as she slept' and fed the family dogs.[9] On TV George Harvey attributed the mystery of it all to the fact that 'mainly ... the things he was doing were all so subtle ... Just, you know, things that weren't aggressive, he was just sort of looking after her.'

Fairlie Arrow went to the police. As her mother recalled the day after the 'abduction' was reported in the media, the police 'sent round patrols but said that, unless they caught this person in the act, there was nothing they could do'.[10] Dorothy Arrow's assessments probably fall short of recognising the help and assistance offered by the Gold Coast Women's Safety Unit. For the police's part, they noted that no complaint about inaction by them on the matter had been lodged, even though making a second complaint was a standard method of actually (and eventually) gaining their attention. Wayward though police action may have appeared it was balanced by the fact that, by the early 1990s, they were sorely tested by hoax callers and bogus solicitations for their help. This must, in turn, be offset against a widely held view that police on the Coast had inherited a reputation for nonchalance from years of perceived inaction where it counted. In the Gold Coast tourist boom of the 1950s such inaction was positively interpreted as contributing to the 'low-key' nature of their work, to the point that 'a policeman is seldom seen at Surfers Paradise [the Coast's economic and style centre] but plainclothesmen move amongst the populace and the owner of an undesirable face is either warned to behave or shifted south of the [Queensland] border'.[11] The perception held until the late 1980s, when problems arose with bag snatchings from or assaults to the persons of Asian tourists, but, by and large, the common view was that, as one commentator noted in 1986, 'one sees few policemen on the beat, especially in Surfers Paradise, [though] police seem to spend a great deal of time catching people in the radar speed zones'.[12] A sense of resignation can therefore be sensed in Dorothy Arrow's conclusion that: 'It's very easy to get annoyed and aggravated with police, but they're only human.' (Indeed, apart from 'busting' motorists and looking after international tourists, little has changed on the Coast, to the point where sex workers there and around it now regularly receive a publication called

Ugly Mugs[13] which details descriptions of violent clients whose activities have largely gone unchecked by police.) In hindsight, popular as well as more specialised perceptions of Coast police 'never being there when you need them' may well have imbued Fairlie Arrow's decision to stage her abduction, on the basis of an assumption that such a view was both widely accepted and historically attested.

Fairlie Arrow described her first confrontation with media representatives after having been discovered at the side of the road at Mudgeeraba as 'traumatic, as traumatic as [my] abduction'.[14] In various media-attentive situations, despite an ABC-TV reporter's assessment that Arrow, in a 2 a.m. news conference the night after her rescue, 'showed no signs of trauma', she attested: 'No, trust me, this is not, I mean I can think of a lot easier [sic] ways to run a publicity stunt than this.'

A 'friend' of Arrow's had, earlier in the affair, given her own account of the 'obsessed fan's' activities inside Arrow's house. 'He kept doing really creepy, weird things,' she observed. 'Doors were left open, things were moved around, stereos left on. Everything was opposite to how we left the house.'[15] Arrow maintained that the fan had kept her, during her two days away, tied to a four-poster bed, blindfolded: 'I never heard radio or television. I didn't have any idea about the massive media coverage.'[16] The silence of the scene, which contrasted strongly with the noisome interventions the 'fan' had previously made at Arrow's house, was now filled; she now said with her own voice: 'I never stopped talking ... I spoke to him about everything, from my singing career to my lifelong ambitions.'[17] Deprived, like her audience, of sight of her captor, Arrow reported that all she knew was that he fed her on 'a diet of sliced apples', then that he had 'a well-spoken Australian voice' and finally (a possible implication that the 'man' was not Anglo-Australian): 'I couldn't think of anything else important about him, except his breath smelt of garlic.' To assist the visualising powers of her audience she declared that 'as [she] was lying down [she] tried to conjure up a picture of what he looked like'.[18]

As things actually stood during these days, Fairlie Arrow was not imprisoned and 'doing time' but in control of her and the media's time – in a state, rather, of self-exile. For between 15 and 17 December 1991 Arrow was reasonably comfortably accommodated in a motel room at Nerang, five kilometres back from the Coast itself, as the story of her abduction unfolded on television. Commented 'flamboyant bachelor' and one-time friend of Arrow, Bob Deering: 'She must have watched every television report on herself when she was in the motel ... and, when she came back, she was a totally different person.'[19]

Resurrected and transfigured, Arrow appeared 'live' on television on 18 December, and doubled the concept in an attempt to discredit sceptics. 'Here I am lucky to be alive,' she said, 'and people are doubting the whole thing.' Correspondingly, she began using the word 'dead' – 'dead time' is anathema to the electronic media – when speaking about her former life. Recalling the early years of a singing career that had begun in Melbourne in 1982, she told reporters: 'I had a career in horses for most of my life. Then I decided I was dead, really. So I answered an ad for a singer and auditioned all bright eyed and bushy tailed.'[20]

The metaphor was reprised after the abduction hoax was revealed in early January 1992, with Arrow declaring that staging the disappearance was 'better than being dead'.[21] The statement could be read in two ways. For those entertaining sympathy for her actions, a redemption of sorts had taken place. ABC-TV had, for instance, on 17 December, made a link between fatal attraction and the public gaze when it quoted George Harvey as saying that he was 'not surprised his wife attracted that sort of obsession'. But others less persuaded may have taken the view that the concept 'no news is bad news' was insufficient grounds for the scam. As 'a friend' sourly noted to a press reporter, it was those who had formerly believed she had in reality been abducted who had suffered a 'death': 'Fairlie had a dream of somehow making it to the top and now her name is on everyone's lips. It doesn't matter who was destroyed in the process. Friendship and love obviously don't mean anything to her.'[22]

Perhaps to respond to and counter this kind of vituperation Arrow was interviewed by Mike Willesee on Nine's *A Current Affair* on 8 January 1992 and suggested a motive for her behaviour quite at odds with earlier explanations. In this interview and in others over the next few days she began to suggest that the scam was, first, intended to gain police activity on the 'fan' and his harassments and, secondly, justified by the sense that the 'fan' was, in fact, a serial killer. 'I just didn't want to be the next person dead', Arrow began, improving on the urgency of the matter by adding: 'I thought, I've got to do something, otherwise I'm going to be the next person who's dead.'[23]

Historically, however, the event submits to analysis more as a composite intertexuality rather than a moment of a series. In 1979–80, for instance, a rapist and murderer known as the Balaclava Man had raped a singer – his sixth victim – at Burleigh, to the Gold Coast's south, 'threatening her with death if she looked him in the face'.[24] Arrow's account that while tethered to the four-poster she tried to imagine what her captor looked like was critically compromised by her later assertion that 'I decided to do it [stage the abduction] the last night I saw him at the window.' The possibility that this appearance at Arrow's window was not enough to provide an identifiable impression might, while providing enough to allay evidence of direct contradiction in Arrow's account, nevertheless have reopened the popular memory file on the killing of Linda Reid in 1983, and subsequent events. Reid was abducted from the car park of the Pacific Fair shopping complex on the Gold Coast and murdered. The attacker struck again the next year. A woman called Faye Harris was, on this occasion, 'one of hundreds of women to have come forward following the report of an assault at Broadbeach involving the man police believe was the killer of shop assistant Linda Reid'.[25] In early 1984, over a 14-week period, Harris' car was broken into, her flatmate tried to frighten a prowler off, Harris saw a man's face peering at her through the glass of her front door and someone climbed through her bedroom window.

Sitting in her motel room at Nerang and watching herself on the nightly television news Arrow could not have been aware of, but may consequently have appreciated, the irony of the fact that her presence there was covertly being observed by the motel's cleaner, who had seen Arrow on TV (just as Arrow had herself) and promptly gave her up to the police. Unable to leave the motel, Arrow was in the grip of her own invention. Beatriz Colomina has written of the theatre box that the person gaining the privilege of occupying such a space has 'become the object of another's gaze [in which] she is caught in the act of seeing, entrapped at the very moment of control'. As Colomina notes, the result of gaining the box seat is that 'it is impossible to abandon the space, let alone leave the house, without being seen by those over whom control is also being exerted'. As in the seduction scene, 'object and subject exchange places. Whether there is actually a person behind either gaze is irrelevant.'[26] What made Arrow's position even more complicated was that she had spliced her own media to another, with which it became increasingly intertextualised.

The event, occurring in the weeks immediately preceding Arrow's own, was the Christine Petersen murder. The trouble began on 6 December 1991 when Petersen, a day short of her 25th birthday, disappeared from her home on the Gold Coast. Attention immediately centred on what part her 'estranged de facto' Lawrence Stehlik might have played in the matter. According to media reports Stehlik, 38, and Petersen had cohabited at his banana plantation near the town of Pottsville for a year before Petersen left the place in the spring of 1991. A well-known model, Petersen had had wide media exposure, but by 10 December with no sightings being reported Surfers Paradise Detective Sergeant Mike Sparke made a plea directly to media organisations: 'Keep this story going.'[27]

In the course of the coverage of the disappearance which followed material evidence rapidly appeared – on 11 December a fishing knife Stehlik had bought was found on the plantation, as was the burnt-out car Stehlik had used to entice Petersen into by telling her it was a birthday present and, next day, Stehlik's own body, shot twice through the head. If, on the morning of her own disappearance three days later, Fairlie Arrow had taken the Brisbane *Sunday Mail* she would in addition have read of Petersen's charred body being finally discovered on the afternoon of the previous Friday. She would also have read that Stehlik had repeatedly phoned his victim as Arrow's own 'harasser' had ('27 times a day to hear [Arrow's] phone message' according to Bob Arrow), and that Stehlik, like the 'fan', was considered by Petersen's friend and boss, model agency owner and former TV identity Pam Tamlyn, to be 'obsessed'.[28]

Where Arrow's explanation to the TV cameras in early January was to be that she thought that she was next in line after Petersen for the attentions of a psychopathic and obsessive serial killer, inconsistencies still existed, not least of them being that Stehlik was already dead. Media reaction was to airbrush the faulty intertextuality, referring both to a third text – the architext of epic Hollywood. And in late 1991 this (as far as the epic of sexual obsession was concerned) meant *Fatal Attraction*. For Petersen, the vehicle for this movement was her work as a model – 'Some people in the Gold Coast's glamour world of modelling claim the murder of the beautiful Christine Petersen was the tragic end of a bizarre *Fatal Atraction* type of love story.'[29] For Arrow, it was her singing career:

> What triggered abduction ... may have been as innocent as a quick meeting of eyes in a nightclub cabaret or a friendly smile, or just a single word. Something ... struck a chord within this watcher's psyche, a chord which sent his obsessive mind plunging over the edge of reality into the dangerous and unpredictable world of fantasy.[30]

This putative scenario is filmic down to the appropriately musical touch in the sound track of a 'chord' synching with a glance, a word or a smile. The reference to *Fatal Attraction* however is totally miscast unless used to explain the *differences* rather than the similarities in the Petersen and Arrow cases. In relation to the former, there is no relation but for the mechanism for the conversion of the Petersen affair into a usable set up, for Arrow's deception lies in the fact of the violent *voyeuse* of the film being a woman and moreover a woman who, while looking all the time as if she might turn out to be a murderer, is herself murdered: it is her *own* fatality the 'attraction' results in. Her death is both a murder (at the hands of her harassee) and symbolically a suicide. As many have observed, *Fatal Attraction* positively proposes a critique of the family and the hypocritical activities of 'family men' that partially justifies the interloper's bitterness and subsequent actions but, in a denouement in which 'power' rapidly de-escalates to a context of physical strength, the outcome is 'a moral' rather than 'moral': this, it is implied, is what happens to women, particularly 'beautiful' women, who insist on their right to their sexuality, their bodies and the right to work and have relationships of their own choosing. And it certainly underlies the extraordinary statement by George Harvey (reported on 17 December 1991) that: 'I can understand why he's done it. She's beautiful.'[31]

'Individual life,' Guy Debord opined in his 1967 *Society of the Spectacle*, 'as yet has no history.' Rather, Debord asserted, lives are historically experienced by way of a procession of 'pseudo-events which rush by in spectacular dramatisations [that] have not been lived by those informed of them'.[32] The celebrity self-abduction, whilst having the arguable effect of momentarily revealing the 'real' of the media's apparatus, hidden most of the time behind its long history of carrying on (even up to and including the operations of virtual reality) the project of realism, also risks a re-territorialisation of the means of the realist effect – and that at the very point where it thought to have seduced and traduced the system upon whose own contrivances it itself ultimately depended. The end of the exercise was, after all, only a knowing glance in the same direction by duper and duped.

Nor is the phenomenon all that new, even if brought to the point of high art by the 'terrorist' affrays and their symbiotic media relations of the 1980s. When, for instance, the minor American film star Marie 'The Body' McDonald disappeared in 1957 (only to reappear shortly after and confess that she had perpetrated a hoax), a founding and classic case of media-oriented self-abduction suggested itself: the infamous case of the self-disappearance of the American radio evangelist Aimee Semple McPherson. Over the five weeks in 1926 during which McPherson sent out messages over her own station that she had been kidnapped by 'two Latin types' and confined in a desert shack in Mexico, the case created an anti-Hispanic furore in the United States. In McDonald's case it was first reported that she had been 'doped and kidnapped from her San Fernando home by a young Mexican and a young Negro'. Turning up 24 hours later after her disappearance on a country road 'sobbing out an hysterical story of abduction, rape and robbery' before confessing her hoax, McDonald nevertheless managed to amend her description of the abductors to 'two Latin types with Elvis

Presley coiffures' to allay virulent antiblack sentiment fanned by her predicament.[33] The solvent of reference to figures that were existent media creations as alibi *and* explanation thus constitutes the 'pseudo-event' both as an appeal to an 'individual history' as default (following Debord) *and* the restitution of the same by an appeal for recognition of an agenda that maintains a solidarity and complicity between the transgressive activity of the media in representing history as itself and the right of any individual to do likewise, using for good reason the fact that a common understanding exists.

'Risk – but in comfort', Paul Virilio epigraphs the chapter 'Unable bodies' in his *Speed and Politics*. The advice is Herman Goering's on, in Virilio's words, how 'to make physical handicaps functional',[34] or, in lieu of the actuality of same, how to fabricate them. Fairlie Arrow's repertoire of legal difficulties, as the hoax and its revelation began to embattle her, turned increasingly to assimilations with other media 'walking wounded'. The plight of Lindy Chamberlain was here a notable invocation: 'They shouldn't have treated her the way they did because she appeared hard and composed. They think I made it up because I am so strong. But that is the way I am. It is just me.'[35]

The last two sentences here, an uncanny anticipation of Noeline Donaher's self-deprecating and oft-quoted words uttered in *Sylvania Waters* before she herself was forced by her rapidly magnifying fame to seek the solace and succours of solitude, were a modest underestimation of Arrow's thespian past. With a mother who had spent long years as a make-up artist with Crawford TV, Arrow had scored acting parts in *Division Four* and *Matlock*. Her acting career was enhanced by an appreciation for actors: 'A fan of Anthony Perkins, she has seen the psychothriller *Silence of the Lambs* several times and often thought of what happened to the victims.'[36]

A day after this interview was reported graphic evidence of what happens to victims was abundantly available by way of incoming reports of the murders of Peter Wade and Maureen Ambrose at their unit in Whelan Street, 'the most notorious street in Surfers Paradise'. In an 'execution-style' operation Wade, who had in the past been linked with starting price bookmaking, and Ambrose, who was a bartender, were the targets of a 'professional hit'.[37] Here, two shots were fired into the front door by a pair of gunmen who had broken into the Delrey Waterfront resort. As the *Courier Mail* report had it on 24 December 1991, after failing to break down the door of the apartment, the hired hands climbed into the ceiling through a manhole in the hallway outside it and proceeded to break through the gyprock ceiling above the main room. The resulting violent struggle saw Wade shot to death and Ambrose likewise (though on initial inspection, her head slumped on her chest, it was thought, given the blood issuing from the region between, her throat had been cut). In an article of 29 December 1991 by Carol Veitch, called 'Crime Coast', the Arrow incident is cited as part of the 'Gold Coast crime wave'[38] of 1991. Tribute 'abductions' modelled on Arrow's began to appear. As the Arrow hoax was being revealed Karen Dixon claimed to have been abducted by 'Asian men'. Later, in March 1992, a Brisbane woman, Jackelyn Grieves, claimed to have been abducted by four strangers. As Greg Roberts wrote in the *Sydney Morning Herald*:

> Like Ms Arrow, Mrs Grieves, who is unemployed, did not flinch before the TV cameras, as complete with bruised face, she told how she had been driving with a friend when a man appeared on the road in front of them.[39]

Police said Grieves had confessed that she had lied. Then, exactly one year after Arrow's own abduction, Joanna Grenside, a fitness instructor who had also worked at Jupiters, commemorated the anniversary with her own disappearance in England. Seized 'at knifepoint' from outside a car park, blindfolded and held captive for 36 hours, she reappeared two days later 'in a disoriented state', according to Hertfordshire police. Arrow, on tour in Darwin, was, according to her manager, 'not amused': 'She doesn't know the lady. She wasn't a friend. She's not interested.'

Itself the product of a text (Petersen), the Arrow affair in turn produced others (Grenside, Dixon, Grieves). As a complex series of puns on the original Petersen scenario, the affair had a structure whose resonances revealed silently held asumptions about fame, spectacularity and the power of publicity that echoed the 'intertextual overload'[40] of films from the early 1980s' period of high post-modernism, especially TV, in which failed or failing entertainers become major forces of history. Parodying and punning on pre/intertexts, inverted references, mismatching of subject and object and the 'pointed inclusive reference', as Stephen Mamber has it, were central, playful devices of post-modernist meta-fiction.[41] Zelig or Rupert Pupkin are everywhere and nowhere; when, at the height of her post-hoax career Arrow played Selina's in full public view, it came, for instance, as news to her solicitors on the Gold Coast: 'If you find out where she is, let us know because she still owes us money', they were heard to say. As the case assumed its full polytropic form, predictably, Arrow's name was punned upon: 'Acting Fairlie',[42] 'Fairlie Shallow'[43] or 'Fairlie Deceitful'[44] adverbialised her forename (playing on the ambiguity in the word 'fairly' as both 'completely' and 'not quite completely'). Likewise the surname 'Arrow' gave rise to 'Slings, Arrows for Fairlie'.[45] Like Woody Allen's Zelig, Arrow's persona now took on a life of its own: a 'seme' or low-level flicker of meaning that both flits through all sorts of contexts and utterances and (in its function as the 'cited') as anacruses to opening gambits of other bits of gossip and scuttlebut. (Barthes refers, for instance, to the tauromachian meaning of citation: 'the *citar* [in Spanish] is the stamp of the heel, the torero's arched back which summons the bull to the banderillos'.[46]

The dissemination of the Arrow 'text', the cutting of the guy ropes that set it free from its legal and juridical moorings, making it 'user friendly' to all in the transition from 'crime' to 'hoax' (or rather, the repositioning of where criminality was to be found, in the realm of false utterance), was predicated on the generation of the various forms of the enunciating 'I' during the couse of Arrow's statements to the press. (Pre-hoax revelation 'I' as in 'I just want to find out who's doing this to me because I don't deserve it, OK?'[47] as against the post-hoax version: 'And if I want something I won't stop until I get it', for instance.) In principle, Barthes wrote in *S/Z*, 'the character who says "I" has no name' as a consequence of their doing so. A fully motivated 'I', on the other hand:

> is no longer a pronoun but a name, the best of names: to say 'I' is inevitably to attribute signifieds to oneself; further it gives a biographical duration, it enables one to undergo in one's imagination an intelligible 'evolution', to signify oneself as an object with a destiny, to give meaning to time.[48]

As things subsequently transpired Arrow enjoyed some success in the wake of the scandal: on 27 January 1992 she returned from a promotional tour in the United States and in April signed a $1 million record deal in a joint venture arrangement between Sydney-based Laser Records and a Los Angeles company, Calibar. In December 1992 Arrow completed her 'World Domination' tour of Australia. Yet, to articulate time as meaning, in the sense that Barthes intends, Arrow's resource – and which she sought to seduce – remained the media itself: a media that is in fact predicated upon a 'unified irreversible time [that] is the time of the world market and as a corollary, of the world spectacle', in Debord's words.[49]

This is finally the paradox of Fairlie Arrow's shoot for stardom. Like the astronomical bodies themselves, stars attract other vast bodies that circulate around them, centripetally drawing them into the 'system' the stars themselves inhabit. And like true sidereal entities, whose light is in fact that of the fire that consumes them, they did, when young, have car accidents, kill themselves or were murdered – the various fates of the James Deans, Marilyn Monroes and River Phoenixes. Arrow's Babylonian exile at Nerang was a simulated star death in this sense. If a name is a destiny, Arrow was a 'shooting star', illuminating momentarily (social, cultural) structures not usually visible.

Notes and references

1. Zelizer, Barbie, *Covering the Body: The Kennedy Assassination, the Media and the Shaping of Popular Memory* (Chicago: University of Chicago Press, 1992), pp. 2–3.
2. Baudrillard, Jean, 'L'ecliptique du sexe', *Traverses*, 17, 1979, p. 146.
3. Carter, Dale, *The Final Frontier: The Rise and Fall of the American Rocket State* (London: Verso, 1988), p. 168.
4. Virilio, Paul, *The Aesthetics of Disappearance* (New York: Semiotext(e), 1991) p. 245.
5. Undated clipping, Gold Coast Public Library, Southport, Queensland.
6. The *Age*, 22 December 1991
7. The *Courier Mail*, 20 December 1991.
8. The *Courier Mail*, 18 December 1991.
9. The *Age*, 18 December 1991.
10. The *Daily Telegraph*, 18 December 1991.
11. *Pix*, 13 November 1954.
12. Jones, Michael, *A Sunny Place for Shady People* (Sydney: Angus & Robertson, 1986), p. 111.
13. *Ugly Mugs* is published by SQWISI (Workers in the Sex Industry), 65 Vulture Street, West End, Brisbane. The December 1994 issue contains descriptions and case histories under such headings as: Fur and Leather Sicko Mug, Gross Unshaven Mug, Should Be Locked Up Mug etc.
14. The *Age*, 22 December 1991.
15. The *Courier Mail*, 22 December 1991.
16. The *Age*, 22 December 1991.
17. The *Age*, 22 December 1991.
18. The *Age*, 22 December 1991.
19. The *Sunday Mail*, 5 January 1992.
20. The *Courier Mail*, 10 January 1992.
21. The *Courier Mail*, 9 January 1992.
22. The *Sun Herald*, 5 January 1992.
23. The *Sydney Morning Herald*, 9 January 1992.
24. The *Gold Coast Bulletin*, 7 March 1980.
25. The *Courier Mail*, 4 January 1984.
26. Colomina, Beatriz, 'The split wall: Domestic voyeurism', in Colomina, B. (ed.), *Sexuality and Space* (Princeton: Princeton Architectural Press, 1992), p. 121.

27. The *Courier Mail*, 10 December 1991.
28. The *Courier Mail*, 15 December 1991.
29. The *Courier Mail*, 15 December 1991.
30. The *Courier Mail*, 18 December 1991.
31. The *Sydney Morning Herald*, 17 December 1991.
32. Debord, Guy, *The Society of the Spectacle* (Detroit: Black & Red, 1983), section 143 (no pagination).
33. *Truth*, 20 January 1957.
34. Virilio, Paul, *Speed and Politics* (New York: Semiotext(e), 1986), p. 61.
35. The *Sunday Mail*, 22 December 1991.
36. The *Sunday Mail*, 22 December 1991.
37. The *Courier Mail*, 24 December 1991.
38. The *Courier Mail*, 29 December 1991.
39. Roberts, Greg, 'The vanishing people of Queensland: An urban myth', the *Sydney Morning Herald*, 9 March 1992.
40. Mamber, Stephen, 'In search of radical metacinema', in Horton, Andrew (ed.), *Comedy/Cinema/Theory* (Berkeley: University of California Press, 1991), p. 79.
41. Mamber, Stephen, 'In search of radical metacinema', p. 84.
42. The *Sydney Morning Herald*, 23 December 1991.
43. The *Sydney Morning Herald*, 3 January 1992.
44. The *Sun Herald*, 5 January 1992.
45. The *Sydney Morning Herald*, 3 January 1992.
46. Barthes, Roland, *S/Z: An Essay*, Richard Miller (tr.), (New York: Hill & Wang, 1974), p. 22.
47. The *Sydney Morning Herald*, 19 December 1991.
48. Barthes, Roland, *S/Z*, p. 66.
49. Debord, Guy, *Society of the Spectacle*, section 145.

11 From Desire to Deconstruction: Horror Films and Audience Reactions

Rikke Schubart

In the splatter movie *Re-Animator* (1985, Stuart Gordon) two young men come to rescue a woman who is being raped by a headless corpse in the morgue, and a tremendous fight follows between the zombies and the young people, heads and limbs flying out the door. Where a first-time audience or an old horror fan would be terrified, scared or at least disturbed, today's young audience cheers and screams with laughter. And in a scene from the truly post-modern and hilarious *Braindead* (1992, Peter Jackson) a young man triumphantly enters a house full of zombies, wields a lawnmower and says: 'The party's over.' While he deals with the bloodthirsty zombies his girlfriend is in the kitchen cutting zombie body parts to pieces in a food processor. Whatever you and I might think of a scene like this the audience is – again – laughing.[1]

Since the fictitious monster entered our homes audiences have been fascinated with the violent breaking of social and sexual taboos, the images of death and violence and the extreme sensations of shock and excitement that are hallmarks of the horror genre. Cultural critics have a hard time understanding the fascination of horror, and the violence especially has always lead to speculation and anxiety about movie audiences – how do we react to the violence of horror on screen (video, TV, movie)? Does fictitious violence lead to aggression in real life? Does it affect our actions and our sense of morals? And is the present young laughing audience proof of final depravation?

Exploring the violence in horror this chapter will look at the various theories applied by media researchers working in the field of reception analysis – the catharsis theory, syringe theory, copy-cat theory and trigger theory. One problem with this research is the plurality of theories and methods. A bigger problem, however, is whether the field of reception analysis offers any valuable insight regarding the meaning and use of violence in horror. Measuring the *effect* of violence in horror is dubious without analysing the *nature* and the *meaning* of violence – which is why reception analysis cannot explain why the audience of a splatter movie react with laughter instead of fear when faced with violence, blood, mutilations and killings. Ignoring questions of aesthetics and narrative, media researchers avoid 'reading' the violence of horror fiction. And the question of 'reading' is, I believe, crucial in horror where violence always carries a meaning located beyond imagery and setting, a meaning under constant change due to the historical development of the genre.

The chapter then turns to genre history, the only perspective able to reveal the radical changes which have taken place in the imagery and meaning of violence in horror since Bela Lugosi refused to drink wine in *Dracula* (1931, Tod Browning) and Boris Karloff came alive in *Frankenstein* (1931, James Whale). Genre history is also a perspective that provides an unprejudiced view of horror, and finally it will help explain the paradox of an audience laughing at horror.

After *Psycho* (1960, Alfred Hitchcock) the horror genre developed from demonic horror to psychological terror and in the mid-1980s the postmodern, fragmented splatter movie emerged with titles such as *The Evil Dead* (1983, Sam Raimi), *Re-Animator* (1985, Stuart Gordon) and *Braindead* – films replacing terror with laughter, sexuality with irony and portraying desires not as repressed sexual nightmares but as parody. In the development from a paranoid to a schizophrenic and finally to a postmodern psychotic horror movie a radical change occurs in audience reception; compared to an earlier audience today's audience has a high consciousness about the media in general and genre fiction in particular, a consciousness which makes it impossible to rework old genre formulas in believable ways. Francis Ford Coppola's *Dracula* (1992) may pretend to be a classic horror story, but in fact openly exchanges the tale of horror with the tale of romance and thus proves regressively premodern rather than post-modern.

'Reading' the violence of the modern horror film is more than ever a question of genre competence and historical perspective, demands that the horror movie meets for its few aficionados but rarely for critics, media researchers or the general public. This is a vast wasteland to venture into and I shall limit myself to placing the modern horror movie in its historical genre context in order to 'read' the funny violence of the postmodern horror movie.

The reception of horror

Opinions are divided as to the impact of fictitious violence. In 1983 the Home Office insisted that:

no one has the right to be upset by a brutal sex crime or a sadistic attack on a child or mindless thuggery on a pensioner if he is not prepared to drive sadistic videos out of our high streets.[2]

In the same year John Mortimer QC commented:

To blame books and films for your crimes is a frequently heard mitigation in court. It may be the roots of criminality lie far deeper and the possibility exists that neither Jack the Ripper nor Heinrich Himmler had ever seen a video nasty.[3]

Media researchers analysing the relationship between fictitious violence, reception and audience reactions in their field studies and laboratory experiments have reached multiple results due to different methods of testing and different theories.

Inspired by Aristotle's theory that the tragedy has a cathartic effect – identifying with the hero the audience vicariously experiences pleasure, aggression and punishment – the *catharsis theory* claims fictitious violence functions as a safety valve, giving the audience an opportunity to let out pent-up aggression.[4] This is, incidentally, the only theory positive towards fictitious violence. The syringe theory, copy-cat theory and trigger theory have it the other way round. According to the *syringe theory* the violence on screen is 'injected' into the veins of the audience, causing violent behaviour in even a non-violent person – think of Dracula inducing his poison into Lucy's pure veins (and yet – isn't Dracula exotic and seducing?).[5] According to the behaviouristic *copy-cat theory* the audience copies the violent acts in fiction and realises them in real life[6] – an argument recently invoked when American feminists protested against Bret Easton Ellis' novel *American Psycho* (1991), holding him responsible for any future murders committed the way he described them. Clearly they did not agree with the conclusion from a report on video violence insisting that

[television and video] contrast sharply to the written word. Reading requires effort. Everything is left to the imagination and the page merely triggers ideas which have to be generated from within. The video film works the other way round. The images are already provided pre-packaged, pre-edited, pre-conceived, pre-run and pre-digested. Because it requires no effort on the part of the recipient, it may be received uncritically and its values internalized without conscious effort.[7]

The feminist protesters didn't see any aesthetic reason why the book should go free while the film got the blame. In the case of the murder of two-year-old James Bulger, committed by two ten-year-old boys in 1993, the copy-cat theory was also invoked: trying to come up with a reason for the inexplicable and repellent murder police theorised that the boys had copied scenes from *Child's Play 3* (1991, Jack Bender), a film rented by one boy's father. The judge commented that 'violent video films may in part be an explanation' and Rupert Murdoch's newspaper the *Sun* (the biggest daily newspaper in Britain) launched a campaign to burn all copies of the film in Britain – although it was not proved that either boy had actually watched the film.[8] (As a result of this debate the British Board of Film Censors in March 1993 commissioned the Policy Studies Institute to initiate the first independent research study in 20 years about viewing habits of young offenders.)

The third aggression theory, the *trigger theory*, argues that fictitious violence triggers already existing aggressive tendencies in the audience ('If it is doubtful, it is dirty,' English Judge Powell commented on the violent video films).[9] And finally yet another theory, the *desensitisation theory*, has it that violence on screen desensitises its audience and makes it accept and tolerate violence in real life as a legitimate way to solve both personal and social problems.[10]

In relation to horror films this research is highly problematic, as a few examples demonstrate: first, a film is often presented to a test group not in its entire length, but as a short extract (see for example Geen and Stonner 1974 and Martin 1993[11]). How is it possible to evaluate a piece of film as a substitute for the whole film? Secondly, the viewer situation is made deviant by the use of manipulation before and after the viewing process – in one case (Geen and Stonner 1974) the test group was divided in two, giving each other electric shocks. Is this measuring the effects of fiction or is it real-life test manipulation? Thirdly, the 'violent' film in question is deprived of its genre context; who would not react strongly presented with a violent programme for the first time – be it news, horror movies, crime stories or action films? (British MPs vomited when exposed to violent scenes from horror movies.[12]) The first spontaneous reaction quickly changes, not as a result of desensitisation but because of experience with the genre. Linked to the problem of genre is also a total lack of differentiation between media genres. The 'violent' extracts a test group is shown vary from a *Tom and Jerry* cartoon to a war documentary, from news to Mexican western movies, from horror films to constructed but seemingly real situations of violence, from especially produced TV samples to a hidden camera and so forth. The biggest problem, however, is beyond doubt the lack of distinction between a sociological sphere (where we find the audience, society and real-life violence), an aesthetic sphere (where we find the horror films) and a psychological sphere (where the two interact). Focusing exclusively on our reaction media researchers seldom bother to watch, let alone analyse, the films. Ignoring the question of our fascination with the violence of horror, media researchers forget to wonder why we willingly subject ourselves to being scared, frightened out of our wits, having sweaty palms, hair on end, heavy breathing and scary nightmares.

Taken as a whole, media researchers insist that violence on screen leads to aggressiveness and violence: 'the evidence accumulated in the 1970s seems overwhelming that televised violence and aggression are positively correlated in children,' concludes the National Institute of Mental Health,[13] and a report from 1985 insists that 'the evidence strongly suggests a causal link between the viewing of violence and violent behavior.'[14] Yet the many theories, experiments and conclusions do not prevent me, a literary critic and horror fan, from being suspicious about the so-called scientific facts of the effects of fiction, a question that has been in dispute since Aristotle (384–322 BC) wrote his *Poetics*. In case we should have forgotten, the issue of horror is fiction, not the real thing, and when we look at the history of popular culture we find that anxiety always accompanied new media; eighteenth- and nineteenth-century critics condemned the popular novel, the 1950s condemned comics, the 1960s and 1970s condemned the effects of television and the 1980s and 1990s have been terrified of video-viewing flexibility and TV-channel plurality. The extreme anxiety with fictitious entertainment and violence and its effect on the mental health of the public is thus not a new phenomenon.

The anxiety of real-life effect is linked to ideology, social taboos and forbidden pleasures or, as Freud would term it, repression, suppression and denial. In the aesthetic field of criticism, however, opinions are divided as to the status and ideology of horror. The New Zealand critic Joseph Grixti accuses the horror film of being the escapist product of a capitalist society: 'Its function is that of taking up within itself determinate fears in order to transform them into other (unreal) fears, with the purpose of saving readers from having to face up to what might really frighten them.'[15] Horror films are not only the 'means of placating a growing unease created by moral and economic conflicts in a changing society,'[16] they are also active in causing misery: 'Depression can be generated and encouraged by the furtive and insistent projection of ill-conceived pictures of reality which ... combine helpless unease with vacuous optimism.'[17] It is not the violence of monsters, vampires, werewolves, zombies, axe-wielding psychos, demon-ridden teenage girls, obsessed houses, giant sharks, rats, worms, spiders, ants, lethal aliens, robots, dolls or pet animals that disturb Grixti (who clearly has Georg Lukacs as his critical ancestor and idol), it is rather the garlic, crucifix, machine gun or whatever other unrealistic means are used to repel the repressed fears. The danger is not aggression, but the depression and passivity that horror allegedly causes in audiences. In opposition to this myopic perspective we find critics with a rather broadsighted perspective insisting that (at least part of) horror is uniquely progressive and subversive, giving reign to repressed pleasures and antisocial fantasies. 'Central to the effect and fascination of horror films is their fulfilment of our nightmare wish to smash the norms that oppress us and which our moral conditioning teaches us to revere,' says English film critic Robin Wood.[18] And in an analysis of the fantastic genre (which includes *Dracula*, *Frankenstein*, *Night of the Living Dead* and other horror fictions) the critic Rosemary Jackson argues that 'what could be termed a "bourgeois" category of the real is under attack ... Undoing those unifying structures and significations upon which social order depends, fantasy functions to subvert and undermine cultural stability.'[19]

Undermining or sustaining stability? Subversive or escapist? The arguments of Grixti, Wood and Jackson are further proof of the complexity of reading and ideologically judging texts. In 1960 critics condemned the psychological horror film *Peeping Tom* (1960, Michael Powell) as being sick and repulsive, whereas director Michael Powell tried in vain to explain that it was in fact 'a very nice, a very tender film'.[20] Often directors are themselves not conscious of a film's 'impact': Alfred Hitchcock was so intrigued by the success of *Psycho* that he asked the Stanford Research Institute to make a study of it (but backed out when told the price of $ 75,000).[21] And *The Texas Chain Saw Massacre* (1974, Tobe Hooper) which most critics read as a repulsive movie, Robin Wood termed 'authentic art, profoundly disturbing, intensely personal'.[22] The problem of reading is also central for the grotesque horror movie; among the titles on an English list of dangerous 'video nasties' is *The Evil Dead*, a film which in my opinion should be read as a subversive and innovative black comedy.[23]

Judging the provocative aesthetics of horror as sick or subversive, authentic or escapist, seems to me beside the point. Horror is social history and the genre's quality has nothing to do with the amount of violence, but with its ability to provoke and remind us of taboos. And, returning to the post-modern splatter movie with its use of the grotesque and the comical, does the laughing audience here accept or reject society's taboos? What role does violence play? To answer that a genre perspective is called for.

A wicked, burning desire

In spite of claims made by modernist critics of mass culture the horror genre is not a product of the twentieth-century entertainment industry. It was not born a video nasty, body-count movie, slasher movie, gore film or splatter movie, and neither did it start out with adolescent boys as its target group. Modern horror dates back to the Gothic novel[24] (approximately 1770 to 1820) at the time of the English Enlightenment, a time obsessed with rationality and progress and exchanging religion and superstition for psychology and science. 'The Devil is certainly nothing else than the personification of the repressed, unconscious instinctual life', Freud[25] has explained, and the irrational fantasies and desires catered for by demons, devils, vampires, werewolves and witches in this period moved from metaphysics to literature.

Gothic combines the sexual theme of the sentimental novel – the 'inverted' love story of a young virgin/daughter pursued by an older villain/father – with supernatural horror. The strong sadomasochistic undertones of the inverted love story was a popular female topic, with the majority of writers and readers of Gothic novels being women.[26] With its fascination for middle-age architecture Gothic set the now classic scene for horror: a female victim tortured in the claustrophobic space of deserted and decayed castles, a space linked with the dark, the night, the dream and the subconscious – a space which we recognise as the living room in *The Texas Chain Saw Massacre*, the bedroom in *Misery* (1990, Rob Reiner) and the cellar in *Psycho* and *The Silence of the Lambs* (1991, Jonathan Demme). The subconscious functions as a nightmarish point of view, 'a distorting lens, a magnifying lens'[27] through which things viewed are permeated with the paranoia of the victim. The distortion let fantasies of sexuality and sadism spring into full bloom with violence, sadism, masochism and, in M.G. Lewis' notorious masterpiece *The Monk* from 1797, incest, rape, necrophilia, torture, murder and other perverse acts.

Gothic made the female body an object for sadistic pleasures and masochistic pain and sensitivity in the same period that the Marquis de Sade wrote his sadomasochistic novels, and clearly eroticism and death are not opposites in this fictitious universe of distorted realities and realised fantasies; they are natural companions. As the Bulgarian-French literary critic Tzvetan Todorov says:[28]

The chain which started with desire and led through cruelty has led us to death. The relationship of these two themes is, moreover, quite well known. Their relation is not always the same, but one may say that it is always present.

The Gothic novel provided the extreme sensations, the distorted vision, the sadomasochistic sexuality, the perverse desires, the vicinity of death and desire, the female victim and the inverted love story, all of which are fundamental to horror. But it took a monster and a woman to bring the horror genre alive, which Mary Shelley did in 1818 with *Frankenstein; Or, the Modern Prometheus*.[29]

The essence of horror lies in the monster. 'Monster' comes from Latin, meaning 'a freak announcing the wrath of the gods' and the monster is psychologically speaking a figure embodying messages from the unconscious, giving life to repressed desires and social taboos. Robin Wood relates the monster to the Other:

> The concept of Otherness can be theorized in many ways and on many levels. Its psychoanalytic significance resides in the fact that it functions not simply as something external to the culture or to the self, but also as what is repressed (though never destroyed) in the self and projected outward in order to be hated and disowned ... Central to [the horror genre] is the actual dramatization of the dual concept of the repressed/the Other, in the figure of the monster.[30]

In other words, keeping track of the Other of modern bourgeois society, horror provides us with an insight into a bookkeeping by double entry.

In his classic study of 'the Uncanny' (*Das Unheimliche*) from 1919 Freud links the uncanny with repressed unconscious fantasies: 'This uncanny is in reality nothing new or alien, but something which is familiar and old established in the mind and which has become alienated from it only through the process of repression.'[31] Our uncanny feelings arise not when we face the unknown, but when we face the previously known and now forgotten.[32] The uncanny originates from repressed infantile fantasies, that originally could be either fearful or pleasurable. Thus Freud explains the fear of being buried alive as a repressed and pleasurable fantasy of returning to the womb, and the uncanniness of dismembered limbs with their symbolising the castration complex – Freud uses as a phallic example a severed hand, a limb horror is littered with from *The Hands of Orlac* (1960, Edmund T. Greville) and *Hands of a Stranger* (1962, Newton Arnold) to splatter movies such as *Body Parts* (1991, Eric Reed), *Evil Dead II* (1987, Sam Raimi) and *Braindead*. Freud primarily identifies the uncanny in literature with the infantile complexes which remain frightening because they refer not to a material but a psychical reality. Together with the castration complex Freud mentions omnipotence of thought; an example of this is the dissolution of limits that follows the monster: limits disappear between death and desire, between human and inhuman, between reality and fantasy, between conscious and unconscious.

An interesting feature of the uncanny is the ambiguity of known/unknown which makes our reaction ambivalent; we are curious and repelled, we feel both pleasure and fear when facing the uncanny in fiction. Thus our reactions to horror are also a kind of bookkeeping by double entry: the supernatural monster is both pleasurable (because of the link to omnipotence of thought in early childhood) and utterly frightening (because unable to be dealt with by our conscious). Ambivalence is fundamental in horror where the audience voluntarily seeks out the dreadful, where we desire the repulsive, where we wish to break the limits of safety, sanity and normality by moving into a world of chaos dominated by unconscious desires. In fact, we would be deeply disappointed and want our money back if not terrified by the movie.

The ambiguity, the unconscious desires and the sexual content is a point of departure media research seldom uses.

Erotic paranoia

In horror the repressed desires, manifested in the monster, are disguised as the ultimate in fears: death. The threat alone is not sufficient to create horror, it must also be carried out. Horror writer and director Clive Barker puts it this way:

> There has to be a sacrifice, probably has to be a lot of loss – love loss, limb loss. It's not that nobody will survive, but those who do survive aren't going to be in quite the same condition that they were in when they started ... They may be transformed in a very fundamental way: they may begin alive and end up dead, they may lose limbs, they may lose their sanity.[33]

The provocative and ambivalent pictures of Otherness in horror are in the genre's first long phase, which I want to term *paranoid horror*, of an overwhelmingly sexual nature, with perverted desires dressed up in sado-masochistic outfit as vampire and virgin, monster and humanity, dancing an erotic pas de deux.

Desires are projected outward on to a clearly external monster which functions not as a Body Double but a Soul Double, a classic doppelganger symbolising the repressed. The fight between man and monster is in this phase a psychomachia, a fight between reason and desires of a sexual nature. The majority of scientific horror either has a scientist 'creating' a monster that threatens humanity and turns against its inventor and kills him (from *Frankenstein* in 1931 to *The Fly* (David Cronenberg) in 1986) or an alien from out of space threatening all humanity (from *Invasion of the Body Snatchers* (1956, Don Siegel) and *It! The Terror from Beyond Space* (1958, Edward L. Cahn) to the *Alien* trilogy (1979, Ridley Scott; 1986, James Cameron; 1992, David Fincher). The demonic subgenre similarly projects our fears and desires outward: the teenage girl Regan is possessed by a demon in *The Exorcist* (1973, William Friedkin), Rosemary is raped by the Devil in *Rosemary's Baby* (1968, Roman Polanski; guess what the result is ...) and a town is plagued by the vampire Barlow in the mini series *Salem's Lot* (1979, Tobe Hooper). The vampire is the symbol par excellence of the sexual nature of horror, and its portrayal in John Polidori's *The Vampyre* (1819), Sheridan Le Fanu's lesbian vampire story *Carmilla* (1872) and Bram Stoker's *Dracula* (1897) leaves no doubt as to the erotic dimension:

> In the moonlight opposite me were three young women, ladies by their dress and manner ... All three had brilliant white teeth that shone like pearls against the ruby of their voluptuous lips. There was something about them that made me uneasy, some longing and at the same time some deadly fear. I felt in my heart a wicked, burning desire that they would kiss me with those red lips ... The girl went on her knees, and bent over me, simply gloating. There was a deliberate voluptuousness which was both thrilling and repulsive, and as she arched her neck she actually licked her lips like an animal, till I could see in the moonlight the moisture shining on the scarlet lips and on the red tongue as it lapped the white sharp teeth. Lower and lower went her head as the lips went below the range of my mouth and chin and seemed about to fasten on my throat. Then she paused, and I could hear the churning sound of her tongue as it licked her teeth and lips, and could feel the hot breath on my neck. Then the skin of my throat began to tingle as one's flesh does when the hand that is to tickle it approaches nearer – nearer. I could feel the soft, shivering touch of the lips on the super-sensitive skin of my throat, and the hard dents of two sharp teeth, just touching and pausing there. I closed my eyes in a languorous ecstasy and waited – waited with beating heart.[34]

Analysing our belief in the supernatural psychoanalyst Ernest Jones traces the origin of these monsters to the repressed sexual desires in our nightmares. 'The sexual idea itself may or may not appear in the conscious belief or fear; it is often concealed by a general apprehension that the creature may throttle one or do some vaguely dreadful thing to one.'[35] Jones also says that the 'latent content of the belief [in the vampire] yields plain indications of most kinds of sexual perversions',[36] a claim supported by the more than 160 screen versions of *Dracula* with thinly disguised perverse fantasies about sexual intercourse with the dead, rape, masochism and sadism.

I drink your blood, I eat your skin

Paranoid horror has (a) a lethal monster which (b) is fascinating and threatening because it symbolises the return of repressed desires, and which c) causes an ambivalent reaction in the audience of both desire and fear. The next phase of horror, which I call *schizophrenic horror*, is characterised by the same three features but with a change in imagery. The monster is no longer necessarily projected outward but as often introjected into our homes, our families and our psyche. Schizophrenia and the psycho are not new symbols of the uncanny, they have been used in literature since James Hogg's *The Private Memoirs and Confessions of a Justified Sinner* (1824).[37] However, since *Psycho* and *Peeping Tom* (both 1960) the theme of the tormented psyche has dominated horror.[38] With a new ironic awareness these films display their psychological and sexual consciousness – in *Peeping Tom* the sexual sadist and voyeur Mark watches one of his victims being carried away by the police. 'What paper are you from?' a policeman asks and Mark replies: 'The *Observer*.'

This meta-reflective irony (the audience is of course as much an observer as Mark is) begins in schizophrenic horror. Being more conscious of sexual perversions and bringing to the fore social themes these films move away from the symbolic sphere of the supernatural and into the origin of the uncanny in the nuclear family, the childhood, the individual's psyche and a threatening society. Though outwardly realistic these fictions are well aware of their status as fictions and realised fantasies and in fact manifest a consciousness about representing the repressed Other.

'I think we are all in our private traps. And none of us can ever get out. We scratch and claw, but only at the air, only at each other, and for all of it we never budge an inch,'

says Norman Bates to his female victim in *Psycho*.

In the traditional psychological horror movie voyeurism and sadism flourish, but with the splatter movie beginning in the 1960s more degenerated perversions see the daylight. The torn-open psyche correlates to the mutilated body, the theme of films such as *The Blood Drinkers* (1966, Geraldo De Leon), *Night of the Living Dead* (1968, George A. Romero), *Flesh Feast* (1970, B.F. Grinter), *I Drink Your Blood* (1970, David Durston), *I Eat Your Skin* (1971, Del Tenney), *Please Don't Eat My Mother* (1972, Carl Monson) and *Raw Meat* (1973, Gary Sherman). The danger in 1970s' horror is not a mere sensual bite in the victim's neck, but being devoured in a cannibalistic orgy. Tobe Hooper's *The Texas Chain Saw Massacre* cleverly combines cannibalism with the degenerated nuclear family and embodies the phallic threat in the maniac Leatherface's attempts to slice open Sally with his chain saw.

The bloody and mutilated body can also represent the force of the psyche being freed from conscious control. In *Carrie* (1976, Brian De Palma) the teenager Carrie reverses the harassments she has suffered in her home and school and transforms herself from victim to victor and monster when she uses her telekinetic powers to destroy the school and kill her mother. Canadian director David Cronenberg explores the sexual dimensions of the perversely monstrous body in his films *The Parasite Murders* (1976), *Rabid* (1977) and *Videodrome* (1983), all of them concerned with a very ambiguous male masochism. In *Videodrome* the main character develops a vagina-like opening in his abdomen, in which a TV company insert their video cassette with the words 'You must open up to us.' The open body, symbolising the activation of repressed desires, is both a fascinating and terrifying possibility.

Yet a third development in the late 1970s' splatter movie is the teenage slasher film that attempts to get rid of symbolism, minimise the storyline and move the perspective and our identification from monster to victim. The ambivalence of dread turns into pure terror as we identify more with victim than victor in the teenage horror film *Halloween* (1978, John Carpenter), which successfully used the technique of a handheld camera switching between the point of view of the monster and that of the victim. The handheld camera and personalised point of view structure the *Halloween* series (now five movies), the *Friday the 13th* series (now eight movies) and (in less degree) the *A Nightmare on Elm Street* series (six movies). Without returning to the earlier sensuality and demonic imagery the teenage horror movies, all identical in structure, have a knife-slashing bogyman killing a group of teenagers and chasing a final girl in the last part of the film – and you must wonder why an audience goes to see a rip-off of the same story. 'Basically sequels mean the same film. That's what people want to see. They want to see the same movie again,' says John Carpenter, the director of *Halloween*.[39] His assertion is underlined by American critic Andrew Britton describing the horrifying experience of watching an audience watch a horror movie (the movie is *Hell Night* (1981, Tom DeSimone), but it could be any teenage horror movie):

> It became obvious at a very early stage that every spectator knew exactly what the film was going to do at every point, even down to the order in which it would dispose of its various characters, and the screening was accompanied by something in the nature of a running commentary in which each dramatic move was excitedly broadcast some minutes before it was actually made. The film's total predictability did not create boredom or disappointment. On the contrary, the predictability was clearly the main source of pleasure, and the only occasion for disappointment would have been a modulation of the formula, not the repetition of it.[40]

Robin Wood was similarly shocked attending *The Texas Chain Saw Massacre*: 'Watching it recently with a large, half-stoned youth audience who cheered and applauded every one of Leatherface's outrages against their representatives on the screen was a terrifying experience.'[41] Both critics are puzzled that the audience takes pleasure in violent acts, predicts them, takes them for granted, thinks them even necessary and, finally, applauds them. The reason lies in the mythic quality these highly repetitive stories achieve, stripped as they are of plot, narrative and character description. The repetitious structure is clearly a wish to control the dreadful events and overcome the feeling of horror, which in the teenage horror movie looks like a modern-day fairy-tale: teenagers abandoned by their parents/the authorities are confronted with maniacal killer/the threat of society which only the resourceful and strong virgin survive. In his analysis of fairy-tales psychoanalyst Bruno Bettelheim describes how children use them as fantasy-dramas about growing up:

> Fairy-tales offer figures onto which the child can externalize what goes on in his mind, in controllable ways. Fairy-tales show the child how he can embody his destructive wishes in one figure, gain desired satisfactions from another, identify with a third, have ideal attachments with a fourth, and so on, as his needs of the moment require.[42]

We might guess that what goes on in the mind of the young teenage audience is the fear of growing up: leaving childhood safety, fighting for integrity in adult society and handling sexual desires. To confirm this argument you need only watch a few of these teenage horror films which all embody the same themes. In his analysis of the horror genre James Twitchell also views horror as a teenage fairy-tale and concludes that:

Essentially, horror has little to do with fright; it has more to do with laying down the rules of socialization and extrapolating a hidden code of sexual behavior. Once we learn these rules, as we do in adolescence, horror dissipates.[43]

Twitchell is in a way mistaken; horror does not dissipate, it just transforms into other fears, other taboos and other imagery.

The heightened consciousness of horror as manifesting repressed desires changes the genre in several ways. The psychological horror movie pictures insanity, social terror and family horror. The splatter movies turn to carnographic horror, cannibalism and mutilation, though differing in their attitude towards sexuality, family, social criticism and psychological awareness. And the discount version, the teenage horror movie, addresses a very young audience with sexual fairy-tales. Schizophrenic horror has in common two features: after 1960 horror moves into our reality, psyche, family and society, and the audience is terrified rather than titillated. As time goes by and the Vietnam War, television and a new phase of capitalism leave their mark on western culture, horror turns more realistic and more frightening.

From psycho to zombie or, is the audience really braindead?

In the 1980s a new horror movie emerged. The teenage horror film may be stripped down to essentials and mythic structure, but the postmodern grotesque splatter movie seems without essentials and mythic structure. Gone is the lethal monster, the maniac, the seducing vampire, the werewolf tormented by guilt and regret. Gone is the pure virgin, the sensitive female victim. Gone is the fear of limits between man and monster, reality and fantasy, desire and death. Gone is the terror of the return of the repressed, whether sexual or social in design. Gone is the audience screaming in panic and fear and with them the essential feature of horror, the ambivalence of fear and fascination, dread and pleasure. Gone is all that constitutes the horror genre. But before pronouncing the genre dead, let's look at what is left in post-modern horror.

In *The Evil Dead*, one of the first of the grotesque and funny splatter movies, a group of young people invoke the spirits of the dead by mistake; one by one the teenagers are possessed and killed by evil spirits until only one man, Ash, is left. His former friends, now demon-like zombies, gather around him chanting 'We're gonna get you, we're gonna get you.' To you and me this would be pretty scary. But in the audience nobody is scared, nobody is screaming in terror. On the contrary they laugh when in the film, indeed quite comically, the camera turns the hero upside down. In the sequel *Evil Dead II* Ash is in trouble in the same cabin in the same desolate woods with the same demons and this time forced to cut off one of his hands with a chain saw because the hand, possessed by demons, is trying to kill him. Again the gruesome scene is turned into a joke: on top of the bucket where Ash has trapped the murderous hand we find *A Farewell to Arms* (by Ernest Hemingway); the hand later makes obscene gestures and picks his nose. And the audience laughs.

Left in the post–modern splatter movie is the violence and the figure of the monster; in fact, most of the meaning of these films is tied to the violence:

> Splattermovies, offshoots of the horror film genre, aim not to scare their audiences, necessarily, nor to drive them to the edges of their seats in suspense, but to mortify them with scenes of explicit gore. In splatter movies, mutilation is indeed the message – many times the only one,[44]

says film critic John McCarthy, famous for the term 'splatter,' an ono-matopoeia imitating the sound of death: in a splatter movie blood doesn't just drip out the side of the mouth, it spurts out of the body with intestines, liver, heart and whatever else may be hidden inside us gushing out on to the floor. That is the meaning of 'splatter', a term referring not to thematics or narrative but to a blood–soaked aesthetics and use of special effects.

In post–modern horror hermeneutic 'depth' and unconscious imagery is replaced with humorous violence. Let us take *Braindead* as an example: the uncanny symbolism of secret desires is openly laughed at in their grotesque and monstrous shapes as zombies having sex, teenagers in love and having to fight supernatural obstacles, a priest being impaled on a phallic statue. Gone is the terror of the nuclear family, of childhood and of social taboos; the dominating mother in *Braindead* is transformed into a gigantic and comic monster, bringing down the house in her attempts to swallow up her son and kill his fiance. The cliches that used to frighten us are made into spoofs: the zombie is reduced to an arse–hole with intestines attached, the German Nazi doctor delivers tranquillisers to calm the zombies and the mother ends up a zombie being fed pudding by her son at the dinner table.

What is strikingly new in post–modern horror is that the split psyche is replaced by a new psychotic vision where nobody questions the bounds of reality or the zombies roaming the street, a fragmentation of reality subverting both the narrative structure and thematics of the text. The sequence of scenes doesn't matter much in films like *The Evil Dead, Evil Dead II, Re-Animator, Braindead, Bad Taste* (1988, Peter Jackson), *Return of the Living Dead Part II* (1988, Ken Wiederhorn) and *Evil Dead III* (1992, Sam Raimi). They are a series of gimmicks, of splatter jokes which may be repulsive but are also funny: a living corpse is frightening, but if we place its head under the arm the scene in *Re-Animator* turns comic instead. And cutting off your own hand is no joke, but if the hand is a little devil, as in *Evil Dead II,* we find ourselves in a comical sphere where the body is uncontrollable. In *Braindead* the disintegrating mother drops her ear in the soup at the dinner table and, with the guests and her son watching in disgust, eats it. As in the *Tom and Jerry* cartoons, the pain is absent and the mutilation unrealistic. But unlike *Tom and Jerry* our pleasure lies in pure disgust and bad taste.

A reflection of the fragmentation of 1980s' horror is the audience's fascination with special effects showing mutilations, deaths, transformations from human to monster and all imaginable grotesqueries. In fanzines from *Inferno* and *Trauma* (from Denmark) to *Chicago Shivers, Cinefantastique, Fangoria, Film Extremes, Gore Gazette, In the Flesh, Shivers, Sleazoid Express, Splatter Times, Splatting Image* and *Starlog*, the special effects become proof of the mastery of designing, staging and fragmenting the body. Body and story are reduced into bits and pieces defying reality and order, free to be rearranged in new chance combinations. Mocking and parodying the hierarchy of the psyche and society, the psychotic horror movie dissolves the order of reality.

Where do we find the pleasure of a text that has replaced ambivalent dread with what Baudrillard, in another connection, calls 'the unclean promiscuity of everything which touches, invests and penetrates without resistance, with no halo of private protection, not even his own body, to protect him anymore'?[45] Why does the audience watch these films? The answer is that pleasure, like violence, has changed in structure: the pleasure of the grotesque splatter movie is found in its attack on sense, morals, social taboos, the control of body and psyche, limits of all kinds; in short, the rules of society are here turned upside down and fragmented into jokes. Baudrillard calls it the end of interiority and intimacy, referring not to the grotesque horror movie but to the plurality of media and TV channels available to the public. However, his words also aptly describe a second source of pleasure which, beside the disintegration of hierarchy, lies in a post-modern textuality that requires a competent audience to make meaning out of the bits and pieces. In fact, the textuality of psychotic horror shares traits with films like *Pretty Woman, Last Action Hero* and other meta- and self-reflective genre films.

The horror audience was always active and competent, expecting certain genre elements. What is new is the competence being expanded to include other texts and genres. Some of the texts referred to in *Braindead* are *Psycho*, *Night of the Living Dead*, *The Evil Dead*, *Evil Dead II* and *Halloween*, but we also meet references outside the horror genre, such as a zombie being cut into a torso as in a scene from *Monty Python and the Holy Grail* (1975, Terry Gilliam/Terry Jones). Other intertextual genre references are the first scene in *Braindead*, a parody on the *Indiana Jones* films, and a later scene which has a priest doing kick-boxing in the cemetery ('I kick ass for the Lord' he exclaims) referring to the kick-boxing films of Jean Claude Van Damme. The audience reading this text is an active audience competent in the history of the horror movie and popular culture in general, an audience behaving as *instinctive semioticians*.[46] The naive spectator titillated and terrified by the paranoid and schizophrenic horror movie has in the 1980s turned into a critical spectator, deconstructing the text with pleasure.

'Two cliches make us laugh but a hundred cliches move us because we sense dimly that the cliches are talking among themselves'[47] says Umberto Eco. In regard to our subject he is clearly wrong. In the horror movie it takes two cliches to scare an audience witless and a hundred cliches to make us scream with laughter. However, the lack of hermeneutic 'depth', the hundred cliches, the intertextual quotations and the deconstructing audience are all characteristics that the grotesque horror movie has in common with Eco's analysis of post-modern textuality.[48] The polysemic text in dialogue with itself, with other texts and with its audience is the result of a genre development which I see as a genre exhaustion. The audience is laughing not just because of the attack on taboos and rationality, but also because it is finally in full control of the text and the Otherness, able to predict and contain it without fear. The lack of fear is of course a response to the laying bare of the unconscious, every taboo, every desire and every repressed fantasy in the post-modern horror movie. It is impossible to guess how Freud would have reacted to these films.

Returning to the audience, violence and research done on reception and effect, we can understand now why horror is constantly charged with breaking down social order. 'A situation is created wherein left-wing revolutions occur or right-wing dictators after the pattern of Hitler may arise and pose as social saviors'[49] one report alarmingly concludes. Because it deals in repressed fantasies, in the obscene and perverse sexuality, the transgression of social bounds, the breaking and shattering of taboos, the manifestation of Otherness buried in modern-day society, the horror genre is, so to speak, born a natural scapegoat, always ready to be slaughtered in times demanding the easy placing of joint guilt and a scapegoat removed by sacrificial bloodshed.

It is understandable that guardians of social order and stability mistakenly link the horror genre with real-life violence and demand that horror fiction be tamed by censorship. But it is hard to have faith that our reactions, conscious as well as unconscious, can be measured by scientists with no understanding of fiction, aesthetics and 'reading', and with no knowledge of the genre. How can we measure the sexually arousing effect of the violence of Dracula and our fascination with it? How do we measure the fear of Leatherface roaming the living room with a chain saw in *The Texas Chain Saw Massacre*? The mad doctor with his head under his arm in *Re-Animator*? Ash catching his sawn-off hand in a basket in *Evil Dead II*? Or Lionel entering the living room with his lawnmower lifted high in *Braindead*?

It is also hard to trust the guardians of social order with the best of intentions. With insight into the history of the genre as a bookkeeping by double entry it is easy to see horror for what it is, a mirror reflecting that which society would prefer to remain hidden. The pictures of Otherness change with the content of social repression, from sexual denial in paranoid horror to insanity, adulthood and social disintegration in schizophrenic horror and finally, in psychotic horror, to an attack on all social, psychological and physical integrity, annihilating fears, desires, neurosis, the unconscious, making the audience mock and subvert all social rules. Would any society argue that such elements be brought out in the open? Yet the last phase of horror, the post-modern grotesque splatter movie, has brought all taboos into bright daylight, disintegrating not just social stability and good taste, but also the text itself and – maybe – the 200-year-old horror genre. And here the laughing audience is indeed scary, not for reasons of real-life violence, but because it indicates the disintegration of the unconscious in modern-day society.

Does violence in the horror genre create real-life violence? Does it trigger latent violence? Does it desensitise us? In 1984 David Hamilton Grant, secretary of the company that distributed the film *Nightmares in a Damaged Brain* (1981, Romano Scavolini, original title *Nightmare*) in Britain, was charged with distributing depraving and obscene material. In court film critic Derek Malcolm defended the film as 'not a classic, but well executed'. 'So was the German invasion of Poland,' the judge responded, and sentenced Grant to 18 months in jail.[50] The reply of the judge is also an answer to our question; discussing psychology, fiction, aesthetics and genre with guardians of social order who intentionally mix reality and fiction is not just naive, it is also forever doomed to misinterpretation.

The horror genre no longer functions as our collective unconscious or (if it ever did) as an emotional safety valve. It will, however, always remain an attack on bourgeois society, provocation being its very nature. Horror is first and foremost a fascinating indicator of the state of mind of modern society. The horror genre is not a social disease we must heal society from; it is, on the contrary, a life-guarding indication of society's mental condition. We have to accept horror, if not as the official story, then as the necessary subtext.

Notes and references

1. I had first-hand experience with the laughing audience on the opening night of *Braindead* in a large cinema in Copenhagen.
2. Martin, John, *The Seduction of the Gullible* (Nottingham: Procrustes Press, 1993), p. 198
3. Ibid, p. 197.
4. See Manning, S.A. and Taylor, D.A., 'Effects of viewed violence and aggression: stimulation and Catharsis', in *Journal of Personality and Social Psychology*, 1975 (Jan), vol. 31 (1), pp. 180–8.
5. See Geen, Russel G. and Stonner, D., 'The meaning of observed violence: effects on arousal and aggressive behavior', in *Journal of Research in Personality*, 1974, 8, pp. 55–63.
6. See Drabman, R.S. and Thomas, M.H., 'Children's imitation of aggressive and prosocial behavior when viewing alone and in pairs', in *Journal of Communication*, 1977, summer, 27 (3), pp. 199–205.
7. Barlow, Geoffrey and Hill, Alison (eds), *Video Violence and Children* (London: Hodder and Stoughton, 1985), p. 160. The quote demonstrates an embarrassing lack of experience with the aesthetics of both literature and film.
8. A year after the murder the two boys, Bobby Thompson and Jon Venables, were sentenced to indefinite detention 'at Her Majesty's pleasure'. It was never proven that either child had actually watched *Child's Play 3*, rented a little less than a month before the murder. The film had recently run twice on Sky TV, owned by the same Rupert Murdoch launching the campaign to burn all copies of the film in Britain, and the moral issues of banning certain films thus appear very ambiguous on behalf of the media.

    The appalling murder of James Bulger shocked the world, and the viewing of a horror film as a motive was presented by the media and (partially) the authorities as a simple and neat explanation to the public (see for example Martin, John, *The Seduction of the Gullible*). Yet two recent Norwegian cases of children murdering children underline the fact that real-life violence is caused by social and familial factors and not, at least not primarily, by media fiction: In 1994 three boys aged four, five and six murdered a five-year-old girl and in 1992 two girls of four tortured and murdered a four-weeks-old infant. In both cases the most active of the assaulting children (obviously too young to watch late night horror movies) were known in the neighbourhood as a child showing aggressive and anti-social behaviour. In one of the two cases the mother of the leading assaulter had for several years asked the social security system for help – in vain.

9. Martin, John, *The Seduction of the Gullible*, p. 217.
10. See Teachman, G. and Orne, M., 'Effects of aggressive and prosocial film material on altruistic behavior of children', in *Psychological Reports*, 1981 (June) vol. 48(3), pp. 699–702; Thomas, M.H. and Drabman, R.S., 'Toleration of real life aggression as a function of exposure to televised violence and age of subject', in *Merrill–Palmer Quarterly*, 1975 (Jul), 21 (3), pp. 227–32; and Thomas M.H., Horton, R.W. and Lippincott, E.C., 'Desensitization to portrayals of real-life aggression as a function of exposure to television violence', in *Journal of Personality and Social Psychology*, 1977, vol. 33 (6), pp. 450–8.
11. Under the headline 'Video Nasty Sickens Euro MPs' *The Times*, 17 November 1983, described how British MPs were presented with ' ... *a Scotland Yard special video stitching together some of the more nauseating sections of the films* available in local family video shops throughout Britain' (my italics), quoted in Martin, John, *The Seduction of the Gullible*, p. 197.
12. Ibid.
13. Quoted in Grixti, Joseph, *Terrors of Uncertainty* (London: Routledge, 1989), p. 127.
14. Barlow, Geoffrey and Hill, Alison (eds), *Video Violence and Children*, p. 165.
15. Grixti, Joseph, *The Terrors of Uncertainty*, p. 173. Although Grixti bases his analysis of the horror genre on the novels of James Herbert and *The Shining* by Stephen King only, he nonetheless extends his reading and rejection to the entire horror genre including movies. The praxis of cursory analysis is only too common with culture-pessimistic critics. For similar arguments see Judith Hess Wright, 'Genre films and the status quo', 1974, in Grant, Barry Keith (ed.), *Film, Genre, Reader* (Austin: University of Texas Press, 1986), pp. 41–50.
16. Grixti, Joseph, *Terrors of Uncertainty*, p. 169.
17. Ibid, p. 74.
18. Wood, Robin, 'Return of the repressed', in *Film Comment* 14, no. 4, 1978, p. 27.
19. Jackson, Rosemary, *Fantasy: The Literature of Subversion* (New York: Methuen, 1981), pp. 26, 69.
20. Stein, Elliott, 'Michael Powell's *Peeping Tom*', in *Film Comment*, September–October 1979, pp. 57–9.
21. See Clover, Carol J., *Men*Women* and CHAIN SAWS: Gender in the Modern Horror Film* (London: BFI Publishing, 1992), p. 11.
22. Wood, Robin, 'Return of the repressed', p. 32.
23. A list of the video nasties appears in Martin, John, *Seduction of the Gullible*, p. 214.
24. Horace Walpole's *The Castle of Otranto*, published in 1765 is generally acknowledged as the first Gothic novel.

25. Quoted in Jones, Ernest, *Nightmare, Witches, and Devils* (New York: W.W. Norton, 1931), p. 154. See Jones for a psychoanalytic analysis of the nightmare, the devil, the vampire and other supernatural beliefs.

26. Tompkins, J.M.S., *The Popular Novel in England 1770–1800* (London: Constable, 1932), p. 120. Among popular female Gothic novels were *Old English Baron: A Gothic Story* (1777) by Clara Reeve; *The Recess: A Tale of Other Times* (1785) by Sophia Lee and *The Mysteries of Udolpho* (1796) by Anne Radcliffe.

27. See Punter, David, *The Literature of Terror: A History of Gothic Fictions From 1765 to the Present Day* (Hong Kong: Longman, 1980), p. 111.

28. Todorov, Tzvetan 1987 (1970), *The Fantastic: A Structural Approach to a Literary Genre* (New York: Cornell University Press, 1970, 1987), p. 135.

29. Or even two genres; some claim her novel is both the first horror novel and the first science fiction novel.

30. Wood, Robin, *Hollywood from Vietnam to Reagan* (New York: Columbia University Press, 1986), pp. 73–5.

31. Freud, Sigmund, Collected Works, volume 14, *Art and Literature* (Harmondsworth: Penguin Books, 1985, 1988), p. 364.

32. Freud also points to another explanation of the uncanny, namely 'when primitive beliefs which have been surmounted seem once more to be confirmed' ('The Uncanny', in *Art and Literature*, p. 372). If you for instance wish someone dead and the person dies shortly after, the effect would be to believe in supernatural powers.

33. Winter, Douglas E., *Faces of Fear: Encounters with the Creators of Modern Horror* (London: Pan Books, 1990), p. 266.

34. Stoker, Bram, *Dracula* (New York: Bantam Books, 1897, 1989), pp. 38–9.

35. Jones, Ernest, *Nightmare, Witches, and Devils*, p. 106.

36. Ibid, p. 98.

37. Also in E.T.A. Hoffmann's many early nineteenth-century novels and short stories, among them *The Sand Man*, and Edgar Allen Poe's *Tales of the Grotesque and Arabesque* (1839).

38. This is what Andrew Tudor claims, based on his own statistics of 900 horror movies in *Monsters and Mad Scientists: A Cultural History of the Horror Movie* (Oxford: Basil Blackwell, 1989).

39. Quoted in Clover, Carol J., *Men *Women* and CHAIN SAWS*, p. 10.

40. Ibid, p. 9.

41. Wood, Robin, 'Return of the repressed', p. 32.

42. Bettelheim, Bruno, *The Uses of Enchantment: The Meaning and Importance of Fairy Tales* (Harmondsworth: Penguin Books, 1976, 1991), p. 65.

43. Twitchell, James B., *Dreadful Pleasures: An Anatomy of Modern Horror* (New York: Oxford University Press, 1985), p. 66.

44. McCarthy, John, *Splatter Movies: Breaking the Last Taboo of the Screen* (New York: St Martin's Press, 1984), p. 1.

45. Baudrillard, Jean, 'The ecstasy of communication', in Foster, Hal (ed.), *Postmodern Culture* (London: Pluto Press, 1990), p. 132.

46. Eco, Umberto, *Travels in Hyperreality* (London: Picador, 1987), p. 210.

47. Ibid, p. 209.

48. See Eco, Umberto, 'Innovation and repetition: between modern and post-modern aesthetics', in *Daedalus*, fall 1985, pp. 161–84.
49. Barlow, Geoffrey and Hill, Alison, *Video Violence and Children*, p. 170.
50. Quoted in Martin, John, *Seduction of the Gullible*, p. 200.

Bibliography

Bentley, C.F. (1972) 'The monster in the bedroom: sexual symbolism in Bram Stoker's *Dracula*', *Literature and Psychology*, vol. xxii, no. 1.
Carroll, Nöel (1981) 'Nightmare and the horror film: the symbolic biology of fantastic beings', *Film Quarterly*, vol. 34, no. 3, spring.
Carroll, Nöel (1990) *The Philosophy of Horror* (New York: Routledge).
Grant, Barry Keith (1984) *Planks of Reason: Essays on the Horror Film* (Metuchen: The Scarecrow Press).
Hogan, David J. (1986) *Dark Romance: Sexuality in the Horror Film* (Jefferson NC: McFarlane and Company).
Lovett, Verena (1989) 'Bodily symbolism and the fiction of Stephen King', in Longhurst, D. (ed.), *Gender, Genre and Narrative Pleasure* (London: Unwin Hyman).
Maltin, Leonard (1994) *Maltin's Movie and Video Guide 1994* (New York: Signet).
Modleski, Tania (1986) 'The terror of Pleasure', in Modelski, Tania (ed.), *Studies of Entertainment* (Wisconsin: Indiana University Press).
Newman, Kim (1988) *Nightmare Movies: A Critical History of the Horror Film, 1968–88* (London: Bloomsbury).
Rubenstein, Marc. A. (1976) '"My accursed Origin"', in *Studies in Romanticism*, no. 15 (Boston: The Graduate School, Boston University).
Schoell, William (1985) *Stay out of the Shower: 25 Years of Shocker Films Beginning with 'Psycho'* (New York: Dembner Books).
Silver, Alain and Ursini, James (1975) *The Vampire Film* (South Brunswick: A.S. Barnes and Company).
Swingle, L.J. (1973) 'Frankenstein's monster and its romantic relatives: problems of knowledge in English romanticism', in *Texas Studies in Literature and Language*, no. 15, spring 1973, vol. xv, no. 1 (Austin: University of Texas Press).
Twitchell, James B. (1980) 'The vampire myth', in *American Imago*, no. 1, spring (Detroit: Wayne State University Press).
Twitchell, James B. (1983) 'Frankenstein and the anatomy of horror', in *The Georgia Review*, no. 37, spring.
Tymn, Marshall B. (1981) *Horror Literature: A Core Collection and Reference Guide* (New York: R.R. Bowker and Company).
Waller, Gregory A. (1986) *The Living and the Undead* (Chicago: University of Illinois Press).
Waller, Gregory A. (1987) *American Horrors: Essays on the Modern American Horror Film* (Chicago: University of Illinois Press).
Wood, Robin (1978) 'Gods and monsters', in *Film Comment* 14, no. 5, 1978.
Wood, Robin (1980) 'Neglected nightmares', in *Film Comment* 16, no. 2, 1980.

Films

Alien (1979, Ridley Scott)
Aliens (1986, James Cameron)
Alien 3 (1992, David Fincher)
Army of Darkness, also called *Evil Dead III* and *The Medieval Dead* (1992, Sam Raimi)
Bad Taste (1988, Peter Jackson)
Blood Drinkers, The (1966, Gerardo De Leon)
Body Parts (1991, Eric Red)
Braindead (1992, Peter Jackson)
Carrie (1976, Brian De Palma)
Child's Play 3 (1991, Jack Bender)
Dracula (1931, Tod Browning)
Dracula (1992, Francis Ford Coppola)
Evil Dead, The (1983, Sam Raimi)
Evil Dead II (1987, Sam Raimi)
Evil Dead III (see *Army of Darkness*)
Exorcist, The (1973, William Friedkin)
Flesh Feast (1970, B.F. Grinter)
Fly, The (1986, David Cronenberg)
Frankenstein (1931, James Whale)
Friday the 13th (1980, Sean Cunningham)
Halloween (1978, John Carpenter)
Hands of Orlac, The (1960, Edmond T. Greville)
Hands of a Stranger (1962, Newton Arnold)
Hell Night (1981, Tom DeSimone)
I Drink Your Blood (1971, David Durston)
I Eat Your Skin (1971, Del Tenney)
Invasion of the Body Snatchers (1956, Don Siegel)
It! The Terror from Beyond Space (1958, Edward L. Cahn)
Misery (1990, Rob Reiner)
Monty Python and the Holy Grail (1974, Terry Gilliam/Terry Jones)
Night of the Living Dead (1968, George A. Romero)
Nightmare on Elm Street, A (1984, Wes Craven)
Nightmares in a Damaged Brain, US title *Nightmare* (1981, Romano Scavolini)
Parasite Murders, The (1976, David Cronenberg)
Peeping Tom (1960, Michael Powell)
Please Don't Eat My Mother (1972, Carl Monson)
Psycho (1960, Alfred Hitchcock)
Rabid (1977, David Cronenberg)
Raw Meat also called *Death Line* (in the UK) (1973, Gary Sherman)
Re-Animator (1985, Stuart Gordon)
Return of the Living Dead Part II (1988, Ken Wiederhorn)
Rosemary's Baby (1968, Roman Polanski)
Salem's Lot (1979, Tobe Hooper)
Silence of the Lambs, The (1991, Jonathan Demme)

Parasite Murders, The (original canadian title) also called *Shivers* (in the UK) and *They Came From Within* (in the US) (1976, David Cronenberg)
Texas Chain Saw Massacre, The (1974, Tobe Hooper)
Videodrome (1983, David Cronenberg)

Notes on Contributors

Mary Eaton is Assistant Principal at St Mary's University College: A College of the University of Surrey. She is the author of *Women After Prison* and *Justice for Women? Family, Court and Social Control*.

David Kidd-Hewitt has taught criminology and law and society at London Guildhall University for over 20 years and is retired Head of the Department of Sociology and Applied Social Studies. He works as a freelance writer and educational consultant and is a member of the editorial team of the ISTD's quarterly journal *Criminal Justice Matters*.

Sue Lees is Professor of Women's Studies at the University of North London. She is the author of *Sugar and Spice: Sexuality and Adolescent Girls* and *Carnal Knowledge: Rape on Trial*. Her research has led to the production of several television documentaries, including *Getting Away with Rape*, winner of the Royal Television prize for best documentary of 1994.

Paul Mason is a lecturer at the Institute of Southampton and the University of the West of England, Bristol where he teaches crime and TV. He is currently completing his PhD on TV and British prisons.

Richard Osborne lectures in cultural studies, mass media and philosophy at London Guildhall University. He is the author of *Freud for Beginners*, *Philosophy for Beginners* and *Radical Philosophy Reader*.

Jim Pines is Senior Lecturer in Media Arts at the University of Luton. He is the author of *Black and White in Colour: Black People in British Television Since 1936* and co-editor (with Paul Willeman) of *Questions of Third Cinema*.

Noel Sanders teaches cultural studies at the University of Technology, Sydney. He has written on Australian crime in its cultural context.

Rikke Schubart teaches film at the Department of Film and Media Studies, University of Copenhagen. She has published several articles on film and popular culture and is the author of *From Frankenstein to Splatter Movies*.

Paula Skidmore lectures in criminology at the Department of Applied Social Studies, Nottingham Trent University. She has written for *Child Abuse Review* and is joint-author of *Prisons Under Protest*.

Richard Sparks is Professor of Criminology at Keele University. He has written widely on criminology as is the author of *Television and the Drama of Crime* and joint-author of *Criminology and Beyond* and *Prisons and the Problem of Order*.

A.E. Stephenson-Burton is currently completing her doctoral research at the London School of Economics and Political Science. She has been a research consultant to the Serious Fraud Office and has lectured at Birkbeck College, Brunel University and Warwick University.

Index